Small School Theatre

This resource uses small schools as a framework for empowering educators and administrators to bring vibrant theatre programs to life, no matter their level of resources. Authored by a seasoned professional in the performing arts field, the book dives into the specific challenges and rewards of establishing, nurturing, and leading a theatrical program. Chapters draw from the author's extensive personal experience as well as insights gleaned from interviews with other successful directors. The chapters are divided into sections for starting, growing, and directing a theatre program, with key takeaways and workbook prompts throughout to provide applicability from first-year teachers to experienced directors and school administrators. Topics include designing curriculum, allocating resources, collaborating among stakeholders, evolving to meet the needs of your school, and more. Practical strategies and inspirational approaches guide educators on navigating program development, fostering student growth, and maintaining program excellence. Whether you're a new teacher embarking on your performing arts journey or a seasoned director seeking to refine your program, this book provides a comprehensive resource to cultivate thriving artistic experiences within your school from the ground up.

David Richard Corkill is Owner and Executive Director of The Performing Arts Community Center, USA. He is a former middle and high school teacher in Texas with 13 years of experience teaching theatre and has directed more than 60 productions and concerts.

Also Available from Routledge Eye on Education
(www.routledge.com/eyeoneducation)

Trauma-Informed Practices for 9–12 Theatre Education
Jimmy Chrismon and Adam W. Carter

Stage It: Making Shakespeare Come Alive in Schools
Floyd Rumohr

Implementing Creative Movement and Theater Across the K-6 Curriculum: Moving Through the School Day
Kelly Mancini Becker

Drama for the Inclusive Classroom: Activities to Support Curriculum and Social-Emotional Learning
Sally Bailey

Immersive Arts Integration: A Step-by-Step Guide to Transitioning Your K-8 School
Jenna Masone and Jennifer Katona

Enlivening Instruction with Drama and Improv: A Guide for Second Language and World Language Teachers
Melisa Cahnmann-Taylor and Kathleen R. McGovern

Acting it Out: Using Drama in the Classroom to Improve Student Engagement, Reading, and Critical Thinking
Juliet Hart, Mark Onuscheck, and Mary T Christel

Small School Theatre: How to Start, Grow, and Direct a Successful Drama Program
David Richard Corkill

Small School Theatre

How to Start, Grow, and Direct a Successful Drama Program

David Richard Corkill

Routledge
Taylor & Francis Group
NEW YORK AND LONDON

Designed cover image: Getty Images

First published 2026
by Routledge
605 Third Avenue, New York, NY 10158

and by Routledge
4 Park Square, Milton Park, Abingdon, Oxon, OX14 4RN

Routledge is an imprint of the Taylor & Francis Group, an informa business

© 2026 David Richard Corkill

The right of David Richard Corkill to be identified as author of this work has been asserted in accordance with sections 77 and 78 of the Copyright, Designs and Patents Act 1988.

All rights reserved. No part of this book may be reprinted or reproduced or utilised in any form or by any electronic, mechanical, or other means, now known or hereafter invented, including photocopying and recording, or in any information storage or retrieval system, without permission in writing from the publishers.

Trademark notice: Product or corporate names may be trademarks or registered trademarks, and are used only for identification and explanation without intent to infringe.

ISBN: 978-1-032-95743-2 (hbk)
ISBN: 978-1-032-95692-3 (pbk)
ISBN: 978-1-003-58630-2 (ebk)

DOI: 10.4324/9781003586302

Typeset in Palatino
by Apex CoVantage, LLC

Dedication

For my theatre students: From the first auditions to the final bows, you gave my life meaning, light, and endless inspiration. Your passion, creativity, and courage always reminded me why storytelling matters. This book is for you.

Contents

Meet the Author . . . . *x*
List of Professionals Interviewed . . . . *xi*
Preface. . . . . *xiv*

Introduction   1

PART 1
Starting a Theatre Program   5

1 **Pitching the Program**   7
   The Benefits of Theatre   8
   Fitting Into the Curriculum   14
   Arts vs. Athletics   17
   "How Much Is It Going to Cost?"   19
   Now What?   21

2 **Elementary School, Middle School, and High School**   22
   Elementary School Level (K–5th)   24
   Middle School Level (6th–8th)   29
   High School Level (9th–12th)   32

3 **Competitive Theatre vs. At-School Theatre**   37
   'Competing' Views   40
   Firm Foundation First   42
   Don't Just Compete   45

4 **Rehearsal and Performance Spaces**   48
   Rehearsal Spaces   49
   Performance Spaces   53

5 **Getting Everyone Interested**   57
   Getting Students Interested   58
   Getting Parents Interested   60
   Getting Colleagues Interested   61
   Getting the Community Interested   63

6 The First Show — 67
Setting the Stage (Before the First Show) — 69
Starting Strong (During the First Show) — 72

PART 2
Growing a Theatre Program — 75

7 Money — 77
Doing a Show for $0.00 — 78
The School Budget — 80
Donations — 82
Fundraising — 83
The War Chest — 84

8 Props, Sets, and Costumes — 86
What to Get? — 87
Where to Get It? — 92
What to Do With It After? — 99

9 Lights, Sound, and Music — 101
Getting What You Need — 102
Using What You Have — 104
Music — 106

10 Advertisements, Tickets, and Programs — 109
Advertisements — 110
Tickets — 113
Programs — 115

11 Picking Shows — 119
Picking Shows Based on the Present — 120
Picking Shows Based on the Past — 120
Picking Shows Based on the Future — 123

12 Traditions and Legacy — 126
Creating Traditions — 127
Traditions to Create — 129
Legacy — 134

PART 3
Directing a Theatre Program — 137

13 Auditions and Casting — 139
Audition Forms — 140
Auditions — 148
Casting — 150
Posting the Cast List and Reactions From Doing So — 152

14 The Schedule — 155
The Pre-Audition Schedule — 156
The First Rehearsal/Read-Through Schedule — 157
Musical Production Rehearsal Order — 159
Production Workdays — 161

15 Rehearsal — 166
Read-Through — 167
Music Rehearsals — 169
Dancing Rehearsals — 171
Blocking Rehearsals — 172
Run-Through Rehearsals — 174
Tech Week — 176
Overall Rehearsal Tips and Tricks — 178

16 The Performance — 181
Performance Things to Note — 182
Show Day Schedule — 186

17 Theatre Class — 190
The Four Quarters — 191
Curriculum and Textbooks — 192
Games — 193
Projects — 194

18 Other Performance Opportunities — 197
Various Opportunities — 198
The Summer — 201

Conclusion: Legitimacy and Excellence — 207

Meet the Author

Born and raised in La Grange, Texas, David has been immersed in the performing arts since the age of three. By age 15, he had already directed his first play, setting the stage for a lifelong passion for theatre and music. He pursued his education at Baylor University in Waco, Texas, and went on to teach theatre and music for eleven years in both Waco and Corpus Christi.

Throughout his career, David has directed more than 65 productions and has performed and directed at esteemed community theatres, including Harbor Playhouse, Aurora Arts Theatre, Temple Civic Theatre, and Waco Civic Theatre. His extensive experience in performing arts education, combined with his deep commitment to fostering creative expression, led him to establish The Performing Arts Community Center (The PACC) in Waco. As the Owner and Executive Director, he has built a space where artists of all ages can explore theatre, music, dance, and film through classes, workshops, events, and performances.

Professionals Interviewed

Brett Boles
Brett Boles is an award-winning musical theatre composer, lyricist, bookwriter, and music director. His original musical *Foreverman* premiered at the New York Musical Theatre Festival (NYMF), earning accolades for Outstanding Orchestrations and the New World Stages Development Prize. He co-wrote an adaptation of *The Curious Case of Benjamin Button* with composer Natalie Tenenbaum, which has been performed off-Broadway at the York Theatre and in London's Southwark Playhouse. His latest musical, *Time Stops*, premiered at the Kravis Center for the Performing Arts in West Palm Beach, Florida, under the direction of Tony-winning producer Michael Moritz, Jr.

Boles' work has been performed by Broadway stars, including Tony nominees Jeremy Jordan, Josh Young, and Kate Baldwin. He co-conceived *From Broadway With Love: A Benefit Concert for Sandy Hook* and has served as a vocal arranger for artists such as Stephanie Mills and Orfeh in the *Concerts for America* series. He is also the vocal arranger for Randy Rainbow. Boles shares his passion for theatre and storytelling through his social media series *The M Tea*, boasting more than 500,000 followers across TikTok and Instagram (including Lin-Manuel Miranda as a follower). A member of the BMI Lehman Engel Musical Theatre Workshop and the Dramatists Guild of America, Boles previously served as Director of Choirs at Hall High School in West Hartford, CT, and now teaches songwriting globally.

Austin Campbell
Austin Campbell is the band director at Logan High School in Logan, West Virginia. A first-year director, Campbell has been involved in music education for 14 years through private lessons and community initiatives. Returning to school specifically to take on this role, he was instrumental in reviving Logan High School's band program after it was left without a director or students in 2022–23. To generate interest, he organized a volunteer marching band for the school's homecoming game, drawing 104 musicians and significant attention to the program. Now leading the program's resurgence, Campbell is committed to restoring and growing Logan High School's band for future generations.

David DeLuca

David DeLuca has been a dedicated band director for 28 years, shaping music programs across multiple districts. He began his career teaching elementary band in Lyford ISD before serving as an assistant high school band director at Columbia-Brazoria ISD. He later worked as the middle school director, drumline assistant, and assistant high school director at La Grange ISD before becoming the head high school director in Hallettsville. Most recently, he has overseen all aspects of the music program in Culberson County-Alamore ISD in Van Horn, Texas, demonstrating his versatility and passion for music education.

Dr. David Guess

Dr. David Guess has dedicated 28 years to choral music education, with a career spanning both church and academic settings. He has served as an adjunct faculty member at the University of Oklahoma and McLennan Community College, as well as the choir program director at Waco High School. From 1997 to 2006, he was the Director of Choral Activities and an Associate Professor of Music at the University of Mary Hardin-Baylor. He earned his doctorate from the University of Texas and played a pivotal role in reorganizing the Central Texas Choral Society (CTCS) in 2003. Under his leadership, CTCS held its first concert in 2012, and he served as both president and director until 2022. In addition to his work in choral conducting, he has taught private voice lessons for more than 32 years, maintaining a private studio since 2010 with more than 28 students.

Carley Hunt

Carley Hunt has been a theatre educator for 13 years, shaping young performers across multiple grade levels. She studied theatre at Tyler Junior College before earning her degree from Lamar University in 2011. After completing a post-baccalaureate teaching program and earning her certification, she began her career in Nederland Independent School District (ISD), where she served as district assistant director, working across three schools as both a high school theatre teacher and technical director. In 2016, she transitioned to Sulphur Springs and Mount Vernon ISDs, where she has continued to teach middle and high school theatre, focusing on competitions and performance-based education.

Eric Staples

Eric Staples has been a theatre director for ten years, bringing his passion for the performing arts to schools of varying sizes. Holding a bachelor's degree in acting and directing, he has spent the past nine years teaching in districts ranging from 5A to 3A. His experience spans all aspects of theatre education, from performance and production to technical theatre, fostering creativity and excellence in his students.

Jeffrey Stirl
With 24 years of experience as a theatre director, Jeffrey Stirl has worked in multiple educational settings, bringing a diverse background in coaching prose and poetry, oral interpretation, theatre, and communication. He began his career as a substitute teacher in Mount Pleasant before coaching and teaching multiple subjects at St. Augustine and Hughes Springs High School in Northeast Texas. He earned his master's degree from Texas A&M Commerce and went on to teach in Gatesville for four years, focusing on theatre and professional communications. He has since worked in various districts, including Pittsburg, Hitchcock, and Clemens High School, guiding students in theatre and competitive speech.

Brian Strohmetz
Brian Strohmetz has been a band director for eight years, bringing his expertise in music education to schools in New Jersey. A graduate of Moravian University, where he studied music education with a focus on French horn, he began his career at Silver Bay Elementary School, directing beginning band and orchestra while also teaching special education music. He later expanded his role to include general music for third grade before moving to the high school level due to district budget cuts. Since 2020, he has served as an assistant director of bands, teaching music technology, songwriting, and choir while also leading the school's theatre and musical productions.

Preface

Theatre in a small school is more than just a class or an extracurricular activity – it's a lifeline for creativity, a safe space for self-expression, and a launching pad for future storytellers. When I first started directing, I quickly realized that success in a small program isn't about the size of your budget or the grandeur of your stage – it's about resourcefulness, passion, and the students who show up, ready to create.

This book was born out of years of firsthand experience directing and teaching in schools where theatre programs had to be built from the ground up or sustained with minimal resources. I wrote this book for the educators, directors, and dreamers who find themselves navigating the unique challenges of small school theatre. Whether you are launching a brand-new program, revitalizing one that has struggled, or looking to take an existing program to the next level, my goal is to provide you with both practical tools and creative inspiration to help you succeed.

The book is structured in a way that mirrors the journey of a theatre program. It begins with the foundation – establishing a vision, understanding the role of theatre in a school, and navigating administrative and logistical hurdles. It then moves into the practical aspects of directing and producing theatre, including casting, rehearsals, stage design, and working with limited resources. Finally, it explores long-term program growth, covering topics such as advocacy, community involvement, and creating a sustainable theatre culture that leaves a lasting impact on students and the school.

What makes this book distinctive is its focus on adaptability and creativity. Many theatre books assume access to professional facilities, large budgets, and a wealth of resources – but small school theatre rarely works that way. Instead, this book embraces the reality of limited budgets, makeshift stages, and multipurpose spaces, offering solutions tailored to those conditions. Special features include real-world examples, practical checklists, and step-by-step guides for everything from building sets on a shoestring budget to navigating administrative roadblocks.

The intended audience for this book includes theatre teachers, directors, administrators, and even passionate volunteers who want to ensure that theatre remains accessible to students, no matter the school's size or funding. It is for those who believe in the transformative power of storytelling and performance, even when faced with obstacles.

Ultimately, small school theatre is about resourcefulness, relationships, and resilience. My hope is that this book not only provides the tools you need but also reminds you why the work you're doing matters. The impact of theatre extends far beyond the stage – it builds confidence, fosters collaboration, and gives students a voice. If this book helps even one educator navigate the challenges of small school theatre with more confidence and creativity, then it has served its purpose.

Now, let's get to work – because no matter the size of the stage, the magic of theatre is waiting to be made.

Introduction

The stage lights dim, a hush falls over the audience, and a world of imagination bursts to life. School theatre is more than just putting on plays; it's a launching pad for creativity, a celebration of collaboration, and a space where students discover their voices. This book is your comprehensive guide to navigating every aspect of building a successful school theatre program, from its exciting inception to its impactful legacy.

Have you ever witnessed the spark of creativity ignite in a student's eyes as they step onto the stage? Or heard the thunderous applause erupt after a moving performance? School theatre is a transformative experience, fostering confidence, collaboration, and a lifelong love for the arts. But where do you begin?

This comprehensive guidebook is your roadmap to building a successful and sustainable theatre program within your school walls. Whether you're a passionate educator with a vision or an administrator seeking to enrich your school's offerings, this book equips you with the tools and knowledge to navigate every step of the journey.

I created this book because it is something I wish I had had in my first year of teaching theatre. The lessons within these pages were a lot of my lessons learned from mistakes and missteps throughout my career. My goal is to help you skip those mistakes, miss those missteps, and go straight to a great program. I had the privilege of interviewing eight professionals in the performing arts to help accent this book with diverse advice, counterpoints, helpful examples, and great quotes. The professionals interviewed for this book represent a wide range of expertise across theatre and the broader performing arts. Collectively, they bring an impressive depth of experience, with a combined total of 140 years in the industry. Their insights lend credibility and depth to the guidance presented throughout these chapters, offering a well-rounded perspective that blends practical strategies with firsthand wisdom. These professionals provided valuable expertise in areas such as directing, acting, technical theatre, arts administration, and educational theatre, ensuring that this book serves as a comprehensive resource for educators at all levels.

I, of course, don't list the schools I taught at, nor do I name real students in my examples. But for some of the examples and context therein, it'll be good to know what types of schools I'm talking about. I've primarily taught theatre at two schools: the first was a small public charter school, which I will call "the charter school," and the second was a small private classical Christian school, which I will call "the private school."

Although this book is entitled *Small School Theatre*, the information within can apply to any size school if applied appropriately. Likewise, the first section is entitled "Starting a Theatre Program," but if you have a program that has already started, there may still be great information in that section to help refresh your program and 'restart' in a way. You can read the book cover-to-cover or pick and choose the chapters that you need the most. Not all of the advice on its pages will apply to your situation, and that is fine. But my goal, after you have read this book, is to help give you the tools needed to start, grow, and direct a successful, legitimate, and excellent theatre program.

From pitching the program to the administration and tailoring it for different age groups to the nitty-gritty of selecting plays, securing funding, and managing rehearsals, this book covers it all. We'll also explore the often-overlooked aspects of marketing your production, from creating eye-catching advertisements to designing programs that enhance the audience experience. You'll delve into the world of set design, costumes, lighting, and sound, and discover creative solutions for maximizing your resources. You'll discover strategies for attracting students of all ages (elementary, middle, and high school) and explore the merits of both competitive and in-school productions. We'll explore how to foster a supportive environment and how to build a tradition of excellence that will inspire generations to come. From the intricacies of auditions and casting to building a cohesive rehearsal schedule, to conducting rehearsals that ensure a smooth performance, this book will be your roadmap to a well-oiled theatrical machine.

One notable omission in this book is an in-depth discussion of social justice issues – a decision made with careful consideration. Addressing topics such as racism, sexism, transphobia, censorship, and broader social justice concerns within a theatre program is undeniably important. However, these issues are complex and nuanced, requiring specialized expertise beyond the scope of this book. Including them could also narrow the book's universal applicability, potentially limiting its long-term relevance. As one reviewer noted, "In a polarized world, this is a huge topic that isn't easily managed by even the most experienced drama teacher." I agree with this sentiment. My primary goal is to provide practical, evergreen guidance that any educator – regardless of their school's cultural or political climate – can apply. That said, inclusivity is addressed in specific chapters, particularly in discussions on auditions, casting, and broadening access to theatre opportunities for all students. Readers seeking a more in-depth exploration of social justice within theatre education may find greater insight in works dedicated specifically to that subject.

Similarly, while I spent more than half of my teaching career in Christian schools, this book maintains a neutral stance on faith-based education. The goal is to ensure that the strategies and insights presented are applicable across all school types, whether public, private, charter, or faith-based. Although faith-based schools often have unique considerations, I have intentionally chosen not to focus on specific religious practices within theatre education. Instead, any mentions of faith-based settings will primarily appear in personal anecdotes rather than as guiding principles for program development. This approach allows the book to remain broadly accessible while still acknowledging the diversity of educational environments in which theatre programs exist. When distinctions between school types are relevant, I will use broad terms such as "faith-based schools" rather than specifying religious affiliations to ensure clarity and inclusivity.

This book is more than just a manual; it's your companion on a transformative journey. With its practical advice, true stories, and insightful discussions on the power of theatre education, *Small School Theatre* will empower you to create a program that not only entertains but also ignites the imaginations and talents of your students, leaving a lasting impact on your school community. So, take a deep breath, step onto the stage, and let the curtain rise on your remarkable theatrical journey!

PART 1
Starting a Theatre Program

1
Pitching the Program

Imagine that you are a social studies teacher at a small school. This small school is relatively new, only having been around for 12 years. Now imagine that although you teach social studies, your college degree, certification, and passion are all in theatre. This small school where you teach does not have theatre in any form and has not ever had a theatre in its brief history. The population of the school has grown so much since its humble beginnings, and now there are 200 students from kindergarten to 12th grade, around 10–15 kiddos per grade. At the end of the school year, you look around and realize that this school needs a theatre program. However, as far as you know, the administration has no plans to add one any time soon. You also realize that if you do not do anything about this, theatre could be missing from this school for quite some time. You take it upon yourself to be the person to pitch the program into existence. You find out that the administration and board are having a major meeting on July 1st. You decide to prepare a proposal in the few weeks between the end of school and this meeting. You prepare feverishly, and the big day comes before you know it. When you arrive at the board meeting, they ask you to take the podium, and you do, with proposal in hand. In front of you sits the elementary school principal, middle school principal, high school principal, superintendent, and all six members of the school board. They all look at you with rapt attention. You clear your throat and begin to speak.

    What do you say?
        How do you convince them?
        What is in your proposal?

This moment has happened one way or another all across the country and the globe. Most small schools that are created do not start with theatre in the curriculum, because it is just not yet a priority. But then, at some point, some of these schools add theatre. Some add theatre for a couple of years, see some less-than-mediocre output, and then decide to take it out. Some add theatre and keep it, but although the output is mediocre, the administration and community just accept it with an 'it is what it is' mentality. Yet some schools get theatre kicked off the right way with the right person, and the interest and quality within the program increases year after year. I certainly hope, since you picked up this book, that you are trying to go with the third scenario and kick it off in the right way. Whether you are that social studies teacher who is trying to start the program, a theatre teacher who wants to improve the program, or an administration official who desires to add a theatre program at your school, regardless of who you are, it all starts with the pitch.

So, back to the main question: How do you pitch a theatre program into existence?

In this chapter, we will answer that question. I'll talk about what you should be talking about in that pitch meeting: What are the benefits of theatre? How can we fit it into the curriculum? How do we balance time between theatre and athletics? And then the all-important final question: How much is it going to cost?

The Benefits of Theatre

Why Join Theatre? Why Add Theatre? Why Theatre?

Every subject, from History to P.E., has had to fight for its right to exist from time to time. Unfortunately, the performing arts have to fight harder than the rest. For those of us who grew up with theatre, studied theatre, taught theatre, and experienced theatre, its inclusion into the school's curriculum is a no-brainer. We understand its benefits because we've experienced them firsthand. However, when trying to add theatre to a school that doesn't have it, you will, more likely than not, be faced with decision-makers who aren't aware of the benefits. In a pitch meeting, unfortunately, you won't be able to show them the benefits firsthand. But you can try to explain what the benefits will be to the students, to the school, and to the wider community, and promise that those benefits will bear fruit sooner rather than later.

Following is an exhaustive yet incomplete list of benefits that you can share with administrators to add a theatre program. However, although you could, I don't think it would be wise to give them every single one of the benefits listed. I think it is important to know what the administration's priorities are. What are the schools' aims and goals? What do they emphasize most?

If the school focuses primarily on college prep, emphasize the points that will help that goal instead of getting in the way of it.

If the school is more geared toward job/career prep, show them that theatre can help in the professional environment, regardless of what area.

Show that whether the school is STEM-driven, state testing obsessed, or even primarily focused on athletics, theatre can add to those goals, not take away from them. Help them see that theatre doesn't have to hinder their primary goal, but rather it can support that goal.

Take any of the following benefits and pitch them to line up with the school's priorities, instead of lining up against them.

Also, the many benefits don't have to be used just for pitching a program. Is a student choosing between Theatre and another elective? Is the administration considering cutting the program? Is an upperclassman deciding whether they want to pursue a career in theatre? In these situations and more, use these benefits as the armor to defend theatre.

Benefits to Students

Teamwork and Collaboration: Theatre is a collaborative effort. Even a single actor putting on a one-person show has help. Remember this: "A play isn't a one-person show even if it is a one-person show!" Who is lighting the stage? Who is helping backstage? Who sold the tickets? Theatre has a lot of teamwork value. Teamwork and collaboration in theatre are primary soft skills for students as they get older. It is vitally important in any industry a student is going into; whether they are a doctor, lawyer, or athlete, teamwork is involved and vital. No matter what field they pursue, they will have to work in a functioning unit toward a common goal. Theatre is a breeding ground for strong teamwork skills. From actors to directors to set designers, a successful theatre production requires a team working together towards a common goal. The ability to come together, have a common goal, and do something you can't do by yourself is invaluable.

Attentiveness: Actors have to be attuned to their fellow actors onstage. They are not directed to just stand in one place and wait to say their next line. They are taught to show the audience that they are actively listening to their scene partner. In real life, we listen with our ears; onstage, we listen with our eyes. Their lines and reactions depend on what others are doing. This translates to better listening skills and the ability to respond effectively in a team setting.

Trust: When you're onstage and reliant on your fellow actors to deliver their lines or hit their cues, trust becomes essential. Student actors will come to know that just as they would help any of their fellow actors out of a bind onstage, their fellow actors would help them right back. Theatre exercises can help build trust and communication with others.

Confidence and Working Under Pressure: Theatre teaches you to manage pressure and perform at your best, even when the stakes are high. This translates to handling stressful situations calmly within tough situations. Working for two months straight for one opening night builds massive opening-night jitters. The more students go onstage and the more they perform, the easier it gets every time they step into the light. Overcoming stage fright and delivering a performance can be incredibly empowering. Theatre builds self-esteem and confidence that spill over into academics and other aspects of life.

Interview Preparedness: One of my colleagues said: "In a job interview in life, they won't ask you to dribble a basketball between your legs. But they will expect a proper handshake, eye contact, and eloquent speaking." Theatre can help with the interpersonal skills needed to speak to others, especially in a job interview setting. Job interviews can be a nerve-wracking experience; however, if a student has been taught how to act confidently onstage, they could very well act as if the job interview is a walk in the park.

Theatre Saves Lives: Theatre can get students on the right path to something that will make a difference in their lives. Not everyone can play sports. Not everyone is academically gifted. Not everyone is musically inclined. Theatre needs to be there to catch the rest of the students from falling through the gaps.

Quality: Theatre emphasizes the importance of creating a quality product. Students won't want to be embarrassed to be a part of a non-legit, lame, half-done production. They will respect the work put in to increase the quality of the product of the production, which can translate into increasing the quality of other products they create – from their English papers to their science projects.

Pride: Students will be prouder of their school and their production, and most importantly, they will be prouder of themselves for being a part of it. Students are rarely able to show off their math test scores, their English presentations, or their science labs. A finished show gives production members something to be proud of.

Engagement: Studies have shown a correlation between theatre involvement and academic achievement. Theatre can improve reading comprehension, focus, and overall engagement in school. If a school has a no pass/no play policy regarding theatre, then students in theatre will have more incentive to study and keep up their grades. Students have proven to be more engaged in school activities, in class, and their education overall, with added participation in a theatrical production.

Communication: Theatre hones both verbal and non-verbal communication skills. Students learn to project their voices clearly, articulate well, and use body language expressively. In this day and age, with phones, social media, texting, and the Zoom phase during COVID, young people's communication skills are worse now than ever. Participating in a theatrical production can sharpen those dulled skills. These skills translate into effective presentations, clear writing, and confident public speaking.

Empathy: Stepping into someone else's shoes is a core part of acting. Theatre exposes students to diverse cultures, backgrounds, and experiences. This fosters empathy and understanding of others' perspectives. Stepping into different roles helps you see the world from different viewpoints. This empathy is crucial for understanding other people and their approaches.

Life Skills: Theatre isn't just about memorizing lines. The arts, including theatre, have benefits for a youth's growing mind. It enhances reasoning, problem-solving skills, and creative thinking. Students analyze scripts, develop characters, and work collaboratively to bring the story to life. In theatre, they are taught skills for regular society. These include discipline, time management, responsibility, and critical thinking.

Self-Reliance: By focusing on a student's own lines and characters, theatre can build the ability to depend on themselves for their needs and wants. After the rehearsal process is done, it is them standing on that stage. No one can say the line for them, no one can find their spot onstage for them, and no one can hit that note for them. They realize that when it comes down to it, they can rely on themselves to pull through. They can better trust themselves to handle tasks, solve problems, and make decisions effectively while also learning to take action without needing constant guidance or support from others.

Self-Confidence: Just like when a student studies overwhelmingly for a test that after having taken they know they aced, full proper preparation for a role in theatre builds self-confidence within the student. Believing in oneself fosters a general sense of contentment and optimism. One is less likely to be weighed down by self-doubt and anxiety, leading to a greater sense of happiness.

Community: Theatre gives students a sense of community. Do you want the students to come to school? If you give them a reason to come to school, they will. It'll encourage other activities and academic pursuits. Sometimes students may hate every one of their classes. If they are in theatre and are enjoying their experience, it might at times be the only reason they want to get up in the morning.

Interdisciplinary Benefits: A theatre program is a fantastic way to bring together different disciplines. Imagine a massive musical production: theatre kids onstage, orchestra and band kids playing music in the pit, choir kids singing backup vocals backstage, visual arts kids admiring their backdrop art from the audience, dancing kids nailing their show-stopping number, and tech kids making it all look and sound great. A production can provide wonderful opportunities for interdisciplinary instruction, team building, and community creation.

Historical Context: Stella Adler once said that "theatre is a spiritual and social X-ray of its time." Example: *The Crucible* to the Salem witch trials, which was a direct correlation to the communist witch hunts of the 1950s. It is important for students and audiences alike to know the context and historical accuracy within the study of all things.

Creativity and Problem-Solving: Theatre encourages creative thinking and problem-solving skills. Students involved in set design, costume creation, or improvisation develop innovative solutions and explore artistic expression. Anyone who has experienced theatre knows that things *never* go perfectly. Something always goes wrong or against the plan. Problem-solving in the moment when a prop breaks, a set tree falls, a mic isn't turned on, an actor is not in their place, a costume rips, or many other possible night-of disasters, is crucial in theatre.

Benefits to the School

School Spirit: Theatre productions can be a unifying experience for the school. Students, teachers, parents, and community members come together to create a shared experience. If a school is not particularly successful in its athletic program, but its theatre one-act-play program is bringing home the hardware, then it will gladly show off its theatre program over the years right alongside those trophies. Have you ever experienced a pep rally for an arts program rather than an athletic one? They exist, and they are wonderful. If your school is sending a theatre group to a big competition, ask to have a pep rally for them just like the football team had. Your theatre students won't know what hit them when they have the whole school chanting enthusiastically for them. This can foster a sense of school spirit and belonging.

Appreciation for the Arts: School theatre exposes the broader school community to the arts. It allows them to witness the dedication and talent of students and fosters an appreciation for the creative process. An appreciation for the arts within a school community can elevate cultural awareness and understanding. As said earlier, exposure to different art forms can broaden perspectives and foster empathy.

Fundraising: Theatre productions can be fundraising events for the school or specific programs. More information about fundraising will be found in the "Money" chapter. However, using a theatrical production to fundraise for a non-theatre cause is a terrific way to increase the school's appreciation for the program.

Community Engagement: Theatre provides opportunities for collaboration with local businesses and organizations, strengthening ties within the community. Businesses can advertise in the program, donate to concessions, provide costumes or set pieces, and appreciate the exposure their participation gets for an audience of hundreds. Some businesses have advertising budgets that go unused. You'd be surprised as to the number of businesses that would be happy to sponsor a show just for the opportunity to put their information in the program.

The Community Face: Theatre is the community-facing part of the school. The math and English classes don't get many opportunities to show what they do to the community. What happens in their classroom usually stays in their classroom and in the gradebook. However, theatre is seen by the school community. What happens in the theatre classroom is shown to the entire world. The arts are the face of the school.

Cultural Understanding: Plays can explore diverse themes and stories, sparking important conversations and promoting cultural understanding within the school community. Many shows grant theatre students and audiences alike the opportunity to reflect on the importance of cultural heritage, to understand and appreciate diversity, to build bridges across cultures, and to highlight diverse cultural differences when it comes to family bonds and intergenerational connections.

Showcasing Student Work: Theatre productions offer a platform for students to showcase their talents and hard work, not just in acting but also in areas such as set design, lighting, and costume creation. This provides a sense of pride for students and their families. You have never seen someone admire the paint job of a set piece more than the parents of the student who diligently painted it or the exact placement of the lights on the stage more than the parents of the student who did the lighting design.

Positive School Climate: Theatre productions can contribute to a more positive school climate by promoting teamwork, empathy, and respect. The shared experience of creating a show fosters a sense of camaraderie and belonging, which can reduce bullying and create a more welcoming environment.

Public Speaking Opportunities: School plays offer opportunities for students who aren't involved in the acting to participate in public speaking roles such as announcing or introducing the show. This can benefit students who might otherwise shy away from public presentations. This is also helpful for students who are desiring to become better at public speaking because that skill is needed in their career pursuits.

Intergenerational Connection: Theatre productions can be a bridge between students, parents, and grandparents. Attending shows together creates shared memories and fosters stronger family bonds. Additionally, involving parents in set construction, costume creation, or backstage work can create opportunities for collaboration and shared experiences. See the chapter on "Production Work Days" about how to make this a reality.

Marketing and School Image: High-quality theatre productions can enhance a school's image within the community. Successful productions can attract positive media attention and showcase the school's commitment to the arts and well-rounded student development. The local paper has to fill the pages every single day. The local news broadcast has to fill four hours of news a day. Believe me, they are looking for stories. Give them a call, and before you know it, the production at your school will be live on the morning news!

Historical Preservation: School theatre productions can be a way to preserve and share local history or cultural traditions. By staging plays based on local events or figures, schools can connect with their community's heritage and foster a sense of place. This is a great interdisciplinary opportunity to collaborate with the history classes to have the students research and write the script for a historical figure-based play.

Fitting Into the Curriculum

So, you've rattled off all of the benefits shown here to the administration. They are overwhelmed by the sheer amount of benefits theatre brings that they could have never dreamed of before. You are sure that they are on board with the idea, but they say this: "That is all well and good, but we just don't think there is enough room in the schedule for theatre. . . . The elective slots are full, and students already have enough to do after school with the existing clubs we have." How do you counter this? What is your next line of defense when creating this program? What do you say to that?

"You Can't Expect Change Without Change"
A colleague of mine went to a mid-sized school and was asked to create a music program from scratch. She said that the administration was enthusiastic about adding music to the school. They seemed incredibly supportive and willing. They wanted music classes as well as music programs after school. The school already had a lot of electives, and their sports programs took up all five weekdays with practices and games year-round. Her new school's administration did not change anything about their curricular or extracurricular schedule upon adding music to the class schedule and after-school schedule. They just tried to shove more food onto their school's already too-full plate. The music classes, as well as the after-school program, therefore, did not have enough students to thrive, and the program struggled. Near the end of the year, the administration still seemed supportive and enthusiastic to get a music program going but told my friend that they wouldn't be changing anything about the next year either. My friend told them: "You cannot expect change without change." That administration was wholly unwilling to do anything to their existing programs to add something new. Administrations can't pair enthusiasm with inaction.

Adding an arts program to an already packed school schedule is a tough concept. But it takes compromise. It takes change. If the administration says there is not enough room in the schedule for a new theatre program, convince them that with a few sacrifices and changes across the board, it is possible.

Compromise
Compromise is the act of finding a solution where both (or multiple) parties involved give up something they originally wanted in order to reach common ground. It involves a balancing act, where each party modifies their demands or expectations to arrive at a mutually acceptable outcome. This outcome may not be ideal for anyone, but it allows everyone to gain something while giving up something.

The act of compromising involves negotiation and clear communication. Each party needs to express their desires and listen openly to the other side. Finding common ground and identifying areas of flexibility are crucial for reaching a compromise. Compromising isn't always easy. It may require sacrificing preferences or stepping outside one's comfort zone. It can also involve feelings of disappointment or frustration if the outcome isn't exactly what you envisioned.

In the prior example, what does the administration want? To keep all of the existing electives in the schedule, make all of the athletic practices and games as plentiful as ever, and add music (but in this case, theatre) programs as well.

What does the new theatre director want? To add a full theatre schedule for all levels and an extracurricular theatre program that rehearses four days a week.

To make it work at first, will the administration be able to keep everything they want? No. Will the theatre director get everything they want? No. It will take compromise from both sides. Both parties need to give up something so that they each may gain something. The administration can perhaps put electives on a bi-year schedule and reduce sports practices to four days a week instead of five. The theatre director can accept that theatre won't be in the full schedule just yet and can compromise down to two rehearsal days per week. It's not ideal, but it can help things work at first.

By being flexible and creative, a theatre program can find ways to squeeze into a busy school schedule and ensure that students have the opportunity to experience the joys and benefits of artistic expression.

Here are some other possible compromises:

Club: Start a small after-school theatre club first. Drama club can be an excellent low-time-commitment way of gauging interest while growing a program from the ground up.

One or the Other: Make theatre only extracurricular at first or make theatre only curricular at first. Some schools have packed day schedules while having wide-open after-school schedules. Some are the opposite. Fill in the gaps where there is room.

Compressed Classes: Instead of a full-semester or yearlong class, consider offering shorter, more focused theatre classes that last a quarter or even a few weeks. This allows students to explore different art forms without a long-term commitment.

Class Rotations: Theatre programs can share time slots with other subjects. Students would rotate through different classes, including theatre, throughout the week. This exposes them to a variety of subjects but keeps the dedicated theatre time manageable.

Before or After-School Programs: Offer arts programs outside of regular school hours before school starts or after it ends. This caters to students who might have scheduling conflicts during the day.

Weekend Workshops: Consider intensive weekend workshops for specific theatre areas like stage combat, choreography, or improv. These focused sessions allow students to delve deeper without a long-term weekly commitment.

Sharing With Others: Administrations can collaborate with other schools or theatre organizations to share staff and resources. This can help reduce costs and spread expertise.

Arts vs. Athletics

The administration seems convinced that they will be able to compromise with the current class schedule and extracurricular clubs to make theatre fit within the school. However, there is one last thing holding the administration back from approving the program. One giant, unyielding, uncompromising behemoth of a program: Athletics. The athletics program at the school brings in a lot of revenue and interest. The students fully participate, and the staff, parents, and administration all support the success of the current athletics program. The administration just cannot envision a future where the athletics program relents enough to let a theatre program grow enough to succeed. The athletics program at the school is, in a sense, too big to fail. What do you say to convince them that theatre deserves a chance? How do you show them that open and supportive communication is possible between the arts and athletics? How do you go face to face and toe to toe with the biggest, richest, most successful program at the school?

Arts vs. Athletics is a tale as old as time. Every school that has ever existed with both arts and athletics has had conflicts between the two. It is, in a way, inevitable.

People often see the many differences between athletics and the arts.
1. The primary focus of athletics is on physical development, honing athletic skills, and achieving competitive success.
2. The primary focus of the arts is on creative expression, the exploration of emotions and ideas, and the development of artistic skills.
3. Winning games or excelling in individual performance are often central goals of athletics.
4. Personal growth, self-discovery, and artistic appreciation are often central goals of the arts.
5. Athletic practices are typically highly structured and involve repetitive drills, conditioning exercises, and game strategies.
6. Theatre rehearsals have more flexibility in structure, allowing for exploration, experimentation, and individual creativity.
7. Athletics evaluations are often objective, based on measurable outcomes such as speed, strength, accuracy, and win-loss records.
8. Arts evaluation is often more subjective, focusing on artistic growth, technical skills, interpretation, and emotional expression.

However, it is important – despite those differences – to think about, focus on, and highlight the similarities between arts and athletics. If administrations see how much the two activities have in common, they just might be more willing to add theatre.

1. Both the arts and athletics require consistent practice and dedication to hone skills, improve techniques, and achieve desired outcomes.
2. Both demand focus and perseverance.
3. Both instill a desire to constantly improve and strive for excellence.
4. Both involve setting goals and working towards achieving them.
5. Both heavily rely on collaboration and teamwork. Similarly, even sports with individual stars depend on teamwork and coordination for overall success.
6. Both require effective communication and coordination. Athletes need to communicate plays and strategies, while artists in ensembles need to coordinate their movements, sounds, and performances.
7. Both contribute to a well-rounded student experience, fostering valuable life skills and a sense of accomplishment.

Let the administration know that, at the end of the day, it is not a competition. The goal for athletics coaches and arts directors shouldn't be to compete for students. There should not be a pushing and pulling back and forth. Above all, we should not want students to have to choose between one and the other. The goal should be that if students want to do both, then the school should allow them that opportunity. Coaches should not put their athletes on the bench if they are in theatre. Theatre directors should not have to give their actors smaller roles just because they are on the basketball team.

This delicate balancing act takes candid, frequent, and amicable communication between coaches and directors.

Candid: Coaches and directors should be encouraged to tell the truth about what they want to happen. Trying to sneak around and go behind each other's backs leads to mistrust and broken-down communication. If both are completely truthful, that will lead to increased trust, which in turn will lead to further compromise.

Frequent: Coaches and directors should not speak to each other only once at the beginning of the school year. If coaches and directors are not communicating at *least* once a week, something is wrong. Although we would love for the students to be constantly communicating openly with their directors and coaches, they will often drop the ball. It is up to us, the adults, to come in and communicate on their behalf. Talk with each other about what's going on. Ask: Why is this particular practice or rehearsal crucial? Are we able to share these students? You can take them for the first half, and I can take them for the second half. Can I have them for this week, and then you can have them all next week? If communication is frequent, it'll build open communication between coaches and directors, which can lead to more successful scheduling.

Amicable: Arts vs. Athletics has that "vs." in the middle for a reason. It is often a competition, a fight, a struggle, a battle. It shouldn't be. Arts and athletics should work together in the best interests of the students. Working together means doing so kindly. Buy the coach a cup of coffee for that week's discussion. Compromise a little more this week so that they might, in turn, do the same for you the following week. Go to their games from time to time so that they might go to your productions from time to time. Coach/Director discussions should never devolve into a conflict. Keep things friendly, and it'll be better for the students in the long run.

"How Much Is It Going to Cost?"

You've convinced the administration! You told them of the many benefits that theatre brings. You explained how it could best fit within the school's current schedule. Lastly, you convinced them that the theatre program and athletics program will work together to share students amicably. However, before they tell you that the theatre program is officially green-lit and before they can shake your hand, the superintendent of the school asks the age-old, spine-shivering, ever-daunting question to end all questions: "How much is it going to cost?"

Later in this book, there will be an entire chapter on "Money" that dives deep into the intricacies of revenue and expenses within a theatre program. In that chapter, it will explain how a director can put on a theatrical production for $0, how to fit within the school's budget, and how to grow revenue and donations. So, in lieu of repeating that information here, we can instead discuss how one should approach answering a question like that when it is posed by the administration.

Your answer should be three-fold: Expenses, Revenue, and Benefits, in that order. You explain the costs, then detail how you will attempt to cover the costs, and then finish with what the investment is for.

Expenses

Instead of giving them specific exact costs right upfront, it is important to keep the expenses discussion general by giving cost ranges instead. Provide cost ranges for different major categories within theatre, acknowledging that exact figures might depend on the chosen play and specific needs. Separate costs into categories like royalties/scripts, props/sets/costumes, sound/lighting, and contest fees/travel (if applicable). Every school's situation will vary wildly based on whether they have a performance space or not, theatre equipment for lights and sound or not, or a store of costumes/props/set pieces or not. It is important to keep it non-specific at first, as you do not want to pin yourself into a corner and not be able to spend more than you said in the initial meeting.

Revenue

After reviewing general expenses, immediately pivot to how those expenses will be covered. Start with cost-saving strategies for keeping show costs low (prop/set/costume donations, parent volunteers, etc.). Also, explain that any props, costumes, and most set pieces can be capital expenses for the school, meaning that they can be kept and re-used, which cuts down on costs in the future. Then, explain the plan for gaining revenue through the show itself (tickets, concessions, etc.). Finally, mention your fundraising ideas for the program to offset remaining costs. Detailed insight and information can be found in the "Money" chapter as well as the "Props/Sets/Costumes" chapter.

If the administration sees that your goal is to cost the school as little as possible while also providing a plan for how to make that work, they will be enthusiastic to say yes to you.

Benefits

Now that you've given a general outline of expenses and how to cover expenses, this is where you reiterate what a school would be getting out of an investment into a theatre program.

Highlight the many benefits seen at the beginning of this chapter.

Emphasize the program's value for the school community. Highlight benefits such as improved student performance, increased school spirit, cultural enrichment, and opportunities for artistic expression.

Frame the program as a long-term investment in students' development, fostering well-rounded individuals with valuable life skills.

Now What?

You have carefully answered the superintendent's question, "How much is it going to cost?" You explained various ranges of costs, how those costs will be covered, and what the school will be getting for its investment. You came prepared for this meeting, and it has paid off. The superintendent extends their hand, and you take it in yours to shake. The program is green-lighted, you are now officially the director, and you have the go-ahead to start crafting what your program looks like.

Now what?

The rest of the first section in this book will explain how to navigate the many decisions that a new theatre program has to make before it even gets to its first show. Read on, and let's get your program started.

 Key Takeaways

1. Upon pitching a theatre program (either to start one or to convince someone to join one), explain the benefits of theatre to a student, including how theatre equips students with a powerful combination of creative expression, communication skills, and collaborative problem-solving, fostering personal growth and enriching their academic experience.
2. Also, explain the benefits of theatre to the school community, including that it fosters creativity, collaboration, communication, and cultural appreciation, as well as enriching the school environment, student well-being, and overall school spirit.
3. Help the administration understand how to fit theatre into the curriculum by providing many examples of compromise that the school can go through to benefit the students in the long run. Make sure they understand that they "cannot expect change without change."
4. Make it clear that there will be as few athletics vs. arts conflicts as possible because you plan to keep discussions with athletic directors/coaches candid, frequent, and amicable.
5. Lastly, when answering a question about how much your program will cost, give a general description of expenses using cost ranges, followed by your plans for cost-cutting strategies, revenue, and fundraising to cover those expenses, followed by highlighting the benefits of a theatre program and why it is a worthwhile investment.

2

Elementary School, Middle School, and High School

Let's follow the journey of two imaginary students. We will call them Glinda and Elphaba.

Glinda and Elphaba are starting in 2nd grade at two different same-sized small private schools. Both girls will end up staying at that school until high school graduation. Both Glinda and Elphaba see a theatrical production at their school that ignites their fascination with theatre. Each had an older sibling (a 9th grader) in the cast of that show, and they both desire deeply to join their sibling onstage as soon as they can.

Here is where their stories diverge.

Glinda's school, Good Witch Academy, has a theatre director who offers theatrical opportunities to students from 3rd grade to 12th grade. The next year, Glinda is able to audition for and get into the spring 3rd–12th grade production of *The Wizard of Oz* as a munchkin. Her now 10th-grade sibling got cast as Dorothy, and Glinda's favorite moments were when she could dance and sing onstage in the opening Oz scene. Glinda's theatre fascination swells, and she is ready for more. She begins a yearly ritual of making sure she is in the 3rd–6th grade summer theatre camp at the school.

Two years later, as a 5th grader, Glinda became the unofficial elementary student leader as she had the most experience in theatre at that school when it came to the 3rd–5th graders in the production. Her senior sibling graduates, and Glinda feels the mantle of responsibility thrust upon her, and she knows that she will carry on her sibling's legacy.

DOI: 10.4324/9781003586302-4

Two more years later, as a 7th grader, Glinda is now able to audition for the fall 7th–12th grade production as well as the spring production. Because of her experience and growing talent, the director in the spring casts her as Annie in *Annie the Musical*. It is her first leading role. Her spark of interest in theatre from just four years ago is now a raging fire. She is beginning to think that theatre is 'her thing.'

Two more years later, as a 9th grader, Glinda now joins the high school theatre class elective. Her high school years are filled with theatre: a daily high school class, the 7th–12th grade major production in the fall, the class's fall comedy play, the 3rd–12th grade major production in the spring, the class's spring drama play, and high school summer theatre camp.

Glinda would go on to earn main roles, production team responsibilities, a theatre camp counselor job, and many awards and recognitions for her achievements in theatre. She, of course, follows her dream to become a stage actress and applies/auditions for a reputable theatre university program. With her vast experience, impressive resume, and stellar audition, she gets into the program easily with a full-ride scholarship. She will go on to become one of the most famous Broadway actresses of her day.

Alright, now, let's check in on Elphaba. Elphaba's school, Wicked Witch Prep School, has a theatre director who only offers theatre opportunities for high school students. Although she wishes she could join her theatre sibling onstage, Elphaba will not be able to as her sibling will be long graduated before she gets to hit the stage. Also, as a side note, the school can't properly put on shows like *The Wizard of Oz* and *Annie* because they don't have a young population of students to fill the roles of munchkins, orphans, and more.

Nevertheless, Elphaba's fascination with theatre is there, and she never misses an opportunity to watch a theatrical production at her school. She enjoys the productions, especially when her sibling is onstage, but without participating in theatre herself, her fascination is steadily declining.

By the time she reaches 7th grade, Elphaba joins the only activity available for her on that campus: volleyball. It turns out she is actually quite good at volleyball, and she quickly rises through the ranks to become a key player. As it is the only extracurricular activity available to her, volleyball, not theatre, becomes 'her thing.'

At last, 9th grade comes, and she is finally able to join theatre in some capacity. Although she could sign up for the theatre class elective, she instead chooses to take the P.E. elective, as she believes it will help with her growing volleyball talent. She is curious, however, as to what theatre is actually like, so she auditions for the fall 9th–12th grade production of *A Christmas Carol*. She gets cast as the Ghost of Christmas Future, the scary hooded figure who she comes to quickly realize has no lines in the play. All she will be doing is putting on some scary makeup and pointing ominously several times. The play experience is somewhat enjoyable, but not what she thought it would be like. Also, the theatre performance weekend prevented her from being at an important volleyball tournament, which was rather upsetting to her. But she does perform, and once it is done, she knows that theatre is *not* her thing. She dedicates the rest of her extra time in high school to volleyball.

Elphaba would go on to become captain of the volleyball team and an all-state player, and she would help her team win a state championship in her senior year. Her number would be retired in the rafters a few years down the road in recognition of her efforts. She gets a full-ride scholarship to play volleyball at the university in the city where she grew up. She would go on to become a member of the U.S. Olympic women's volleyball team.

Glinda and Elphaba had similar beginnings to their theatre fascination but wildly different outcomes. It was all because of what their school offered so far as theatre opportunities were concerned.

As a side note, please don't think I am saying that liking volleyball, playing volleyball, and going to college for volleyball is a bad thing at all! I don't disparage anyone for following their dream and doing what they like to do. However, as this is a theatre book and not a volleyball book, I just used volleyball as the antagonist in this imaginary story.

It is important to give students as many opportunities to pursue what they are interested in as possible. Not just theatre but music, art, sports, reading, history, math, etc. The more options we offer as early as possible, the more they will learn in that field, the more they will have experience in that field, and the more they will be able to excel in that field.

In this chapter, I'll give you examples of theatre opportunities you can provide from kindergarten to high school so that your school can offer growth and experience in theatre to stoke the flame of fascination for every student there.

Elementary School Level (K–5th)

Each section in this chapter will be split up into three different kinds of theatre opportunities per level: Curricular, Extracurricular, and Summer. In the following chapter, "Curricular and/or Extracurricular," as well as "The Summer" chapter in Part 3, I will dive deeper into the details of those different opportunities. This chapter will just serve as an overview of what to do at each level and why.

In addition, as with every chapter in this book, the information will vary in its applicability for each different school's situation. Although some of the ideas offered might work in a lot of places, that does not mean they will work at all schools. Take what you like, and leave what doesn't work.

Finally, the overall assumption is that the students in this imaginary school stay at that school from K–12th. I know that in life, it isn't always that way, and some students change schools or move. However, with this hopeful assumption that they are staying at the same school for their whole educational career, these ideas will include hooks to keep students coming back year after year. Small schools – private schools especially – have a tough time keeping students once they transfer to middle school and even more so when they transfer to high school. Other schools in the area, particularly large public schools, often offer opportunities that aren't available at the small private school. However, it is our job to provide some opportunities that will keep students coming back to the same school year after year.

Curricular

Year-long, everyday theatre classes at the elementary level are tough to execute well. Theatre fundamentals given at that young of an age need to be re-taught again and again year after year. Elementary school is a time to expose students to all of the different opportunities that will be awaiting them when they reach middle and high school. This doesn't just mean theatre; they should be shown music, art, sports, speech, foreign language, and their elementary years. They should be shown and experience the gambit of educational life so that when they do reach middle school and high school, they will have a better understanding of what they want to focus on when it comes to choosing classes and electives.

Theatre, as well as those other opportunities, if given at the elementary level, should be given either partial year or partial week.

Partial year: Provide theatre class for only one six-week (or nine-week) period. Then, when the next period comes along, students take art, then music, and so on. This exposes them to theatre for enough time so that they can get their feet wet and experience it enough to gauge their interest, for the future.

Partial week: Provide theatre class only one day out of the week instead of all five. This is an elective block schedule where on Monday, 1st grade would go to theatre, then Tuesday – art, then Wednesday – music, and so on. This allows the same staff member to teach all of the levels without filling their daily schedule with 12 classes. The theatre teacher in this scenario would teach 1st-grade theatre on Monday, 2nd grade on Tuesday, 3rd grade on Wednesday, and so forth.

In these theatre classes, the students should spend about 25% of their time on fundamentals, another 25% on games/activities, and the remaining 50% on performance.

Fundamentals: You don't want to inundate them with the fundamentals at such an early age. It can sometimes bore students and have them lose interest in the long run. Cover enough to improve their eventual performance, but don't get bogged down in it. The majority of them are not going to Broadway at five years old. Meet kids where they are to benefit them the most so that they can be successful.

Games/Activities: Elementary kiddos love games (no WAY!). This is what will keep their interest, keep them hooked, and keep them coming back for more. There are hundreds of theatre skill games for elementary school students that will not only teach them theatrical skills but also keep them enjoying the experience.

Performance: Every theatre class at any level should include a performance. Period. Imagine just teaching some fundamentals, playing some games, and then the class ends. What do they have to show for what they've learned? In art classes, they get to create artwork; in music classes, they'll put on a concert. Likewise, theatre class needs a performance. Depending on how long you have the students and how many days of the week determines how long the performance should be and what format it should take. If you have them for fewer weeks and only once a week, then a ten-minute play should do it. However, if you have them for nine weeks or a semester and more than one day a week, you can get closer to a 20–30-minute play. You don't want to give them too long of a production at this level curricularly, as the stress of maintaining a really long production at that age might cause them to become disinterested.

Core Class Plays: Elementary students can also experience theatre in their core classes. Class plays in history, English language arts (ELA), religion, and more can be great tools to not only teach them the class material but to flex their theatre muscles. Core class plays should be done in addition to elementary theatre classes; however, they should definitely be done if there is no elementary theatre class. If there are no theatre classes, these core class plays might be the only opportunity they get to try out theatre. As a theatre director, you should try your best to be present at as many of these class plays as you can. It helps with course integration and interdisciplinary cooperation but also helps you see which students have natural early talent.

It's good to expose young elementary students to theatre. Brainstorm other ways to make this possible. Bring the high school to the elementary school for performances: storytelling, puppet theatre, and reading skills. It's good to do little plays, but when they rehearse and perform the little plays, what are we trying to teach them? Theatre? Reading? Stage Presence? Acting? Confidence? Teamwork? How about all of the above?

Extracurricular

The model at Glinda's school in the introduction is my recommendation for extracurricular elementary theatre opportunities. If it is a small school with only one theatre director, only a limited number of productions can be directed and performed. As you will see later, the upper school needs to have its own production, but it is also important to include the elementary school as well.

One full extracurricular theatrical production for elementary students per year helps them experience theatre at a bigger scale while also providing opportunities for the upper school at a different time of the year. In the example, it said a 3rd–12th grade spring production, but based on what your school has going on when, it might be better for your situation to put it in the fall.

Third grade is the youngest grade that should participate in this school-wide production, and it should be full length and not just include 3rd through 6th but go all the way up to 12th grade.

> **3rd Grade:** Why not K, 1st, or 2nd? Any elementary teacher will tell you that a mountain of change goes through the elementary kiddos in just a handful of years. The difference between a 7/8-year-old 2nd grader and an 8/9-year-old 3rd grader is vast. Second graders are still in the younger half of elementary school and still have some of the habits and tendencies of their K and 1st-grade counterparts. Third graders, on the other hand, generally are starting that journey toward late-elementary maturity. They have more of a grasp on their actions, can be more independent, and tend to follow theatrical direction better than their younger counterparts. When including the younger classes (K–2nd), you run the risk of putting on just another silly, lame production (see the chapter on "Legitimacy and Excellence" for more on this topic).
>
> **Full-Length:** If you're going to put in the time to do an extracurricular production, it should be a full-length production. By full length I mean a long one-act (60+ minutes), a two-act play, a one-act junior musical, or a two-act musical. There will be a deeper dive into the differences between the types of productions you can pick in the "Picking Shows" chapter, but for now, this extracurricular production may very well be your school's biggest production of the year, maybe even its biggest event. It is a great fundraising opportunity, a community builder,

and a giant centerpiece for your theatre program. It would be a shame if the biggest event of the school year was just a dinky 35-minute one-act play. Giving the elementary students a full-length production specifically will show them different theatrical opportunities beyond what they may have experienced in classes growing up thus far.

3rd–12th: Imagine it, an eight-year-old acting side-by-side with an 18-year-old. A 3rd grader next to a senior. A theatre amateur learning from an experienced actor. These productions stretching from 3rd–12th grades are a huge opportunity for growth in the theatre program at your school. First, it is a huge community event that brings together the elementary, middle, and high school campuses. Second, it is a spotlight on your program for the school as a whole. Third, you can perform productions that you otherwise wouldn't be able to do properly if it was just a high school production. As mentioned in the intro, shows like *Annie* and *The Wizard of Oz* are great for age-spanning productions. The elementary students are the orphans, munchkins, and flying monkeys, and the high school students are the adults, witches, and mains. Can *Annie* and *The Wizard of Oz* be done at just the high school level? Sure. But I assure you when you cast an age-spanning production, it is so much easier for the audience to suspend their disbelief, and therefore they will enjoy the production infinitely more.

If there is no room in the curricular schedule and there is some room in the extracurricular schedule but not enough for a full production, that's where the idea of a drama club comes in. There are lots of great models online for drama clubs and theatre organizations that can be held from elementary all the way up to high school.

Summer

Offering theatre opportunities to elementary students outside of class and outside of extracurricular productions is important to growing program interest. Perhaps a student couldn't do an extracurricular production, but they love theatre. What else can they do? Perhaps a student is in *love* with theatre already and wants to improve their skills, where else should they go? Summer Camps are excellent opportunities for short, quick, crash courses for theatre knowledge and skills.

Note: When I say "Summer" and "Summer Camps," this does not necessarily mean it has to happen in the summer months. These opportunities can be offered during winter break, spring break, or even on weekends throughout the school year.

Although more details on the types of summer opportunities will be shared in the "Summer" chapter, for elementary specifically, hosting camps can significantly increase students' buy-in to the theatre program at your school. A short weekend or weeklong camp is just enough time to have fun, get excited, put on a show, and then keep the excitement sustained afterward.

For the elementary ages, it is recommended to keep the camps to the elementary level. If you include K, 1st, or 2nd grades, I wouldn't go any higher than a K–3rd combined camp. If you start with 3rd grade, I wouldn't go any higher than 3rd–6th grade combined camp. The reason for this is to be able to differentiate for the specific grade levels and increase their skills in this crash course better across the board. With a camp that would span K–12th, you would only be able to play games, do activities, and perform plays that kindergarteners would understand, which your high schoolers will easily grow bored with. However, this is an excellent opportunity to have some of your high school theatre leaders step up as 'camp counselors' and help out in teaching the lower school kiddos.

If all of the recommendations are applied at your school, your elementary students from 3rd–5th grade will experience theatre in the following ways throughout the year:

1. Class plays
2. A small production to be completed within a 1–9-week theatre class
3. A full-length production as a spring extracurricular for 3rd–12th grade
4. Summer camp crash course and production

If an elementary student is interested in theatre, they have plenty of opportunities to stoke that interest. If an elementary student has not yet experienced theatre, they have a lot of opportunities to start.

Middle School Level (6th–8th)

Curricular

Having a full year-round middle school theatre class depends to a large extent upon how big your school is and what the elective schedule looks like. Adding theatre classes to the different levels in school is not like it is with band/orchestra. With band or orchestra classes, when adding them to a new school, one would likely start with 6th grade the first year, then 6th and 7th grade the second year, slowly adding one grade per year over seven years until the

6th–12th grades all have it. With theatre, you'll want to try to add them to a school in reverse. Start with high school classes, then if those are successful and your theatre program is growing, add them in middle school.

Note: With the following recommendations (although I am denoting "middle school" as 6th–8th grades), the models used only refer to 7th and 8th grades. The reason for this is that at the school where this model took place, band class was mandatory ('bandatory,' in a manner of speaking) during 6th grade. It was also a full class year-round, so it did not leave room for a theatre elective. Also, the school was split into grammar (K–6th), logic (7th/8th), and rhetoric (9th–12th). Your school may differ with grade levels and who is considered to be in middle school. If you feel like these recommendations can work for your 6th graders, go for it!

With elementary school, I advised a partial-year class rotation schedule with having theatre either for one six-week period or one nine-week period a year. When it comes to middle school, more solid electives start to take shape. This is where the band and orchestra will throw their hats in the ring, so it is important to ensure that theatre still has a place at the table. A common compromise with middle school is a semester elective course. This can pair really well with choir electives if those are offered at the school as well. Middle school choir is the best time to separate the students based on gender for vocal changes and developments. It'll give the students a chance to sing in an all-boys choir or all-girls choir before they come back together in high school for SATB (soprano, alto, tenor, bass). So, when that idea is combined with theatre, in the fall, the boys take choir while the girls take theatre. Then in the spring, they swap. Other compromises can be made to make sure that theatre is on the schedule. If the administration is balking at the idea of adding theatre, compromise and reduce a yearlong course down to a semester or even a nine-week course if you have to. Anything is better than nothing.

You will want to differentiate the middle school theatre classes from the high school classes if you have both. As you'll see in the "Theatre Class" chapter, with high school classes it is recommended to have a full one-act performance every semester. With middle school theatre, those full performances should instead be replaced by more fundamentals, more games, more activities, and perhaps an in-class smaller performance. Within the class, they can also learn the fundamentals of production help by assisting with the extracurricular production or even teching for the high school class's production.

A student can read and speak well for the most part by the time they get to 6th grade. At that point, they can start learning the acting techniques, keep it surface level, growing each year.

For the middle school smaller play in class, invite the high school class and other theatre students to come by and watch.

As for core class plays, by the time middle school comes around, in-class plays are few and far between. Try to encourage the core classes to continue the practice of having history and literature-based plays in the classes like they hopefully did in elementary school. As they are in middle school now, the content can be deeper, the scripts can be longer, and the output can be better.

Extracurricular

The model of extracurricular theatre presented in the elementary school section was this: one full-length 7th–12th grade theatrical production in the fall and one full-length 3rd–12th grade theatrical production in the spring. If you stick with this tried-and-true model, theatre students who have been at the school for years and are now entering middle school will be excited to perform in the big fall play as well. Being in the upper school production will make them feel more mature, more motivated, and will have them watching the upperclass students as role models even more so as they are not as far away from them now as they used to be.

For the fall 7th–12th grade production, the plays will be able to be (although they don't have to be) more mature, more advanced, and more difficult. You would choose plays here that you wouldn't choose for the elementary students to be a part of. Some examples would be serious historical content such as *The Diary of Anne Frank* or *Number the Stars*, deep thought pieces such as *The Crucible* or *The Giver*, and common romances such as *Grease* or *Bye Bye Birdie*.

When it comes to middle schoolers in the 3rd–12th grade production in the spring, their role placements are based on the production, sure, but mostly, they are based on where they are in their development. Middle schoolers go through the most physical changes out of any grade level. You can have a 4'11" high-voiced 7th-grade boy next to a classmate who has already shot up to 6'1" and has had his vocal change. Middle schoolers in the 3rd–12th grade production allows flexibility. They are able to blend into the smaller roles with the elementary kiddos sometimes, and likewise are able to blend into the larger roles with the high schoolers at other times.

Also, with the 3rd–12th grade production, I would set the first year that a student is able to be a stage tech/lighting tech/sound tech, etc. for 7th grade. Techs need a sense of duty, maturity, and focus, and having elementary-level techs spells disaster. Introduce middle schoolers to the teching world when they get to 7th/8th grades, of course with having high schoolers as techs as well to help guide them and show them the ropes.

In some states, middle school is the first opportunity for students to compete in one-act-play competitions and other theatre skill-based events. Usually, the middle school competitions are the opposite semester as the same high school competitions. If your school has the time, room in the schedule, and resources – and taking on competitive theatre doesn't take away from the success of the program at home – competitive theatre can be a beneficial addition to the middle school extracurricular opportunities if done well. More will be discussed about competitive theatre as well as how and if to implement it in the next chapter.

Summer
Introduce a 7th–12th grade summer theatre camp (or winter or spring break, etc.). This provides the opportunity for the middle schoolers who are just now about to become 7th graders an introduction into the upper school, and it gives those just entering 9th grade a glimpse into high school leadership. For the most part, 7th graders will be able to keep up with the games and activities that a 12th grader can. If you are struggling to get enough people for camps, combining grades like this will increase your numbers. On the other hand, if you have too many people signing up, so much so that a lot of them would be without roles, or it would be too much to manage all at once, then consider splitting it into 7th–9th and 10th–12th or something similar.

Some of your most trusted 7th–8th grade leaders can also serve as counselors for the lower-grade camps if the need is there.

If all of these recommendations are applied at your school, your middle school students will have twice as many theatre opportunities as their elementary counterparts. They'll be able to participate in two extracurricular productions, be enrolled in a possibly longer and more in-depth theatre class experience, possibly compete with a play, begin flexing their muscles as techs, and not only participate in a theatre camp but help with one as well. With small schools, although some students leave for other middle schools, sometimes this is the time when a lot of new students enroll as well. With these middle school theatre opportunities, you are providing those new students with plenty of theatre to fill their year.

High School Level (9th–12th)

Curricular
Depending on the size of your school and the number of students interested in theatre, high school theatre classes can take lots of forms. There are introduction to theatre classes, acting classes, improv classes, technical theatre classes, theatre production classes, and more.

With a small school, it is unlikely that you will be able to offer more than two different theatre electives; however, if you have the population and resources, by all means, make it happen. The ideal model for high school theatre classes would be to divide it into two levels: Theatre I and Advanced Theatre. Both of these classes would be year-round and either every day of the week or approximately 180 minutes in a block schedule.

Theatre I: This foundational class is available for 9th–12th graders. Theatre I can serve as the all-encompassing year-round theatre class experience. Whether the students experienced theatre in many ways throughout elementary and middle school or this is their first experience, we have to get them all caught up to speed. More details about the structure of these classes can be found in the "Theatre Class" chapter. Suffice it to say, these classes will be filled with fundamentals, games, activities, projects, and two productions – one comedy and one drama.

If this is the only theatre class available in high school, then you will need to change up the curriculum a bit every year to accommodate those students who have taken theatre every year in high school while also making sure the new students get the essential information.

Students do not have to advance to advanced theatre after completing this course. They can choose to instead take Theatre I again if they aren't ready or willing to go to the advanced course.

Advanced Theatre: A student must have first taken Theatre I as a prerequisite for Advanced Theatre. It will therefore only be available for 10th–12th graders. Building on the foundation they got in their first theatre class, this class delves deeper into specific acting techniques, introduces students to the backstage workings of a production, and can also include playwriting and directing.

This class will usually be smaller than Theatre I and will consist of your most dedicated and gung-ho theatre kiddos. This class can also be a tremendous help for students who are seeking to pursue a career in theatre or acting.

Like with Theatre I, if you have students who take this class repeatedly, you'll need to change up the curriculum to make sure they are doing different things year after year.

Of course, every school's schedule is different and what is ideal and what is reality doesn't always line up. I said earlier, "Anything is better than nothing." That is true when it comes to high school theatre classes. If you are only able to get them for a semester, that's fine, take it and craft the best semester course you can. If you are only able to have one kind of theatre class for all four years 9th–12th, that's fine, but just make sure to differentiate the content to have four years that aren't identical. Taking a theatre course again shouldn't be like taking US History 1877–present again.

It shouldn't be the same lessons every year. Do different projects, focus on different skills, play different games, and mix up the productions. Keep it fresh for them.

Extracurricular

High school is where students are provided with the most extracurricular opportunities of their lives. They are bombarded with sports, clubs, and competitions, not to mention all of the obligations outside of school. Theatre should not have to be hidden behind the rest. Often athletics is the behemoth drawing their attention the most. As said in a previous chapter, we should not want the students to have to choose; we should allow them the opportunity to do as many electives as they want. High school students' passions and skills are solidifying, so by the time students reach 9th/10th grade, most will know if theatre is 'their thing.' However, that doesn't mean excluding students who haven't been in theatre before. I once had a senior boy who had never stepped foot on a theatrical stage before in his life. Spring of his senior year he auditioned for the big musical and earned the leading role! You never know where there are those diamonds in the rough.

As said in the prior two sections, let's stay with the extracurricular model we have: 7th–12th grade extracurricular production in the fall and 3rd–12th grade extracurricular production in the spring. High schoolers in both of these productions will be your leaders, your on-stage adults, your main characters (for the most part), and will hopefully be role models to all students younger than them.

Just as most students know whether or not theatre is 'their thing' by the time high school comes around, students who do think theatre is 'their thing' also know whether being *onstage* is 'their thing' or not. Some students absolutely *love* theatre but cannot even fathom stepping onstage into the light. Those will be your best, most passionate techs! Now, this is not a hard-and-fast rule, because I had a student who was a tech from 7th–10th grades, with stage fright at an all-time high. But after another student had to drop out of a role, the former tech kid stepped into the role at the last minute and did an excellent job. High school students will not only help as techs, but they can also be the heads of running the production side of things: light booth, sound booth, etc. A student leadership team or production team are more opportunities to add at this level.

Without diving too deep into competition theatre here (see the next chapter for more), high school is where competition theatre reaches its peak. If your school is adequately prepared to participate in competition theatre without lowering the quality of the program at home, this can be a great addition to a student's resume, trophy shelf, and letter jacket. A recommendation if there is competition theatre: Let's say the one-act competition takes place February through April in the spring. Does this mean we cancel the 3rd–12th grade production? No. Just move the production to late May, so that way, by the time the one-act competition is over or almost over, the students can begin rehearsals on the big extracurricular production. Even if there is overlap, a little bit of conflict is better than canceling something outright. If, for whatever reason, competition forces high schoolers to not be a part of the extracurricular production, then worst-case scenario, the production can be 3rd–8th grade only.

Summer
As with middle and elementary programs, summer/winter/spring breaks can be filled with extra theatre opportunities for high schoolers in the form of camps. Depending on your numbers, you may need to combine high school with middle school. However, if you have the numbers and the interest, you can have many different varieties of theatre camps at this level, including Musical Theatre, Improv, Playwriting, Production, and more.

If you have a student or students who are exceptionally passionate about theatre and are possibly considering a future in theatre, giving them an opportunity to direct a theatre camp is also an option. You as the adult would be there to supervise, of course, but the organizational skills, planning skills, and creative skills that go into planning a week or two weeks of a theatre camp could be done by an upperclass student well. This option is also great if you are unwilling or unable to plan/direct a theatre camp yourself, but still want one provided at your school.

High school is also the time that the most camps are provided by local colleges and organizations. Make sure to look around your city and state for those opportunities and post them so your students can be aware of all that is available.

If all of these recommendations are applied at your school, your high school students, if they do it all, will have their calendar filled year-round with theatre. They'll act in, tech in, and/or lead in two extracurricular productions, possibly take various levels of theatre classes during the school day year-round, compete with competitive one-act plays, become leaders and production team members, participate in, help with, and even direct a theatre camp, and more. If all of these elements are in place, the elementary students and middle school students will be keenly aware of the amount of theatre opportunities that the high schoolers have and will therefore be excitedly waiting for 9th grade.

Key Takeaways
1. For elementary school students, provide theatre in the form of partial-year, partial-week classes that are filled with games and activities, core class plays, extracurricular full-length plays starting in 3rd grade, and elementary-exclusive theatre camps.
2. For middle school students, provide theatre in the form of half-year classes, possibly separated by gender and traded with choir, which increases the fundamentals and encourages more core class plays at that level. Also add a second extracurricular play in the fall, beginner tech positions, possibly middle school–level competitions, and upper school theatre camps.
3. For high school students, provide as many theatre opportunities to them as possible, including full-year classes of varying studies and levels, leadership opportunities within productions, camps, and classes, state-level competition theatre, and different theatre camp varieties.

3

Competitive Theatre vs. At-School Theatre

Let's take the scenario from Chapter 1 and turn it around. Imagine you are a social studies teacher (with a theatre degree and certification) at a 12-year-old school. However, this time the administration approaches you instead of the other way around. Here is what the superintendent says to you:

"Hey there, we saw that you had a theatre background, and we have a favor to ask you. In the fall we want to start a theatre program, and we want you to be the director of it."

You are beyond excited. This is a dream come true.

They continue: "For now we only want to go to one-act-play competition. Back in my day at my 5A school, we had a great one-act-play program, and they went to state almost every year. I think it'll be good for our school if we go and create something like that and compete."

You are less excited now. You know (because you read this book) that starting a competitive theatre program without first having a solid foundation of a theatre program at school is a recipe for disappointment. Though you too were in one-act-play competition in high school, and are familiar with the territory, you still have your doubts about long-term success and growth.

However, in this scenario, you feel like you are not in a position to argue. It's just the end of your first year there, and you still want to stay in their good graces. So, you say, "You got it!" and get to work.

Unfortunately, by the end of the next year, you realize that your worries have become a reality. You begin to look back at what happened and why it happened:

The athletic and art competition organization that your school belongs to offers two different semesters of theatre competition: ensemble one-act play in the fall and solo and duet acting in the spring.

In the fall, you work hard at recruiting students to audition, but only six show up wanting to participate. Since theatre is brand new at this school and most of the students have never done it in any form, it's no wonder that most were wary and stayed away from jumping in and going to compete in their first-ever play. However, the show must go on, and you know that some amazing one-act plays can be done with six students. You begin rehearsals. You quickly start to realize that your actors are struggling quite a bit with rehearsals. You had chosen a simple drama, but because these students hadn't been trained in class or after-school plays, they were not keeping up with the material. It would be as if you took six students who had never played basketball a day in their life and threw them on the court expecting them to already be good at the sport. Of course, they wouldn't be. They don't have the fundamentals, they haven't been coached, they didn't grow up with it, and they've never competed in a game before.

You try your best to direct your small six-student company, and before you know it, competition day comes. Since the competition is in the middle of the day on a Tuesday, none of the other teachers or students at your school can attend to support the students, and only three of the six students' parents were available to travel to watch their child's play. One person who was able to attend, though, was the superintendent. You see him standing in the back of the auditorium, excitedly waiting for his school's theatre premiere. Your group performs fourth out of the six schools in your district, so they get the opportunity to watch the first two schools' performances before going backstage to get ready. The first two schools, who had been participating in one-act play for decades, performed exceptionally. Your students are in awe of the talent and execution. The students, besides being in awe, are now growing concerned. They were excited about their performance, but now that they've seen some of the competition, some are not too sure.

It is now your school's turn to perform. They set up the stage as rehearsed and begin the play. You watch, proud of their courage and their improvement. The play ends and is clocked at 38:29 – 91 seconds to spare. So now you wait. After disassembling the stage, getting out of costume, and coming back to the audience, your company gets to watch the sixth and final performance. It wasn't as good as the first two, but still was pretty good.

Results time: The judges announce the district runner-up (third place) followed by the second and first-place schools going on to bi-district. Your school is not one of the top three. You and your students are bummed, but it wasn't entirely unexpected. You, as director, are handed the judges' sheets in an envelope and you head for the bus. As everyone is loading up, you look at the judges' scores of your school (scored from 1 = best and 5 = worst), and your heart drops: 5, 4, 5. They got sixth place out of six. You know you have to tell the students, but you also know this will discourage some of them, perhaps from participating in the future. The cast is devastated, and the bus ride home is nearly silent.

The following week, the superintendent looks over the judges' sheets and, although discouraged, has hope for the individual events for the spring. They ask you to 'keep your chin up' and 'we'll make it happen next semester.'

Unfortunately, when next semester's interest meeting for the individual acting events arrives, only three students are in attendance, three of the six original cast members in the fall production. The other three were discouraged by the dismal outcome and didn't want a repeat of that again, so they decided not to continue with theatre. Those three unfortunately also spread their feelings to their friends, at such a small school, which means everyone heard about it, so no new students decided to join for the spring. Nevertheless, the show must go on, right? One of the spring students does a solo acting piece, and the two others decide to do a duet. The contest comes and goes, and for the same reasons as the fall production, none of the students placed. The students lacked the fundamental knowledge, training, and experience it takes for a difficult event such as that, which some would say is even more difficult for an individual than one-act play. You see the repeated disappointment on the students' faces and get the sinking feeling that none of them will be trying again next year. Well, whether they were or weren't, it doesn't matter, because at the end of the year, you meet with the superintendent, and he cuts the program. He cites budget issues and staffing assignments as the reasons, but you know it is because of his expectations versus reality. They have cut the theatre program after just one year. This will likely prevent theatre from being added to the school in any form for many years to come.

Competitive theatre is tough, especially for a director, students, and school that has not done it before. I gave you that (admittedly long) scenario to highlight the importance of building the foundations of theatre at home (at school) first before trying to compete. However, if competitive theatre is done properly and in the right timeline, it can have many benefits for the students and the school as a whole.

In this chapter, we will dive into competitive theatre and at-school theatre. We will compare and contrast them, highlight the pros and cons of both, and then discuss how (and when) to implement them in a new theatre program.

'Competing' Views

I interviewed a lot of directors for this book. Wonderful, talented, experienced directors who I consider experts in their field. They provided me with a wealth of knowledge that is peppered throughout this text. However, when it came to my interview question about "competitive vs. at-school," their answers were all over the spectrum from "you *must* compete" to "you *must never* compete." Here are some of their answers, separated based on pro-competitive vs anti-competitive.

Pro-Competitive
1. "It motivates the students."
2. "It helps the director with hard and fast deadlines."
3. "It is good to see other shows and grow."
4. "I recommend they participate in them, there are advantages for the kids, opportunities there."
5. "It goes back to the Greeks, they had play festivals and competitions, goes back thousands of years, we continue it with one-act play, film has the Oscars, TV has the Emmys, and theatre has the Tonys."
6. "We have an innate competitive nature. If a person is walking faster than you then you'll pick up your pace."
7. "A lot of kids today need validation, and they can get it by competing sometimes."
8. "If you want to compete in those programs, with competitive theatre there should be a level of professionalism, work ethic, respect. Until you get in the competitive mindset it's hard to understand the professionalism."
9. "It's a nice evaluation, other subjects have standardized tests, so why not go and have some other people watch us and put it into context."
10. "There are benefits of competitive theatre: providing students with something to work towards, a concrete goal beyond a school performance, a chance to meet other schools and groups and make connections, get outside input for improvement and possible accolades for the program that may make recruitment easier as you build the program, etc."

Texas-Specific Pro Feedback
As I am a director in Texas, a lot of the directors I interviewed were also from Texas, and some gave Texas-specific answers. Texas is not only incredibly competitive when it comes to sports, but it also is when it comes to competitive academics and fine arts

through an organization called University Interscholastic League (UIL). If you are from a state that is similar to Texas, this feedback could be for you. If your state is not as heavy into competition, ignore these.

1. "Yes, if you're going to be in Texas, you might as well compete."
2. "People in high school move around Texas for football, it will benefit them in the future sometimes that's the case too."
3. ". . . if starting high school in Texas, yes you have to, we small schools and big schools too, within the fine arts live and die on UIL. UIL is what we get our budgets from, it's how we get directors, it's how we get noticed in the community, it's how we get kids a part of our program."

Anti-Competitive
1. "Never been an advocate of competitive in the fine arts. There is no set thing that makes one better than the other. In a race, this person ran faster than that person, and there is a clear winner. But with a song, someone might say that's the greatest song ever written, one might think it is trash. It is subjective."
2. "The administration is not looking at the quality of the show, just did we place or not."
3. "Theatre is different, if the judge doesn't want a farce, they don't buy in."
4. "I'm all for adjudication, give me feedback where I can improve, but competitive doesn't make sense in the theatre realm sometimes. How can I improve, it's all subjective."
5. "Festivals are important, getting feedback in that sense. But don't chase trophies, don't just commit everything you have to bring home a little bling for the school."
6. "If you want to start trying competitive theatre, do some solo and duet events first. Have students perform duet acting scenes, solo monologue performances, speech, theatrical design, and film to get started before committing the whole program for a semester."
7. "Here's my motto for right now: 'Why be a C minus at everybody else's game when we can be an A plus at *our* game?'"
8. "It runs the risk of damaging morale if it doesn't go well. If you decide to compete, you will need to make sure you prepare the students emotionally for that potential outcome and build resilience as an ensemble."
9. "I would not advocate for competitive theatre *at first*."

These competing views sum up the reasons to do competitive theatre as well as the reasons not to. When all is said and done, it is up to you. I'm going to give you the pros and cons as well as the warnings and guidelines. Every school's situation is different. Your administration might be giving you no choice but to do competitive theatre. Your administration might not have the resources to do competitive theatre. You might be all for it but going into a program that has never had it. You might be completely against it but going into a program that has been wildly successful with it.

Take all of the these pro-competitive and anti-competitive quotes. Take all of the following pros, cons, warnings, and guidelines. Sum them up with your situation, and make your own judgement call. After all, isn't making a judgement call what competitive theatre is all about?

Firm Foundation First

Although my interviewed colleagues disagreed on whether competitive theatre was positive or negative overall, nearly all of them agreed that if you are starting a brand-new program, it is not a good idea to start competitive theatre right away until you have built a firm foundation.

The introduction scenario was chock full of reasons why a brand-new theatre program should not jump into competition right away:

> **Back in My Day:** In that scenario, the superintendent said: "For now we only want to go to one-act-play competition. Back in my day at my 5A school, we had a great one-act-play program, and they went to state almost every year. I think it'll be good for our school if we go and create something like that and compete." There are lots of reasons why just this one proposal from the superintendent is flawed in your potential situation.

This is a small school, not a 5A school, and they couldn't be more different.

"They went to state almost every year?" Is that what you and the rest of the administration are expecting? State? On average it takes a director 12 years of directing one-act plays to learn the know-how and inner workings of the competition organization to make it to state for the first time. Are they okay with waiting 12 years for it?

"For now, we only want to go to one-act-play competition." Why? Generally, competing in one-act competition is more expensive than at-school theatre when travel and competition costs are taken into consideration.

I'm Still New Here: In the intro scenario, it said, "You feel like you are not in a position to argue. It's just the end of your first year there, and you still want to stay in their good graces. So, you say, 'You got it!' and get to work." Whether it is the end of your first year, the middle of your fifteenth year, or even before your first year begins, do not ever feel like you are not in a position to argue. Remember, *they* hired *you* to direct theatre. They have appointed you as the resident expert in theatre. You are here to produce the most successful program you can, using the resources that you have. Present your case, and explain to them that there are other ways of doing things.

Build Interest First: From the scenario: "Only six show up wanting to participate. Since theatre is brand new at this school, and most of the students have never done it in any form, it's no wonder that most were wary and stayed away from jumping in and going to compete in their first-ever play." In most cases, you will find that with a brand-new theatrical program, the students will be very wary of participating at first. They don't know what it is like, and for most students, the thought of going up onstage and doing *anything* in front of their peers is a nightmare. You might think that you'll still get only six if you have at-school theatre too? Maybe, maybe not. Some don't want to or aren't eligible to compete. Some would not sign up for an unknown one-act play but would gladly sign up for a fun production like *Alice in Wonderland*. However, if you're going to have a lack of participation, it's better to start small in a classroom setting or a drama club setting and build from there.

Fundamentals First: ". . . because these students hadn't been trained in class or after-school plays, they are not keeping up with the material. It would be as if you took six students who had never played basketball a day in their life and threw them on the court expecting them to already be good at the sport." Why would anyone expect a first-year school and theatre program to do well on a competitive stage? There are exceptions to this rule, of course, but overall, competitive theatre is hard to get a foot into the door of advancing. You'll see in the "The First Show" chapter that the expectation for the first performance will be high, and it is possible to be successful and legit. However, the first competitive show and the outcome thereof can have negative effects on the future of the program, especially if they don't do well. If you have a normal at-school first show of, say, *Alice in Wonderland*, the crowd is mostly packed, they clap enthusiastically, the kids have a blast, and it is considered to them a success. But if after months of preparing a competition play as their first-ever performance and then getting last place? It would be hard for anyone to consider it a success. Build the fundamentals first. Coach them first.

Small Competition Audiences: ". . . none of the other teachers or students at your school are able to attend to support the students, and only three of the six students' parents were available to travel to watch their child's play." This is an all-too-familiar reality with competitions. Competitions are usually on weekdays during the day. The rest of the school can't attend because they are still in school. Some of the parents can't attend because they can't get out of work. It is tough for students to have their first-ever performance if hardly anyone they know sees it. They'll wonder what is the point of performing if no one they know is there to see it.

The Results: ". . . (Scored from 1 = best and 5 = worst) – Your heart drops: 5, 4, 5. They got sixth place out of six. You know you have to tell the students, but you also know this will discourage some of them, perhaps from participating in the future. The cast is devastated, and the bus ride home is nearly silent." Imagine that these students hadn't had a single theatre class before. No drama club, theatre camp, or theatre production either. Imagine that their first theatrical experience is three judges they don't know saying that they were the worst in the whole district. What do you think those students will now think of theatre? This is a really tough first impression to shake off. If there had been a few years of building up the foundation and a group of students already *loving* theatre before going to competition, if they then get last place, they will still have that foundation of love of theatre and will be more alright with the outcome.

Individual Results: For the individual and duet competitions in the scenario, ". . . none of the students placed. The students lacked the fundamental knowledge, training, and experience it takes for a difficult event such as those, which some would say is even more difficult for an individual than a one-act play." Individual competitions can be a great resource for individual growth in acting skills and a powerful addition to any aspiring performer's resume. However, without a foundation in theatre skills through a class, camp, club, or production, what are the expectations? With a one-act-play company of six or more, at least when they don't place, they don't place *together*. When an individual doesn't do well, it hurts more. The disappointment without a foundation and love of the program will likely lead to a program exodus.

In addition to the introduction scenario of this chapter, there are some other things that administration, parents, and/or students might say to you to advocate that competitive theatre must happen in a program's first year. Here are some of the things they might say and how to counter them.

> "The sports do it, so theatre can too!"

Sports are inherently competitive, theatre is not. Theatre is entertainment. Also, each sport gets to play dozens of games a year whereas theatre only gets one 'game.' It isn't a good comparison.

> "We've done it in the past, so we need to continue it."
> "That school did it in the last three years with the last director, so I have to continue it this year."

This is the most common scenario I hear from theatre teachers starting at a new school. Don't let that reasoning force you into competition. Stand your ground, tell the administration of the risks and consequences of investing so heavily into competitive theatre, and tell them of the benefits and vision for an at-school theatre program. You aren't telling them that you'll *never* direct competitive theatre, you're just saying that you need to build a solid foundation at home first before going out into the world. It's a building year (or few years).

> They don't have experience with excellent at-school theatre productions, so all they know of or have experience with is competition.

Show them. Give them that experience. Remember this phrase: "They don't know what they don't know." If administrators (or students, or parents) are used to mediocre, lame, and little productions, then that's all they will expect. It is your job to show them another way. It is your job to let them know what they don't know.

So, if you are being asked to direct a new theatre program, advocate these thoughts to the administration and ask them to be okay with holding off on competing in theatre at least at first. Ask for a few years of building a foundation of at-school skills, and then after two or three years, you promise to give competitive theatre a try. Some administrations only think year to year, but if you give them a zoomed-out five- to ten-year plan, they might get on board with you.

Don't Just Compete

Let's say you get your firm foundation built. You've grown the program through at-school productions, theatre classes, clubs, camps, and more. The population of your program has grown exponentially, as has the community interest in it. You feel like the students have developed the skills and experience needed to compete successfully. You decide to sign up your school for competition. Please do not think I am anti-competition theatre. There are so many benefits to competitive theatre, some of which are:

1. Being offered scholarships
2. Receiving individual accolades
3. Developing skills
4. Performing in a high-pressure environment
5. Receiving feedback from experienced professionals, which can help them identify areas for improvement and develop their craft
6. Exposing actors to a wider audience, including college scouts, casting directors, and other theatre professionals
7. Building college applications
8. Motivating actors to work harder and strive for excellence. The goal of winning a competition can push them to put in the extra effort to deliver their best performance.
9. Watching other schools and growing from their example

However, the point of this section is that once the decision is made to compete in theatre, to not let it become *all* of what your program is about. Unfortunately, some programs focus on their one-act-play competition year-round. If their competition is in the spring, all fall they are studying scripts, and in some cases starting rehearsals, and then all spring every day of the week is dedicated to the competition, and then whenever they are eliminated either early on in March or making it all the way to State in May, they then start studying scripts again and the loop restarts. There should be so much more to a theatre program than just the competition. If you have competitive theatre, have it be an option, one of many for your students. Some may only want to compete; great, you have that possibility for them. Some want to compete and perform at school; cool, make sure you have both at that point. Some, however, may not like competing and will only want to perform at school, so make sure that there is still a focus on those students as well.

If a director's heart and soul is in one-act-play competition, the students will know this by the way they direct everything else. Even if you have other theatre opportunities throughout the rest of the year, if half of your mind is already on one-act play, that will show in your directing, and the non-competition parts of your program will suffer.

Generally, one-act-play competitions are in one semester or the other. Let's say it's in the spring for high school and the fall for middle school. So, for the fall, make sure the high school is doing a major at-school production and that the middle schoolers are able to be a part of it or to at least help with it. Then for the spring, do the opposite, make sure the middle schoolers can have an at-school production and that the high schoolers have other opportunities in addition to one-act play.

Some school administrations – and in some cases, some directors – don't even care about the outcome of the competition. They are somehow okay with coming in last place every year. They just want to say that they are competing. Why would this be okay? Why do something if you aren't going to do it at a high level? Why not strive for the highest? Why not strive for excellence? There will be more information on this topic in the "Legitimacy and Excellence" chapter. But suffice it to say, if your school is competing, take it seriously. Learn the ropes and rules, go to the conferences, and do what you have to do to be successful. If you get fourth place, alright then, make sure you get third or higher next year. If you get to bi-district, okay, but make sure next year you make it to region. Always strive to improve your program year after year. Don't accept stagnation. Don't stick with the status quo.

 Key Takeaways
1. There are many pros and cons to competitive theatre; analyze them alongside your school's and program's situation, and then make an informed decision about whether to compete or not.
2. If the program is brand new, it is advised not to compete at first. It is important to build a firm foundation of fundamentals, interest, and experience first.
3. If your program is competing in theatre, do it at the highest possible level, not accepting year after year of failure, while also not making the competition the only part or most important part of your program.

4

Rehearsal and Performance Spaces

"All the world's a stage."

That is the famous quote from William Shakespeare's play *As You Like It*. But it is also an apropos reminder for a theatre director who is trying to find a place to rehearse and perform with little to no options on their campus.

I was rather lucky at the private school to arrive at a campus that had a building with a full dance studio in it as well as a building converted to a stage performance space. Sure, the stage had some issues, but it just took some creative adapting to overcome them. The building also had some great equipment set up in it as well. (There will be more about the equipment in that space in the "Lights, Sounds, and Music" chapter.)

However, not all theatre directors who try to start a program on their campus are so lucky. At some campuses, the only available spaces larger than a classroom are either the cafeteria or the gym. And when I say "available" that doesn't mean they are always . . . "available." More often than not, the spaces we use to rehearse in small schools are being used by other classes, sports, or organizations. We have to learn to share and to be creative with the schedule. So, if those campuses' performance spaces are the cafeteria or gym, that means that it likely can't be used for rehearsal, as it'll be used for other things most of the time. So, you have to find a place to rehearse most of the time in another space. What should that rehearsal space look like? What can you do to make it adaptable to the performance stage? When should you transfer the production to rehearse to the performance stage before opening night?

DOI: 10.4324/9781003586302-6

Some schools are in the process of expanding and are interested in making some spaces for the performing arts. But how big should they make it? What should they put in it? What else should it be used for? The main question you need to ask yourself when potentially advising them on building is: Are you building these spaces for the present or building them for the future? In general, small schools grow quickly, especially ones just getting started. So, do you build for the school population and potential audience you have now? Or do you build for the one you hope to have in the future?

The smaller a theatre performance space is, the fewer the people who come to your shows (duh). But think about it. If you only have a space that can hold 50 audience members and you perform three shows, the maximum number of community members you can have to see your show is 150. The community will get used to this, and soon, some families in the community won't even try to go to shows because they know those precious 50 seats should be for the students' families and loved ones. But say you build a space that has 200 seats; your school might not be ready for a space that size, but it might be one day. And even if it never is, imagine you have seating for 200 and three shows, but if only 100 people show up per show that is still 300 people who get to see the show rather than half that much with the smaller space. Would you rather perform for a filled audience of 50 people or a half-filled audience of 100 people?

In this chapter we'll talk about finding, building, growing, adapting, filling, and getting the full potential out of rehearsal and performance spaces for theatre.

Rehearsal Spaces

What is the ideal rehearsal space? Answer: the same stage that you'll be performing on. However, in small schools, this is not always feasible. The space you perform in is often only available the week of the performance, if that. Also, when we talk about 'rehearsal spaces,' I'm including a theatre classroom space as well, and holding theatre class on a large auditorium stage is also not realistic. So, in this part of the chapter, let's assume that you cannot rehearse on the same stage as the performance space. Let's walk around campus together to find spaces, create spaces, and possibly build spaces.

Finding Rehearsal Spaces

A Space with Space: The ideal theatre classroom and non-stage rehearsal space is one with lots of . . . *space*. If you are being given a tiny classroom, try to find something bigger. The less space there is, the less your class and production will be able to do in it. Advocate for your program and make the administration understand the importance of space in theatre. That being said, do not let limited space hold you back. If you have no choice but to use a too-small space, make the most of it, get creative, and do what you can. Do what you can with what you have.

Pillars and Flexibility: Also, pillars or columns are sometimes found in classrooms, especially in older buildings. Steel pillars sticking right in the middle of a theatre space are also not ideal, so try to stay away from those spaces. The theatre classroom and rehearsal space should also be very flexible and transformative. You should be able to have all of the student chairs in a big circle one minute, then placed in rows like an audience in front of the class stage the next.

No Desks! If you are using or being told to use a normal-sized classroom with student desks filling it, find something else. If you cannot find something else, get the desks out of there! A true theatre classroom should not have desks in it. If the class curriculum involves the need for a desk, it should be rare, and you can borrow another empty classroom with desks in it for those occasions.

Noisy Neighbors: A theatre classroom can get quite noisy sometimes. With the games, activities, projects, and performances we do regularly, there will be yelling, screaming, singing, chanting, and more. Try to stay away from normal classroom spaces that are near or sharing a wall with a 'normal' class. I've even seen s a big open area typically found in elementary schools where two classes were going on at the same time in the same space separated by a few free-standing walls with nothing to keep the noise going from one side to the other. The theatre class was constantly 'shushed' by the Spanish teacher who shared the room. If your class or production team is 'shushed,' stifled, or prevented from projecting 100%, the class activities, rehearsal, and eventually the performance will suffer. Avoid paper-thin walls and shared spaces. The ideal for this situation is a separate building.

Creating Rehearsal Spaces

Painter's Tape Is Your Best Friend: Using painter's tape on the ground of a rehearsal space to draw an exact-sized replica of the performance stage is key when you are not able to use the performance stage until tech week. You first take a measuring tape to the performance stage and start measuring and creating a blueprint on paper. Then with a partner, go to the rehearsal space and map and measure it out exactly. "But what if the rehearsal space is smaller than the performance stage?" Tape it out in chunks. One time a performance group of mine was performing a play on a very large church sanctuary stage that was 45 feet by 32 feet. Unfortunately, our rehearsal space was only 22 feet by 16 feet. So, with three different colored painter's tapes, I taped out the three thirds of the performance stage. The center part went down first, then stage right in another color, then stage left. It made for some creative blocking, but once the students knew "We are on the purple tape now, that's stage left," when they finally got to the performance space, they recognized where to go immediately. If you can rehearse your musicals in dance studios, taping out the performance stage space in front of the mirrors is an excellent way to get the choreography down.

Little Bitty Stage: This idea is especially useful for the theatre classroom space. If you have plentiful space in the theatre classroom to still have activities and put this stage in, it can be a terrific addition. One classroom I taught in had these handmade black wooden risers that were 4 feet by 8 feet. I put four of them on the ground to create a 16-foot-wide, 8-foot long, and 1-foot-tall stage against the wall in the classroom. This denoted a specific space for in-class performances. So, the students knew that if they were going to perform something, they would be up there. The whole class games and activities were in the large middle stage – less space, but any performance or presentation was up on the stage. It's only one foot high, but the students really felt a difference between just normal classroom space and a real stage.

If It Looks Like a Theatre . . .: Once you have found a space, try as much as you can to make it look like a theatre space. Paint the walls black. Tack large black or red bed sheets in a pattern on the wall to make them look like stage curtains. Have some art students create murals of the theatre masks or other theatrical artwork. Either paint one wall bright green or tack up a bright green sheet to create a green screen wall for potential filming possibilities. Adding to the Little Bitty Stage from above, hang a mini room of curtains on the sides of the stage in the front to create a quasi-backstage area where the audience can't see the performers who are about to step onto the stage. There is a wealth of great posters, educational materials, and theatre learning cutouts that, if put up professionally, properly, and with purpose, can be a fantastic addition to a theatre classroom.

Building Rehearsal Spaces

If you have the fortunate opportunity to have a say in designing, creating, and building a new rehearsal space for theatre, where do you begin?

The Big Boys: Whether in your city or the nearest big city, look up the newest built and biggest middle school or high school in the area.

Call them up and ask if you can come see their theatre spaces. Theatre classrooms have been growing and developing over the last decades. If you haven't seen some of the latest examples of brand-new theatre classrooms built in the 2010s or 2020s, do yourself a favor and go take a look. These will be typically in 5A or 6A schools. One example of a brand-new model that is being used all over is the theatre classroom black box space. This is a 40-foot by 50-foot tall room that is painted all black and has railings near the ceiling for curtains that can slide all the way around the class if needed. There are theatre lights all around the ceiling, a green room, two dressing rooms, and two large storage rooms attached. Not only that, but a door to the room also opens up and follows a ramp up to the large cafetorium stage. This room is used for the theatre classes but can also be used for black box theatre performances.

Performance Stage Adjacent: In the next section, we will discuss how best to create a performance space, but if you have the liberty to build a rehearsal space, do whatever you can to keep all of the theatre spaces on campus together and attached. The theatre classroom, dance studio, green rooms, dressing rooms, performance stage, and theatre director's office should all be accessible to one another by a short walk. Advocate to have all of the theatre areas together so that you and your performers are not wasting time walking across campus for ten minutes to get to the auditorium.

The Above Advice: If you can build your own theatre rehearsal space, try to take the advice given in the Finding Spaces and Creating Spaces sections:

1. Have a lot of open space.
2. Make sure there are no pillars in the middle of the space.
3. Ensure that chairs and furniture can be easily moved around the space flexibly.
4. Have absolutely no desks taking up space in your space.
5. Don't be within hearing distance of other classes, preferably having your own separate building or separate wing.
6. Use painter's tape (or if the stage and rehearsal space is permanent, use paint) to draw out the performance stage in the rehearsal space.
7. Create a stage area in the classroom to denote performances vs. normal activities.
8. Fill the room with things to make it as legit as possible.

Performance Spaces

Finding Performance Spaces

Colleague Relationships: This is where it is super important to be cordial, amicable, and helpful to your colleagues on your campus. This is where relationships come into play. More often than not, the space you will be performing in will be used by someone else. Is it a gymnatorium? You'll have to talk to the coaches. Is it a cafetorium? The food staff. Is it an auditorium? The choir and band director. Is it a cafegymatorium? You'll have to talk to everyone. I even had a stage space during one of my jobs that was also used by a church on Wednesdays and Sundays.

You have to work with these people to get a schedule that works for everyone. This is where compromise comes in. You won't be able to have the space as much as you want, but they also won't be able to. It's a back and forth, a give and take. Help them with their events and they'll help with yours. Give them their time when they need it, and they'll hopefully give the time to you when you need it.

What's There Already? If there isn't any form of an official "atorium" on your campus, where are the best places to find for your performances?
- Cafeteria: Cafeterias are usually the largest open spaces on any campus. The downside is that they are filled with tables and chairs, but if you coordinate it right, those chairs are turned into the audience, and you find a space for a stage either in the middle in the round or on the wall for a proscenium show.
- Gym: Gyms are also very open but are unfortunately one of the busiest rooms on campus year-round. Trying to navigate around all of the P.E. classes, athletic practices, and sports games, you will have a tough time finding a performance date, let alone some time to rehearse.
- Outside: Outside has all the space in the world, but I would advocate staying away from outside performances as much as you can. There is a time and a place for them, but do not make it a habit. Sound is next to impossible with an outdoor performance, and the audience usually cannot follow what is going on. A big pro to outside performances is teaching your students about projecting their voices.
- Sanctuary/Chapel: The worship place at a lot of private schools usually either is a church or resembles a church. Church altars can be transformed into stages and pews into audience seats.

- Theatre Classroom: If there is just not a space available or you have little choice, sometimes the best option is what you have been using for rehearsal. If you hopefully found an ideal space described in the last section, a large open theatre classroom can be transformed into a performance space if needs be.

Go Searching: The perfect space is not going to find you. You have to find it. Some campuses just do not have performance spaces worthy of your performance. Well then, it's time to go out of campus and look around town. Churches, other schools, and community theatres all are suitable places to borrow or rent their space for your performance.

Creating Performance Spaces

Build Your Nest: The ideal situation for any theatre company is to be able to move into the theatre performance space fully and not have to worry about moving things around or cleaning up their stuff for other organizations. At a small school, this usually won't be the case. You'll have to clear the room and stage for the other classes, chapel, sports, what have you. However, if you have a workspace you can be in that you can stay in and know how to utilize it efficiently, it will save you so much time in the long run. Sometimes it takes 30–60 minutes to set up a space and then another 30–60 minutes to break it all back down. Try to advocate that you can 'move in' to your performance space for at least tech week so that you are not spending precious rehearsal time setting up and tearing down.

Black Box Gym: Most schools will have a gym. Aside from the scheduling issues stated earlier, if you can acquire the gym for a performance, you can get really creative as to how to use it for a great performance. You can have the audience in the bleachers and the actors on the floor. But have you thought of it the other way around? The audience is on the floor and the bleachers as the stage. This can make for some unique blocking and can work well with some pieces. Also, if you leave the bleachers out, you can set up a black box in the center of the gym court with the audience sitting in chairs all around. Get some lighting trees or even lamps with extension cords and you are off to the races.

No Excuses: Don't make excuses. Nobody has time for excuses. You will never have a perfect situation. Plan around what you have. Don't spend time 'wishing' or saying things like, "Well, if we only had 'x', then we could do it." Get creative. Build staging out of tables and chairs. Build a stage with your own two hands out of some two-by-fours. It is all about ownership. Advocate for your program. Fight for more. But at the end of the day, you have what you have, and you have to make the best of it. Strive for excellence. Strive for legitimacy. If you do, the rest will follow.

Building Performance Spaces

Function Over Form: If you are lucky enough to get to design and build a new theatre space, know that money is not ever going to be unlimited. There will be a budget, and the powers that be will not want to go over the budget. You will seldom have enough to create the perfect space. So, if you could spend money on one of the following two things, which do you choose to spend on: (1) how the performance space looks or (2) how the performance space works? A thousand times, spend on how the performance space functions over what its form is. Some administrators and those helping build the space worry too much about how the auditorium looks for the audience. You, as theatre director, need to advocate for your program and ensure them that how the theatre *works* is much more vitally important. The money should be going toward the stage functionality, the lighting, the sound, the tech, and the backstage spaces. It doesn't matter if you have the most beautiful room in the world; if the production team is not given what they need to make a great show, then it won't be a great show.

Tech Over Size: Again, if you could only choose one, do you choose to spend the majority of the money on creating a bigger stage space or on the lighting/sound/equipment for the stage space? Always invest in the tech over a larger stage. Some of the best performances I've ever seen have been on tiny stages. It is not the size of the stage that counts as much as what you use to light it, to make it sound good, and to make it work well for the production. There will be more specifics on tech in the "Lights, Sounds, and Music" chapter, but if you are given the choice between a bigger stage and better mics, lights, sound equipment, communication devices, lightboards, soundboards, software, and projectors, put the money toward what will make the production look and sound great. You should much rather want to direct a show on a small stage with great equipment than on a large stage with old or cheap equipment.

Build for Where You Want to Be: As said in the intro, don't build an audience space that will pack the house the day it opens. Build a larger audience space than you'll be able to fill today but that you'll hopefully be able to fill tomorrow. The hope for any small school is growth, and if you can only get 100 people in your audience today, build for an audience of 200. If the audience thinks there won't be room or that it'll be too crowded, some will choose not to come. Be optimistic about how many people can eventually be in the audience. A larger audience space can also help with school presentations and outside-of-school events.

Back to the Big Boys: Like with the rehearsal spaces, go see what the large public schools are building new nowadays. Some 6A theatre spaces rival big-city Broadway venues. But even aside from looking at the big boys, take inspiration from schools your size as well. See what the other small and private schools in the area are doing. Some have had to be creative with the spaces they have created. You'll likely not have a blank check to create the biggest, most grand space anyone has ever seen. So, see what the little guys are doing as well, and create the best you can with what you have.

Key Takeaways

1. Find, create, and build a rehearsal space and theatre classroom that has lots of space, no pillars or desks, which doesn't disrupt other classes, with a painter's tape replica of the performance stage, modeled after newly built big school spaces, and that is adjacent to the performance space.
2. Find a performance space on campus, such as the cafeteria, gym, or chapel, with open and friendly communication with colleagues or off campus such as a church or other school.
3. Create unique performance spaces where you don't need to move in and out every day, transforming areas such as the gym into a black box theatre, and at the end of the day, don't make excuses for not having the perfect space.
4. If you have the opportunity to build a performance space, make sure to invest in how it works over how it looks. Invest in the tech that makes it look and sound good rather than how big the stage is, that has a larger audience area to prepare for the future, and is modeled after some of the new additions in your town, both at the big schools and the small ones.

5

Getting Everyone Interested

So, your program has now officially started. You've pitched it to the administration, and they approved it. You've figured out the blend of curricular and extracurricular theatre and you've decided to refrain from competitive theatre at first. You've also developed a program filled with opportunities for all three levels from elementary to high school that will expand one year at a time and have secured a proper rehearsal space and performance space. Everything is set and in place. You are ready for the first day of school.

The first day of school comes and students discover that there is now a theatre program at the school . . .

STOP. There's your first big mistake. If you get to the first day of school and people in your school community don't yet know about the new theatre program, you are already behind the ball and set up for failure. Let's try this again, shall we?

Everything is set and in place. It is the end of the last school year, and you make announcements to the whole school community at every level about the impending theatre program coming in the fall. Excitement and anticipation grow. Then you get to the first day of school . . .

STOP. There's another mistake. You announce it at the end of May and then wait until the first day of school to say anything else? Do you know how much students and parents forget over the summer? From the top!

Everything is set and in place. The announcements have been made at the end of the school year informing the students. Throughout the summer, you do a social media blast on the school's website, begin signing up students for

DOI: 10.4324/9781003586302-7

theatre class, and have a theatre interest and information meeting a couple of weeks before school starts. The first day of school comes, and although the returning students are aware and excited about the program, brand-new students and parents at the school have no idea that the school was adding a theatre program . . .

STOP. Yet another misstep.

You got the returning families to learn about the program, but you didn't advertise it to the potential and incoming new families? Some families consider the fine and performing arts to be a crucial part of the education of their children. If those families are deciding between two private schools in town, and one has a program and one does not, guess which one they'll go with?

You can have the perfect program set up. You can have everything scheduled and put into place ready for success. You can even have the best, most high-tech, greatest performance space in town. However, if you don't have anyone interested in the program, none of that matters. One of my favorite phrases that I sometimes say at the end of a production to the audience is, "We thank you, the audience, most of all because, without you, we would just be people dressed up singing and dancing in an empty room." How do you fill up the room? More importantly, how do you fill up the stage?

In this chapter, we'll talk about how to best and most effectively get people interested in not only a new theatre program but any theatre program. We'll figure out how to get the students on the stage, the parents to help behind the scenes, the colleagues to support their students, and the whole community in the audience.

Getting Students Interested

The student section of this chapter will be split up into two sections: Brand-New Program and Already Established Program. I'll first explain some strategies for getting students interested in a new theatre program in its first year, then explain programs that have already been around for a while. Note: Some of the strategies will work in both cases.

Students: Brand-New Program

Unlike an already established program, a new program usually doesn't have the luxury of gearing the students up for theatre in the years preceding 6th grade (see the "Already Established Program" section). However, except in some rare cases, your school administration (and hopefully you) will know the theatre program will be starting at least the school year before it starts, if not before. So, let's say the administration and board give you the green light to start next year's theatre program in January. That gives you roughly eight months to prepare, but that is also eight months of recruitment. This information should not remain a secret to the rest of the community; it should be told to as many people as possible as soon as possible. So, you have eight months, what can you do to maximize student interest?

>**Admin Inform Prospective Students:** In some small schools, once the spring rolls around, it is the time to find new students to sign up for the following school year. This usually involves paperwork, a tour, and an interview. During that tour and interview is a crucial time for the admin, or whoever is giving the tour and/or interview, to inform the incoming students about the new program. Also, on the tour, they can make it a point to stop by your room (if you are working there at that point) so that you can explain the program in even more detail.
>
>**Initial Announcement:** As soon as the green light is given, the students should be told. The announcement should be school-wide to get the community interested. The announcement should be as big and official as possible, with all the bells and whistles you can think of. It should feel like you are about to open a whole new building for the school next year.
>
>**Visiting Theatre Performance:** Invite another school or theatre group in the area to come and perform for the school to show what a theatre program can turn into. The bigger and more impressive the show, the better. You can also have your students travel to another campus or theatre for a show. Bonus points if the show is something the students will be familiar with, such as *The Lightning Thief*, a Disney show, *Hamilton*, etc. If the students can see the potential of what good theatre can be, they'll be more interested in jumping in.
>
>**Summer New Student Interest Meeting:** This is a chance to call all of the incoming new students together to catch them up on everything they missed. They will have likely missed all of the above, so it is crash course time. In this meeting, you can tell them the plan for theatre and all that it will entail. This meeting will be admittedly less involved than all of the above. However, it is very important that the new incoming students are as informed as current students.

Students: Already Established Program

Any of the suggestions in the "Brand-New Program" section can be adapted and used for an already established program. However, the goal will be less about informing them of the theatre program's existence and more about showing them what they have already seen and heard. Here are some suggestions for how to get students interested once the program is already up and running.

Incentivize Theatre Exposure: This one will take a bit of help from the classroom teachers. Do we want the younger students to be interested in theatre? Well, give them a reward if they go expose themselves to theatre. Extra credit for going to the high school show. Drop a low grade for going to a community theatre play. Extra recess for anyone who can bring a ticket stub and program from any theatrical performance. Have them go out into the world and watch what theatre can be. They'll get something extra for it, but they'll also see what theatre has to offer.

Improv Night: Host an open improv night where students can participate in fun, low-pressure games that showcase their comedic timing and creativity. This is a great way to break down inhibitions and show the fun side of theatre.

Backstage Pass Tours: Offer guided tours of the theatre space, showcasing the technical aspects like lighting, sound, and set design. Let students see the magic behind the curtain and pique their curiosity about the different areas of theatre production.

Monologue Slam: Organize a competition where students perform monologues from their favorite plays or movies. This allows them to focus on acting and get comfortable onstage.

"Theatre for a Cause" Event: Choose a social issue students care about and organize a short play or performance night where proceeds go to a related charity. This taps into their desire to make a difference and showcases the power of theatre to address real-world issues.

"Meet the Cast" Q&A Sessions: For upcoming productions, host Q&A sessions where students can interact with the cast and crew. This personalizes the experience and allows aspiring actors to ask questions and see themselves onstage one day.

"Theatre for All" Workshops: Offer introductory workshops in acting, improvisation, or stagecraft that are open to students with no prior experience. This is a low-pressure way to introduce them to the basics and spark their interest.

Getting Parents Interested

There is an old phrase in education: "If the kids are happy, the parents are happy." Well, that phrase works the other way around as well. If the parents are happy about an opportunity that their kid can do, then they will be enthusiastic about letting them do it. Your students' parents will come from all different backgrounds and experiences. Some may have been sports stars in their day, some may have just been focused on academics, and others may have some theatre experience.

As for parents who weren't in theatre before, they'll need as much help and guidance as the students to learn the ropes. They might know next to nothing about theatre, as perhaps some of their schools also didn't have a theatre program. Bring them along in the process. Have them attend an instrument petting zoo with their own kid, for example. Imagine a dad and their son trying to buzz on trombone and trumpet mouthpieces together and making strange buzzing noises together. You'd better believe they are going to be talking and laughing about that shared experience later.

For those parents who have had theatre experience, you want to use that to your advantage in having those parents help encourage the students who might be on the fence. So, at an interest meeting with the parents invited, ask if any parents have been in theatre. Have them tell the room what plays they have been in, what roles they played, and what kind of experience they had overall. If kiddos, especially their own, see that their parents were a part of this too, they'll be less reticent to join. You could even invite a few experienced parent volunteers to perform a scene in front of the kids.

Regardless of whether their parents were in theatre or not, they should still be informed of all of the benefits of theatre (as discussed in Chapter 1). If the parents are made aware of the long-term academic, physiological, and social benefits that come with participating in theatre, that will be your best hook for getting them involved.

The bottom line with parents is this: You as the director can tell them everything, you can explain theatre until your face turns blue, and you can bring them to every interest meeting you host, but the one thing that will go the longest way to getting them on board, enthusiastic, and 'pulling out their checkbook' is seeing the excitement and enthusiasm in their child's face. For tips on getting that excitement and enthusiasm, re-read the last section on "Getting Students Interested." As you will see with the other sections in this chapter, interest in theatre starts and ends with the students. Get them interested, and the rest will follow.

Getting Colleagues Interested

Three students named Angelica, Eliza, and Peggy walk into their history classroom with their favorite teacher, Mr. Hamilton. Angelica, the school's basketball star, is spotted by Mr. Hamilton first: "Hello there, Angelica! I was at your game last night. You played so well in the post! Keep it up and you'll go on to play for Baylor!" Angelica, filled with pride and appreciation, takes her seat. Eliza, the first-chair violinist in the school orchestra, is next: "Hey, Eliza! I was at your concert this weekend. You did so well! I don't know how you played all of those fast notes; you have some real talent, young lady!"

Eliza, smiling from ear to ear, thanks her teacher and takes her seat next to Angelica. Peggy, who's in the school's new theatre program, passes Mr. Hamilton's desk: "Good morning, Peggy. Please take your seat, we are about to begin." Peggy, disappointed, takes her seat with the others. Peggy and the new theatre program had their big first show the past week, but Mr. Hamilton wasn't there to support.

Teachers are asked to do a lot. (Understatement of the year?) During their normal school hours from approximately 8–4, they work extremely hard, with little reprieve, for not enough pay. Why then, should we expect them to take their precious little free time to come back to the school after p.m. to go to a game, concert, or play? Here's why: It helps them, their classes, and their students. If a teacher doesn't go to anything provided at the school, they won't know what is going on with the kids, they won't really understand how busy the students often are after school, and they won't be able to connect with the students by having shared an experience. Also, if teachers don't know what is going on outside of the classroom, there may be problems inside the classroom. Imagine a teacher scheduling a major test the morning after a game where the students were out until 10 p.m. Imagine a teacher assigning extensive homework on the night when half of their students will be in the theatre. Imagine a teacher having a big group project due the morning after the band concert the students have been preparing for for three months.

Explain these scenarios to your colleagues. Tell them of the many benefits of going to see their students' games, productions, and concerts. Are you expecting them to be at every single basketball game or every concert? No. But as each theatrical performance comes along, that is where you need to encourage your colleagues to take the time to come see their students perform. This is especially important in the first few years of a program. Your colleagues have likely been to one of their students' sports games, but going to a musical might be completely foreign to them.

Here are some things you can do to help encourage colleagues to become interested in theatre and theatre performances:
1. Post the show flyers in the teacher break rooms. (As I will talk about in the "Advertisements, Tickets, and Programs" chapter, post an *annoying* amount of very professional-looking flyers. When teachers can't look anywhere without being able to see a flyer, they will not be able to use the excuse, "I didn't know about the show!")
2. Announce the show a few times in staff meetings.
3. Have students personally invite their teachers. (This one goes a long way.)
4. Chat with colleagues about it during lunch or in passing.

5. Get the performances scheduled and into the official calendars before the beginning of the school year so that they are on every teacher's desk calendar all year round.
6. Create a theatre performance calendar, similar to a football game schedule poster that the athletics department makes, to put right alongside the sports schedule. (This one will show visually just how many opportunities they have to catch a basketball game (12–20 games a year) right next to a theatre schedule's few opportunities (only two to four shows a year).
7. Make sure to have yourself or a student make the announcements for the show on the intercom (or TV, or YouTube live cast, or however you do announcements) in the days leading up to it.

It is your job to make sure everyone knows about a show, using as many means as possible. It will ultimately be up to them if they come. However, to echo what I was saying at the end of the parents section, you, as director, can make all the announcements possible, make an even bigger calendar than all the rest, and even post a hundred flyers in each teacher's classroom, but the one thing that will go the longest way to getting teachers interested in theatre and enthusiastic to attend shows is seeing the excitement and enthusiasm on the faces of the students they teach every day. The best advertising beyond all else is an excited student walking up to a teacher and personally inviting them to the show.

Getting the Community Interested

A director I knew who had a great legacy of starting, growing, and flourishing a program at a small school in town decided to change jobs. They were hired by the administration at their new job in early March to become a director at a private Catholic school just down the road. This century-old school had a program in the past, but it had dwindled to nonexistent less than a decade before. It was his job to rejuvenate and rebuild the program, a task he felt like he was up for. Class wouldn't start until the fall, but the director knew how important it was to get the word out to the community as soon as possible. The director asked the administration to make an announcement of their hiring, including a picture and bio. He also asked if he could come make some announcements and possibly hold a few interest meetings later in that spring semester. Lastly, the director requested that he could record a neat video preview of the program. including music, effects, and the director introducing themselves to the community and explaining all that would be coming with the program.

Unfortunately, the administration got too busy in the spring to accommodate his requests. Then once summer came, the administration was still too busy either wrapping up the last year, prepping for the next year, or on vacation. Finally, one week before school started, the administration posted a "Meet the New Teacher" post on Facebook for the director alongside six other incoming teachers. The post got buried amidst the others and was barely a 'blip' for informing the community of the restarted program. By the time the fall semester was halfway through, most of the community was still not even aware that the performing arts were back at the school, let alone that there was a show coming up.

In this true-story example, the administration did that new director a massive disservice. Instead of going into the school year on the right foot, ten steps ahead, and set up for success, he was on the back foot, ten steps behind, and set up for failure. The new program would end up not continuing the following school year.

When I say 'getting the community interested,' who do I mean by that? Who is the 'community'? Well, the community is, in a word, *everyone*. It is the students who aren't in theatre, the other parents of the school (the ones who don't have kids in theatre), the administration, the staff, the faculty, the alumni, the board members, and anyone else tied to the school in some way. So, even if we get a sizable number of students into a theatre show, all of their parents to come to the show, and every colleague of yours to be there too, the audience will still be mostly empty. How do we fill the seats? How do we make the theatre performances a community event?

> **All of the Above:** Everything listed above in the student, parent, and colleague sections applies to the community as well. Announcements, flyers, posters, and calendars are for all in the community to see. Perform the tasks of getting the students, parents, and colleagues interested, do it in a wide over-arching way, and the rest of the community will have the chance to follow.
>
> **Social Media:** Social media, for all its faults, is the way word is spread in this day and age. Hopefully, your school has some form of social media, if not several. Your theatrical performances and opportunities should be 'blasted out' on all the school's social media accounts. If the person in charge of them forgets to do them or is unwilling to send so many, offer to do a 'social media takeover' of the accounts for the week leading up to the concert.
>
> **Preview Performance:** There will be more information on this in the "Other Performance Opportunities" chapter, but in summary, have your play cast perform a scene or your musical cast perform a song or two

from the musical at a community event: a pep rally, lunchtime, chapel, or fundraising event to get more interest for the concert. The community is already at these events. It will be hard to ignore a 30-person ensemble chorus line high-kicking proudly on the stage. They'll have no choice but to take notice.

Letter to the Board: I've found that there are two types of school boards out there: (1) the board that has its ear to the ground, is very involved in the community, and is very visible at school events; or (2) the board that just meets once a month, doesn't know much about what is going on so far as the day-to-day is concerned, and can hardly be spotted at any school events. If your board is in the first category, then you will have an easier time getting them interested and involved in the theatre program. You'll likely see them around and at other events and can invite them to shows yourself. However, if your board is more in the second column, it might take more to reach them. It is important to get the board 'on board' because if the board of the school knows about the program firsthand, that means possibly more money, more support, and program longevity. A neat trick I learned is to have your students write a 'letter to the board.' Say there are six board members: There should be six different letters from six different students (or groups of students). Their letters should be personal invites to a show, along with words of appreciation for their work and support in getting the theatre program up and running. The school will have the board members' addresses. Put the letters in envelopes, put postage on them, and send them on their way. A personally written letter nowadays can go a long way.

The Wider Community: Let's say you get every student, parent, colleague, administrator, and board member of your school to your concert and there are *still* seats left unfilled (that darn 3,000-seat auditorium . . .). Who do you go to next to fill the rest of the seats? The wider community, those who are outside of your school. This is particularly important when it comes to major performances that will be particularly well done or special. Take the flyers and put them in local businesses and coffee shops. Have the area schools, and particularly their theatre directors, announce the performance and offer extra credit for going to it. Put an ad in the local paper, magazine, or city website. Send your students on an 'advertisement spree' around town, where they invite members of their churches, colleagues of their parents, extended family members, and more.

There are lots of ways to get the word out there, it just takes time and effort. But if you put in that time and effort, you'll fill up that 3,000-seat auditorium before you know it.

Key Takeaways
1. When the program is approved: announce early, announce often, and announce to everyone.
2. When starting a new theatre program: make sure the students know the logistics, the ins and outs, the expectations, and what the future may look like before day one of the school year.
3. Get the parents on board by informing them about theatre just as much as the students, let them know the many benefits for their students, and most importantly, if you get the students interested and excited, the parents will be too.
4. Let your colleagues know of the benefits of attending their students' shows and let them know when the performances are scheduled, using any means necessary including, most importantly, a personal invitation from the students.
5. Make sure the school community and wider community are aware of the theatre program and the performances using social media 'blasts,' giving preview performances, sending personal written letters, and going on 'advertisement sprees' around town.

6

The First Show

"This should be the worst performance of this show you do."

That is a phrase that I tell my theatre company during the rehearsal of their first full run-through of the production. It is not to say that the performance will be *bad*, per se, but that they should always strive to improve every single time they do it.

The same goes for you directing shows as a director. Each show should be better than the last one. You learn from your mistakes, double down on the things that went well, and improve every time.

We know that when opening night comes, the students are going to be nervous. However, we also know that the director will be as nervous as them – or even more so in some cases. This is the big premiere! This will, for lack of a better phrase, 'set the stage' for the future of the program. The director knows that if things go poorly, the program – and potentially their job – might be in jeopardy.

For you veteran theatre directors out there, you might be thinking back to your first show and cringing at the thought of all the things your present self would have done better. But just because you cringe, just because it could have been done better, does that necessarily mean that it has to be bad?

The first show is not the end-all-be-all, it is not life-or-death; however, it is especially important for a theatre program that is just getting started. Therefore, you should work as hard as you can and as long as you can to make that first show as good as it can be at that time with the resources and people you have.

DOI: 10.4324/9781003586302-8

Which episode of a television series do they spend the most time on? Is it the series finale? Wrapping everything up in a nice bow with a satisfying ending. Or how about the episode with the most special effects in it? Trying to emulate Hollywood movie-style effects with a tenth of their budget. The answer is the pilot. The first episode of the series. Producers, writers, and creators spend months, even years, developing just the very first episode. In that business the pilot is make-or-break. There have been far more pilots than there ever have been full television series. Those creators have just 22 (or 42) minutes to convince the network execs, the critics, and the audience watching that this show is worth going on to the second episode.

The same goes for late-night talk show hosts. Take James Corden, for example. Corden was named the new host of "The Late Late Show" on September 8, 2014, but his world premiere pilot episode wasn't until March 23, 2015. That means that he and his producers had six-and-a-half months to prepare their show, but most importantly, to prepare their first episode. James Corden was relatively unknown when he became the host. So not only would the first episode be a premiere of what type of show his version of "The Late Late Show" was going to be, but also a premiere of him as a person to the country. The pilot consisted of, amongst other things, Corden and Tom Hanks singing and acting their way through Hanks' career, cameos from many stars, including Billy Crystal, Simon Cowell, and Arnold Schwarzenegger, and a piano-backed ballad sung by the host to close out the first show, solidifying the show's emphasis on performative segments. Corden had a great premiere, and viewership grew over the years – flocking to his unique, fun, and funny take on late-night comedy.

Now, had Corden not had a great first show, does that mean that he would have been instantly cancelled? No. But it would have taken longer to get the audience members back who turned off the show after the first episode. Back to normal television series: Have there been successful shows that had less-than-successful pilot episodes? Yes. But what made Corden's first episode good, and what can make your first show good, is the potential for positive growth. The pilot episode of the show might not be the best episode of the series or even the season, but the producer and audience see it for its potential and can see that it has a firm foundation on which to grow. Your first theatre production needs to accomplish the same things: It needs to be solid, have a firm foundation, and show the whole school community that it has the potential for positive growth.

In this chapter, we will discuss how important the first impression of a theatre program's first show is, show how to properly set the stage for success, and consider several tips, tricks, and ideas on how to start your program off strong.

Setting the Stage (Before the First Show)

Let's say you have a one-night-only opening night of your show. That means you have two hours to convince the students, parents, administrators, and community what your program can do. Two hours. But how many hours did you put in to prepare for those two hours?

In theatre, we have a couple of months to get a show ready. But your preparation for this first show should not start on day one of rehearsal. Your preparation for your very first show should start the moment you are hired as director. The thoughts, preparations, ideas, advertisements, and legwork that need to be put in to get everyone ready for that opening night are going to be more than any of your other shows. Here are several things you can do to help set the stage for your first show.

> **Put in the Extra Hours:** Work exceedingly hard to get this show ready. The work-life balance is always tough throughout a career. You'll want to take it easy generally to not get burned out too early. However, with your first show, you'll want to put in a lot more extra hours to make sure everything is as perfect as can be. For your first show, you will likely not have the extra help and assistance and parent helpers that you'll accrue throughout your program. Therefore, a lot will be left up to you to finish, whether it be designing sets, building props, painting a backdrop, or setting up the green room. Work overtime. Work until it is done.
>
> **Research the Past:** If this is your first year in an already existing program, blow them away, and show them something new. You should do your research by talking to the previous directors and current administrators, and looking through past yearbooks to see what shows they have done in the past, what they were like, what they had and didn't have, and make sure to try to improve on what was there before while still holding the traditions that the students might still hold dear.
>
> **Your Pilot Episode:** This is your pilot. The first show is something you should be thinking about the moment you are hired. Spend the money, time, energy, and resources to make it as good of a first impression as you can.
>
> **Tradition . . . Tradition:** This is the time to know what traditions you want to put in place. It is harder to add things steadily over the years, but if you have certain things in your first show, it's something in your program you can say: "We've had it since our first show!" Things like tickets and programs (see that chapter for more), unique concessions, pre-show entertainment, reception before or after, and more.

Recognizable Title: Just like your hooks for the students, the first show should be a hook for the community as a whole. You shouldn't pick a completely unknown (except to theatre insiders) play as your first show. It should be something the community can recognize by names such as *Peter Pan*, *Snow White*, *A Christmas Carol*, *Alice in Wonderland*, *Robin Hood*, or *The Three Musketeers*, to name a few. There will be more information about selecting 'hooking' shows in the "Picking Shows" chapter.

Now Hear This: Get copious amounts of advertisements out there to set expectations. Create posters, flyers, and social media campaigns to generate interest in your production.

Community-Wide Audience: Make sure the whole school is invited, even if it is just a high school production. Make sure the elementary school and middle school are fully aware of the show and that they also know that they are more than welcome to come and enjoy the program.

Plan Audience Seating: Make sure the performance space is set up perfectly to accommodate your audience. Think about people getting up and sitting back down. Think about how the actors might need to navigate to the stage from the audience. Think about sight lines and obscured views.

Spend the Most: The first show is not the time to pinch pennies. You should spend more money on your first show than any other show that year. In typical years, once your program gets going, usually the 'big spring musical' is the most expensive. However, for your first year, it is important to spend the money to make a good impression. Spend the extra money on props, sets, costumes, and anything else that makes the show look and sound good. Do this even if it makes your program's budget go in the hole. It's okay, you'll build it back up the rest of the year with revenue and donations (see the "Money" chapter).

What Did They Say? Make sure your actors can be seen and heard. There is nothing worse than going to a show that should be amazing but because of mic, sound, light, and/or music issues, the actors can't be understood by the audience. It'll make a bad impression right away that your shows can't be understood. Take a look at the "Light, Sound, and Music" chapter for more tips.

All Ages: The first show should be something for all ages. You will have the opportunity to direct shows that have more mature themes in them in your program, but don't do it for your first one. Stick to a rated G or PG show for your premiere to the community. That way the elementary school will be able to join with no problem.

Extra Credit: If the content of the play is somehow connected to another class either historically or via literature, communicate with your history and/or English teaching colleagues about the show. You can encourage them to offer an assignment or extra credit for their students to see the show. Also, offer extra credit to your theatre students who are not in the show to come and watch it and report on it to you. The more students that come, the more parents come, and then the more interest grows in your program.

You Are Cordially Invited: Personally invite the administrators to the show. A lot of directors would rather not have the administrators in the audience for several reasons. They might be nervous about what they might think, nervous that they would be nitpicking the show apart, and more. It is vitally important that administrators come to your shows, however, especially in your first year, and here's why. Imagine that the administrators don't come to any of your shows throughout the whole year. Then at the end of that year, they choose not to renew your contract. That wouldn't make sense. How could they make that kind of judgement call without having seen the product of your labors? If they are at the shows, there is no excuse in that case.

You Are Coachially Invited: Invite the coaches. That's right, they should be there too. If the athletic coaches see the product of a theatre production's hard work and see how much the students (especially the athletes in the production) are enjoying it, they might be more flexible when it comes to letting students leave practice to go to rehearsal.

What First Show? Although this is your first show, it should not look or sound like a typical first show. Meaning, if someone were to come watch the show and not know it was the first show of the program or the first show of your direction at that school, they wouldn't be able to tell that, and they might think that this program has been successfully running for years. Just because it is your first show doesn't mean it's okay to squeak by on a few things. Don't let things go in the hopes of getting it together in future shows. You should leave the audience in awe of how you staged such a well-put-together production in just your first two to three months there. Strive for top-notch quality production value. Even with limited resources, endeavor to put on a visually appealing and well-rehearsed performance.

Ready? This goes without saying about any of your productions, but make sure it is going to be ready on time. There is nothing worse than all the hype, build-up, advertisements, and excitement to end up with a show that is stumbling across the finish line. Make sure you have crafted your schedule so that your production will certainly be absolutely ready for opening night. See "The Schedule" chapter for more.

Starting Strong (During the First Show)

You got hired and started working on your first show right away. You worked through the summer, into the fall, and for months to get this one-night-only first show ready. But now it is here, the two hours that you have been planning for six months.

Here are some tips and tricks to help make your first show more memorable, more legitimate, and more successful.

The Carrie Curse: First impressions are everything in the performing arts. Broadway critics send out their thoughts on the show the day of their opening night. Some professional shows have closed within two weeks because of a bad first impression – the most infamous example of this was with "Carrie The Musical," which closed its doors after just three days back in 1988. Do not underestimate the power of a first impression. It is the first time people will be seeing you, hearing you, seeing your program, hearing your program. Impress them. Exceed their expectations. Don't settle for anything less than an audience in awe.

Anything Is Not Better Than Nothing: If this is a brand-new program, you'll likely be showing them something they haven't seen before. The bar is lower generally in a brand-new program. You are presenting something that has never existed before. That means that anything is better than nothing, right? Wrong. You don't want the administration and community to regret having started the program. Yes, sometimes a bad show is worse than not having a program at all.

Good Vibes: The students will know you having worked with you for months, but your colleagues, the administration, and especially the parents will be going to that first show to see what you're made of. Your students have likely been reporting back to their parents after rehearsal on how things are going. Hopefully, they are reporting back good things. But hearing secondhand from their kids versus actually seeing for themselves are two different things. Make sure to keep a good, positive, and energetic vibe.

Caffeine Kick: Make sure you have energy for the show, especially for the moments you are onstage speaking. Whatever gets you that extra boost, whether it is coffee, Red Bull, candy, soda, etc., drink it, eat it, and get that energy boost. When opening night comes, you'll be exhausted. You don't want that exhaustion to come through for your first show because the people seeing you and hearing you will either think that is how you normally act or that doing this show almost killed you, both of which you want to avoid.

What Else Is Going On? At the show, speak about your program, what you have been doing, and what you plan to do. Make sure that everyone has the dates to put in their calendar for everything you are doing for the rest of the year.

Y'all Have Fun Out There: Make sure your students in the production have a wonderful time over the course of the show(s). They should have food provided to them, fun warm-ups before the show, recognition in the program, and a fun, stress-free environment in the dressing room from start to finish.

Hello! My Name is _____: Introduce yourself to the crowd. This being your first show is the first time the audience may be able to see you speak. Take the time either before the show or afterward to introduce yourself to the community by perhaps giving them a small bio journey of how you got there, your philosophy on starting/building this program, and your experience with this show specifically.

Set Babies to 'Silent': Set audience behavior expectations right away. If this is not a new program, the audiences at that school may have some bad habits regarding what they can and cannot do in the audience during a show. Audiences are getting worse and worse when it comes to proper audience etiquette nowadays, and so it is up to us to try to nip it in the bud. Make sure the proper audience etiquette is displayed in the program, on the pre-show slideshow, and in the pre-show announcement. Proper policies on cell phones, cameras, talking, clearing the aisles, getting up, getting back in, and anything else need to be spelled out for all to see, hear, and understand.

Don't Forget to Hit Record! Record and take photos of the show for posterity's sake. With my very first show, I had so much on my mind that I didn't even think to record it. To this day, I have no evidence that that show happened except for a few photos some parents sent me. If your program lasts five years, ten years, or 30 years, you'll want to have that first show's video and photos to document how far you've come.

See You on Monday! Let the students go home after the last show. You'll see in the "Production Workdays" chapter that you'll need to schedule a post-production workday the week after the production closes. You want the students to be able to just get out of costume and head out with their family to enjoy a late dinner or dessert to discuss how the show went. You don't want the families to have to wait around for 30 minutes to an hour t for their student to be done breaking down the set or dressing room. Let them go for the night, and they can take care of it next week.

That Was Perfect . . . But How Do We Make It More Perfect? What your first show is will be the standard, the control by which they will judge the rest of the shows that year. As the intro says, your first show should be your worst show. You should always strive to improve. There will be things that go wrong in your first show that you will hopefully fix for next time so that new things go wrong. You should try to avoid making the same mistakes twice. After the show, make sure to note the things that went wrong and what to improve upon right away when it is fresh in your mind. Then, four months later, when you get started on your next show, pull those notes out and remind yourself of what to do or what not to do.

 Key Takeaways

1. Before your first show, plan more thoroughly, work more hours, spend more money, invite more people, and prep more diligently so that you can set the stage for success.
2. During your first show, make a good first impression by having energetic and positive vibes, introducing yourself, letting the community know what else your program is doing, as well as how to behave properly at a show, and making sure the students are having a good time and can go home with their families shortly after the show is over.

PART 2

Growing a Theatre Program

7

Money

The first musical that I directed at the private school was the full version of *The Wizard of Oz*. Whether you have directed theatre productions a lot or not, try to guess how much that show cost the school to put on. Take a guess.

Think about everything involved:

- Performance rights
- Scripts
- Accompaniment tracks
- Over 200 costume pieces
- Nearly 50 props
- Massive set pieces, including a house that can spin in a tornado onstage
- And everything else involved in the production

How much did it cost?
$0.00

That's right. The full production of *The Wizard of Oz* didn't cost the school one single penny.

If you want to make your administrator's day, say: "It won't cost the school anything!" Believe me, you'll get show approval faster than you can say "Merry Ol' Land of Oz!"

In this chapter, I'll explain how I put on *The Wizard of Oz* and most of my productions for no cost to the school, and then show you how you can do it too.

Doing a Show for $0.00

How can you do a show at no cost to the school?

The short answer is: Your show revenue through ticket sales and concessions needs to reach or exceed the cost of the show.

The long answer is a bit more involved. Let's break up the short answer.

Ticket Sales

You need to find a magic number of a price for tickets that is not too low and not too high. Not so low that you aren't missing out on potential revenue, and not so high that it is preventing some audience members from attending. When a program is just starting out, ticket prices are generally lower than they end up being later. I started at $5 for general admission, but after several years of the program's success, tickets had gone up to $15 for general admission with $20 for premium seating. However, when starting out the program, you don't want to get the community used to cheap tickets or you'll have a riot on your hands when ticket prices shoot up. Steady, growing inflation of the price over the years, matched with program growth and better shows, and it should be fine.

The price of the tickets also depends on what type of show you are putting on. You cannot charge the same for a one-act straight play as you would for a full two-and-a-half-hour musical production. Some programs charge a flat ticket fee regardless of what type of show it is. This means that either the cheaper show is overvalued or the more expensive show is undervalued. If your community sees that the ticket price fluctuates based on what type of show it is, they'll be more appreciative of the value of the show.

As mentioned previously, and as will be discussed in the "Programs, Tickets, and Advertisements" chapter, having different tiers of tickets can be a good way to bring in a bit more revenue. The way I did it was by having the first two rows be premium seating for $5–$10 more per seat. The rest of the seats from row 3 on back were general seating at the normal price. This way those parents or other theatregoers who insist on having a great seat won't need to worry about lining up early.

Try to work on ticket prices with the basics of supply and demand in mind. If your show sells out way before opening night, ticket prices are too low. If you are having trouble filling the seats for your shows, ticket prices are too high. The goal should be to sell out at the door the night of the show.

Concessions

A concessions stand can be a great supplement to nightly revenue for your shows. Some think of concessions revenue as just a little extra added on top of total revenue, but with a few tweaks here and there, it can rival ticket sales, and in some cases outpace ticket sales revenue.

The simplest concessions stand model is just candy and soda cans – all for sale for $1. Profit margins are about $.50 per item sold, and it'll be just a minor supplement to overall revenue.

The more you charge, the more you'll make in profit, but the less you'll sell simple economics. For simple snacks and drinks, $2 or $3 at most would do well on a show night. Any more and you'll be rivaling football stadium prices.

An important thing to keep in mind when doing a concessions stand is the *sound* the snack – and especially the snack wrapper – will make when the audience member is eating it. At my first show, I offered popcorn from a popcorn machine. Popcorn is always a huge hit and can raise concessions sales a lot. However, I, without forethought, got crinkly popcorn bags. By the time the show started, the audience's combined popcorn bag crinkle noise was competing with the actor's lines. From then on, I got the standard paper red-and-white-striped popcorn boxes.

The more you spend to get fancier foods and drinks ready for the shows, the more you'll make. The adage that you have to spend money to make money applies well here. However, if you are ramping up your concessions, you can make some capital expenses that will be a lot upfront but will last you for years.

Things like:
- A popcorn machine
- A pretzel heater
- A hot dog roller
- Chili and cheese heater
- Slushie machine
- Etc.

It would be rare, but if your campus allows sales of alcohol, beer, wine, and special wine cocktails, that can double concessions revenue instantly.

Having 'food-food' like hot dogs, nachos, etc. at your concessions stand needs to be known by the community beforehand. That way they know that they don't need to eat beforehand and that they can instead eat at the show.

Coffee is a huge hit, and having a stand with specially made coffee drinks can be a big boost to sales.

Having special show-based foods available for your concessions stand is also a great way to boost sales. For my show of *Narnia*, I provided actual Turkish Delight, which people bought just out of sheer curiosity. Other examples: for *Alice in Wonderland* – tea, for *The Hobbit* – lembas bread, for *A Christmas Carol* – figgy pudding, etc.

Cost of the Show

A lot of the specifics about how to control the cost of the show will be in some of the following chapters. However, comparing the cost of the show to the revenue you make from the show is an important factor in what prices you set for tickets and concessions.

But before you calculate those things, you need to figure out what your goal is: Do you want the show to break even? Do you want to have to spend only $1,000 for the show? Do you want to make money on the show to put in the war chest? Once you figure out whether you want to spend less, break even, or make a profit, then calculate ticket prices and concessions based on the cost of the show.

If the show is low-cost, ticket and concessions prices can in turn be lowered. Conversely, if the cost of the show is higher than normal, ticket and concessions prices can be raised. Usually, if you explain to the audience the extraordinary costs of the show – whether it be from the show rights, number of costumes, or intricate set – then they will more often than not be okay with the raised prices. This goes back to adjusting the price of the show and not keeping it the same regardless of what show you put on.

However, if you have a 'spend low earn high' strategy, which is using the shows themselves as fundraisers for the program, you would keep the ticket and concessions prices high while ensuring that the cost of the show stays low.

The School Budget

School budgets for theatre programs vary wildly based on your school's situation and your program's situation. However, whatever the situation, you always need to be advocating to the board/'powers that be' the need for additional resources for your program. Don't ever just give up; year after year, go back to them to try to get more. Your budget should reflect your philosophy and vision. If it is a competitive program, you'll see that reflected in the budget. If it is a big musical program, that will be in there as well.

There are plenty of argument points on your side of the budget talks that you can use as armor in those discussions.

Comparative Programs: How much does athletics get? Band? Choir? Make sure that your program's budget is comparable.

The Board: What does the board want? What do they want to see the program do? They won't invest in something they won't believe in. Show them the program's potential and they'll begin to imagine higher highs.

Half/Half: Tell them that you plan to cover a portion of the program costs through revenue, fundraising, and donations. If the board sees that you aren't just taking from the school budget and that you're pitching in on your end, they'll be more willing to dig deep.

The Proof Is in the Pudding: If your program is successful and has been putting on excellent and legitimate productions, then make sure the board knows about it. They should have been at the shows, to begin with, but whether they were or weren't, the budget talks remind them of the show with pictures and videos while discussing the potential for even better shows with financial help.

Capital expenses: if you are planning on buying things for your program that are going to be used for multiple years, this needs to be talked about in your budget discussions. If you are about to invest in a sound system that costs way more than a yearly budget allows, explain that that sound system will be used for a very long time – for not only every theatre show but other school events as well. If they believe they are getting a lot out of the investment, they'll be willing to increase the budget for it.

Specificity

Try to make your budget less specific. The more specific the line items in your theatre budget are, the less flexibility you will be able to have with it.

Example 1

Costuming Budget: $500, Props Budget: $500, Sets Budget: $1000

What if your show is very costume-heavy and doesn't involve very many props and only minimal sets? With a budget like this one, you won't be able to spend as much money on your costumes as you need to, and you'll have extra money left over in the other two categories.

Solution: Combine this line item in your budget to be a Costume/Props/Sets line item for $2,000 total. That way if you need to spend $1,000 on Costumes, $250 on props, and $750 on sets, you can!

Example 2

Lights Budget: $250, Sound Budget: $250, Computer Tech Budget: $200, Mic Budget: $300

With a separated budget like this, what if your lights are all set for the show you have, but you do need more mics for the additional actors? What if you need to buy a whole new sound system? That $250 will not go far.

Solution: Combine all of these line items into one 'tech' line item for $1,000 total. That way you can spend the money that year on what you need to.

Example 3
Budget per show: $3,000

Some theatre budgets out there are like this. There is a flat budget per show all included. The problem with this is what if you have one really cheap show and one show that costs a lot? The cheap show will either have money left over or will needlessly spend more. The show that costs a lot will not get all of the resources it needs because of the cap.

Solution: If the budget is put together like this, go ahead and combine it into one big line item 'theatre shows' = $6,000. That way if you want to save $5,000 for the big spring musical, you know you have $1,000 to spend on the fall show.

Concerning cash money, be above board. Make sure you have good controls. Never cash a personal check out of cash money. If collecting cash, don't fool with it ever. Don't keep cash in an insecure location in the theatre room.

Donations

Do not think that you can just hold out a hat and ask for donations and that you will get a plentiful bounty. People in your community need to know that they are donating to something great, something useful, something with potential. Getting families to open up their wallets, especially in a private school where they have already opened up their wallets a lot, is no easy task. Your program needs to be inspiring and useful to the community at large. Prove that your program is helping the students. A large portion of donations to the arts are what are you doing for kids. Parents are willing to give money now to things that are good for their kids.

Asking for money is a humbling thing, but it comes with the territory. Do not be afraid to ask for money. The worst that can happen is that they say no. This is another area where relationships come into play. Personal benefactors you know, not only in the school community but also from your personal history, can be a great resource for donations. For every event you hold, there should be a donation bucket/basket/hat on the way out. That donation bucket should also be announced near the end of the show to remind people. Not only do they need reminding, but they also need to know what the donations are going for. "If you like what you saw tonight and want to see more shows like this but bigger and better, consider donating to the theatre program on your way out."

Write grants. Grants are great ways for programs to get donated money for longevity. There are several great programs to reach out to, such as The

National Endowment for the Arts, (Your State) Commission on the Arts, The American Rescue Recovery Grant Program, and the American Theatre Wing's National Theatre Company Grant. Grant writing is tedious and takes a lot of effort to keep up with, but the outcome can be well worth it.

Reach out to banks and other local businesses. You can request $500 on the spot to put the business in the program. Some businesses have a set advertising budget, and they are looking for ways to use it. Have a business sponsor a show. Put their business logo on the wall. Have company-donated drinks and snacks for concessions when they might want their new products to be tried by the masses. Major local partnerships with companies, businesses, and colleges in your town can be a great resource to get your program some money.

Fundraising

Find the right fundraisers for your organizations. If it's something important to the kids, they will find a way to find the money. To build a program that they're proud of, they need to be visible, in front of people, and they will find a way to make it happen.

Fundraising is more difficult nowadays because there are more rules on it than there used to be. Some schools have a rule you can only do one or two fundraisers a year. You'll need to also make sure to follow the rules when doing bake sales during school, as you'll be competing with the cafeteria and most likely going against the nutritional values.

Here are some classic and unique ideas for fundraising for your program:
- Bake sale
- Coffee bar
- Candy/popcorn/pies, etc. sales
- Car washes
- Face painting at football games
- Haunted house every year (We hung black tarps pulled taut onstage and made walls. Students acted out all the characters, added spider webs, and for $250 created a haunted house that made over $1,000.)
- Selling poinsettias in the holiday season or lilies around Easter
- Pre-Show Auctions: Auction off the chance for an audience member to make a cameo in Act 2 or for the actors in the show to perform a song of the winner's choice during intermission.
- Auction and Silent Auction: Having people and businesses donate trips, items, and more to be sold at an auction can be a great

fundraiser for your program. These auctions can be during one of your shows, but they can also be separate events. If you want to get really fancy with it, have it at an alternative location like the local country club and have real professional auctioneers host it. Include a meal, tables, drinks, and a silent auction going on at the same time. A massive fundraising event like this can change the course of your budget for years.
- Singing Telegrams: Have students buy the chance for your singing actors to go sing a love song to their crush in their class around Valentine's Day.
- Themed dinners
- Merch/swag sales
- Raffles
- Peer-to-Peer Fundraising: Set up a crowdfunding campaign on a platform like GoFundMe and encourage your members and supporters to share it online.
- Themed trivia night
- Costume contest
- Scavenger hunt
- "Sponsor a Set Piece" program
- "Adopt a Costume" program
- Matching grants
- Murder Mystery Dinner Theatre
- Improv night
- Stage readings
- Online streaming event
- "Donate the Change" campaign partner with a local business to allow customers to round up their purchase amount to the nearest dollar with the difference donated to your theatre program.
- "Backstage Pass" program

The War Chest

When revenue is high, expenses are low, fundraising is flourishing, and donations are up, then at the end of the year, you will usually end up with more money than you had going in. That money that is left over needs to go into a special "war chest" specifically for your theatre program. The term "war chest" typically refers to a large reserve of money an organization accumulates for specific purposes, often unforeseen ones. It's built up in advance, similar to how a country might stockpile weapons and supplies in preparation for war.

Some school budgets aren't built this way, and you'll need to figure out if this is the case sooner rather than later. Some school budgets instead go off of the model "if you don't spend it, you lose it," which causes programs to spend money needlessly. Try to convince the powers that be to create an account, fund, or tracked line item that the extra money for your program goes into.

If you are successful, that war chest will grow year after year. Then if you have a major purchase in mind, that is when you dip into these reserves. The purpose of the war chest can also be for unforeseen circumstances, so this would be in the case if something major broke or needed replacing. However, using this money on major expenses like a new sound system, lighting system, mics, or an extraordinarily expensive show can help your yearly budget from going to $0 on day one.

If the war chest accumulates enough, there can be an argument made for major overhauls of theatre facilities. Updating, furnishing, outfitting, or even building a new dance studio, dressing room, backstage area, stage, or auditorium can be helped by using the extra money you receive in the war chest.

Don't let the money sit in the war chest for too long, however. If you have the money in there, it should be spent on something to improve your program within a matter of years.

 Key Takeaways

1. Put on a theatre show at no cost to the school by having your revenue through ticket sales and concessions reach or exceed the cost of the show.
2. Always advocate to the administration for an appropriately sized and less specific budget that is comparable to other programs, matches the board's vision with your own, will be matched by your own revenue and donations, and covers capital expenses.
3. Although asking for money is humbling, do so by speaking to personal benefactors, writing grants, reaching out to local businesses, and always having donation opportunities at every event you host.
4. If your school's budget is set up to do so, try to end the year with a profit and put that profit in a 'war chest' to be used for major expenses in your program's future.

8

Props, Sets, and Costumes

When I first arrived at the private school to begin to see what theatre things they had in storage, I wasn't sure what to expect. So far as they told me, the school had done "a handful of shows" over the last decade. I went searching in the theatre storage closet – nothing was there. I went searching in the other spaces in the theatre building – still nothing. After some inquiry, I finally found their storage of props and costumes in a small under-the-stairs, concrete janitor's closet in a separate building on campus. Here is what I found: two medium-sized totes filled with a random assortment of props and masks haphazardly placed, and two flimsy cardboard boxes that contained 20 folded-up costumes. Most of the props and all of the costumes were from a production of *The Chronicles of Narnia: The Lion, The Witch, and The Wardrobe* that the school had performed seven years prior. (I ended up choosing *Narnia* as our second production there because they already had a majority of the props and costumes to save a considerable amount of money in the first year – see the chapter on picking shows for more detail on using already owned costumes to influence show selection.)

There were several things wrong with what I found and how I found it stored: (1) Although they had performed "a handful of shows," the props and costumes in storage were primarily just from one of their shows; they did not keep things from other shows. (2) Packed away in a small closet: too small, too remote, too hard to access, and in my case, too hard to find. (3) Packed into totes and boxes: how could I see what costumes there were or what props they had without opening up the boxes and taking everything out? It wasn't out in the open, it wasn't labeled, it wasn't inventoried.

Five years later, here is what those two totes and two boxes turned into: an entire 60-feet-by-45-feet third-floor storage area filled with thousands of costumes, props, and set pieces, all sorted, organized, neatly stored, hung up, and inventoried. There were 150 feet of costume storage bars hung from the ceiling, and each bar was packed with dozens of costumes. There were shelves, file cabinets, tables, boxes, and totes all labeled and filled with everything from five years of productions.

I turned a small handful of costumes and props into a theatre director's dream storage room in just five years. In this chapter, I'll tell you how I did it and how you can too by analyzing (1) what to get, (2) where to get it, and (3) what to do with it after.

What to Get?

Props

When you think of props compared to sets and costumes, props seem less important, less visual, and less vital. Don't underestimate the power of good props, and more importantly, the power of bad props. I would argue that props can be a major indicator of a lame, not-well-put-together show. If you have a major sword fight happening onstage, but your three musketeers are wielding big, too-colorful foam toy swords, it will be hard for the audience to buy in to what is happening. If you have a play set in the 1940s, but you have an olive-green phone from the late 1970s on the desk, more parents and grandparents will notice that than you think. If you have a show's focus and centerpiece being a prop, like the Arkenstone from *The Hobbit* or the rose in *Beauty and the Beast* but you only provide the audience with a small plastic gem and a plain carnation, you will have stopped well short of excellence.

Here are a few tips on all aspects of acquiring and using excellent props in a theatre program:

Script Breakdown: This is the foundation of getting started with props for a show. Read the script carefully, making a list of every single prop needed. Don't forget background items that help establish the setting.

Prioritize: Review the prop list you created and categorize props by necessity, especially if you don't have a lot of money to work with. Are some essential to the plot or character development? Can others be substituted or creatively represented?

Handmade vs. Already Made: There is a big debate when it comes to handmade props in theatre versus something that already exists.

A lot of factors play into this decision, including cost, accessibility, and whether or not the item actually exists. However, the bottom line is that you need to acquire the *best* prop you can. Don't settle for something less good. If the one at the store isn't good enough, make a better one. If the one your team tried to make isn't what you had in mind, go buy one instead.

Prop Table: Backstage during the show, you should provide the students with a prop table. This table should be sectioned off with tape where each prop goes so that you and the techs can instantly see what is missing and begin tracking it down before the show starts. It gives the students a simple solution – once you are done with that prop, put it back on the table.

DIY Magic: Get crafty! Upcycle, paint, or repurpose existing objects to create the perfect prop. Think outside the box and unleash your inner artist.

The Power of Illusion: Sometimes, a convincing stand-in can work wonders. For instance, a lightweight replica of a heavy object might be sufficient for the purposes of the play.

Printable Solutions: For specific signs, labels, or documents, consider creating high-quality printables that look authentic from a distance.

3D Printing: 3D printing is the latest technology that is reaching theatre everywhere. If you or your school has access to a 3D printer, make specific props that require intricate details or that don't exist otherwise. The 'toner' for 3D printing is somewhat pricey, but it might be a fraction of the cost of the real prop you're printing.

Safety Always Comes First: Never compromise on safety when dealing with props. Ensure that they are appropriate for their intended use and pose no risk to actors or the crew.

Painting: Clever painting and spray painting on props can turn an otherwise ordinary item into the exact item you need for your show. If you are re-using the prop, you can always paint back over it.

Sets

The set is your production's costume. It is the first thing your audience will notice about your show and the biggest indicator of whether the show looks good visually or not. Audiences can spot a poorly put-together set more than any other aspect of the show. Sets done well are also rather expensive, especially if you have multiple sets per show. If your budget only has enough room for one full stage of sets, then you will have to take that into account when selecting the show – ensuring it only has one scene worth of sets. The set comprises a lot of different pieces: backdrop, built set pieces, wall hangings, rolling pieces, platforms, and more.

Here are some tips for acquiring proper sets for your productions:
   The Power of the Triangle: A large standing rolling triangular prism set piece is a great way to quickly and easily switch sets without moving much onstage. They are two feet wide and eight feet tall on all three sides. When placed up against a side wall or perpendicular to the stage front, the audience will only be able to see the front-facing side of the triangle. One quick 33% rotation and you're already in another set. These types of set pieces can vary in size, but all are equally useful for a quick set switch.

   Pink Insulation Foam Boards: This is some of the best, most versatile, and cost-effective ways to get large set pieces made. At any home improvement store, they have 8-foot by 4-foot by 1-inch pink foam insulation boards usually for 12–15 dollars a slab. They can be easily cut into any shape with a razor blade and can be painted any color you need. They work well as set walls as well as standing set pieces like trees and cartoonish-looking things like fire hydrants or mailboxes. They can also be flipped to the other side, so painting one set wall on one side, then in the scene change, just flip it around and you're already in another room.

   One Backdrop to Rule Them All: If you get a quality piece of large canvas cloth the size of your stage's back, you can paint that thing for years creating a new backdrop for every show. Some shows don't call for a backdrop, but I feel that having one is always better than just leaving it blank to the curtains. If your show is set in London, even if you aren't outside a lot, having the London cityscape as your background can really enhance your production.

   If You Look Long Enough: The perfect set pieces that are exactly what you want and are in the time-period of the show are out there. You just have to look long enough. Take the time to search for the perfect set pieces that fit your show. Don't settle for a green metal teacher desk when you need a wooden presidential desk. Don't use the white plastic cafeteria chairs when you need a comfortable recliner. Don't have enough money to buy these things? Borrow. Ask enough people in the school community and someone will have what you are looking for and will likely let you borrow it for the run of the show.

   Expensive Art Is Actually Cheap: You need the *Mona Lisa*? Well, unless you have a contact at the Louvre that will let you borrow it, you'll need to find a copy. Amazon, Etsy, and some other sites sell canvas prints of famous paintings for rather cheap. From the audience's perspective, they look like the real thing. If you are looking for a non-famous painting but something that still looks rather impressive, head to thrift, secondhand, and antique stores. They usually have large artwork for a fraction of what they used to sell for.

Castors Are on a Roll: Castors are your friend, but in certain cases, they can also be your enemy. Spend a little bit of extra money getting silent rolling castors. It's really tough during scene transitions to hear the loud, squeaky rolling of the new set pieces coming onto the stage. Castors to get new set pieces on are especially important when you either don't have many techs and/or your techs aren't old enough/strong enough to carry large pieces. Keep all your castors from show to show. Consider every single set piece you have and whether they would benefit from castors or not.

Measure and Draw: Prior to selecting your set pieces, get a scale diagram of your stage drawn on paper. Cut out scale set pieces from other sheets of paper and you can visualize the space of the sets on the stage. Mood boards and other types of sketches are important to creating the vision before executing building.

Lighting Round: Here are some "this goes without saying" tips, but I'm saying them just in case this is your first rodeo. Only paint the sides of sets that can be seen by the audience. Avoid trip hazards. Ensure everything is completely and properly secured when it is on the stage so that it does not fall. If an actor needs to climb onto a set piece in the dark between scenes, make sure they have adequate lighting so that they don't hurt themselves.

Costumes

Audiences have keen eyes when it comes to costumes. After all, they see clothes every day. They know when something is legit, and they can spot when something is a cheap replacement. You can find amazing things online that look like the real deal, but costumes are not just about how it looks. You will also have to consider how it fits the actor, how easy it is to get on and off when considering quick changes, how the actor will feel when wearing it, and more.

Here are the tips, tricks, and advice when it comes to getting costumes for your show:

Prioritize Your Mains: If you are working with a limited budget for costumes, prioritize the main characters that have the most stage time.

This is especially important if you have a large ensemble. Consider who is on the stage the most seen by the audience and put the bulk of your budget's power toward them.

Closet Costuming: Ask your students to provide their costumes out of their own closets. This is mostly effective for shows set in the modern day. However, when you ask your actors to dig into their closets, you may be surprised at what they come up with.

Costume Bag: In addition to their costumes, provide a bag for your actors. This bag is to put their miscellaneous smaller costume pieces in. Ties, belts, socks, suspenders, jewelry, and more can go in this bag that is hooked on with their costume's hanger. I always used those reusable grocery bags that you can find at the grocery store for a dollar a piece. They are durable, big, and last a long time.

Plastic Hangers Over Wire Hangers: Wire hangers are sharp, bend easily, and are increasingly harder to find. Plastic hangers are not sharp, don't bend, and can be found everywhere for very cheap. You can currently get an 18-pack of plastic hangers for $2 at Wal-Mart. They also come in several colors, so if you want to color-coordinate your actors' costumes with different colored hangers, you can.

Reversible Belts: A lot of belts are available where the buckle can rotate around and the other side of the leather can be used. You can find them in many colors, including black/brown, black/blue, brown/grey, etc. Getting double-sided belts increases your likelihood of reusing them for future shows.

Wash, Wash, Wash Your Clothes: After a production is over, make sure you have a plan in place to wash every costume piece your students touched. Even if you need to take every piece home and do it yourself, it needs to get done. Parents are often keen on helping with this task and will do it for you. However, in addition to after the show's run, if your students have been wearing the costumes a lot for tech week and even before, they might need washing before opening night. You'd be surprised, but a stinky costume can actually affect your actors' performance.

Head-to-Toe: A costume is not just a shirt and pants. You need to consider every single piece of clothing that students wear from head-to-toe: hat, wig, jewelry, shirt, gloves, belt, pants, socks, and shoes. You don't want Romeo in a perfect Shakespearean costume wearing Nikes. Great costume shoes can be found at secondhand stores for cheap.

Costume Fitting: Schedule a fitting to ensure costumes fit well and actors feel comfortable in them. Be open to adjustments based on their feedback.

Costume Parade: Once costumes are complete, hold a costume parade with you and other production members to see how everything looks together under stage lights.

Beyond Period Accuracy: While historical accuracy is important for some shows, prioritize how the costume reflects the character and story.

Where to Get It?

Now that we've taken a look at some tips on what kinds of props, sets, and costumes to get for your show, let's consider the many places where you can get them. This part will be separated into four sections in the order in which you should search for your costumes. First, you'll try to get donations from the community, then you'll check with the local theatres that may be willing to let you borrow some, then you'll see if creating your own is feasible, then the endless possibilities of the internet, and finally in-person stores.

Donations

This will be the cheapest route when it comes to acquiring props, sets, and costumes. However, just because it's the cheapest, that doesn't mean it's the easiest. Sure, scrolling on Amazon for an afternoon and then clicking "Buy" and then it shows up two days later is easy, but it's not cheap. Acquiring what you need through donations takes knowing people, fostering relationships, building parent trust, and advocating for yourself and your program.

The most-used phrase in education is "beg, borrow, steal . . ." Well, don't steal. But begging is sometimes necessary for getting the things you need for the show on the cheap.

Prior to a production getting kicked off, it is important to know your needs. Make a detailed list of all the costumes and props you need. Include size ranges, colors, periods, and specific details for each item.

Hit up the faculty e-mail. "Anyone have a couch we can borrow?" "We need costumes from this time period." The worst they can do is say no or not answer.

Post on your school's social media some pictures of what you are looking for. Even families that aren't involved in theatre will see it and might contribute.

Lumber prices have gone up lately. Put on the school's social media if families have lumber just lying around that they'd be willing to part with. People often have projects that have leftover wood that just sits in their storage shed for years. Tell them it doesn't matter what it is and that you'll take it and will find a use for it.

Certain programs make sure students are responsible for providing their own costume and props. This is similar to a band making students purchase their instruments, sports making students purchase their own uniforms, or robotics teams making students purchase materials. Some don't like this approach, and others jump on board. Some can't afford it. Students tend to take care of it more if it is their own stuff.

You can hold certain non-show-specific events to fill up your prop, sets, and costume storage. Holding a "spring cleaning" for the school community is an opportunity for families to clean out their closets, garages, and attics, bring it all to the school, and you'll store it all for future shows.

Announce what you need at performing arts events and other school-wide events. Get onstage and tell the community about the show and what you are on the lookout for. Not only is this a great way to advertise the show, but it is a good way to talk to people immediately after you speak and get their information. Sometimes people forget when it comes to an e-mail or social media post, but if you tell them all in person, they might come meet you at the side of the stage and say they have what you're looking for.

Hold a Production and Parent Meeting. Once the cast list comes out, hold a meeting with all the cast and crew members as well as their families. This is a good chance to tell them about the logistics of the show, but it can also serve as an opportunity to tell everyone what you are looking for right when the production is getting started. This allows for buy-in from the students and families. There might be props, sets, and costumes that you were 100% intending on buying, but the production families might say they have exactly what you need, and you just saved some money right there.

With donations, be open to receiving costumes or props that don't perfectly match your vision. With some creativity, they might be adaptable for your production.

Offer a pick-up service. Make it easy for people to donate by offering to pick up the items yourself.

Lastly, be courteous and professional. Thank everyone who donates, regardless of the size of their contribution. Even offer a shout-out or ad in the program for large donations.

Other Theatres

After trying to acquire all the donations you can for your show, the next step is to reach out to other theatres in the area to see if they have what you are looking for. This is especially helpful if they performed the show you are about to perform. They will likely have a lot of the props and costumes for that show and might even be of better quality than you could have come up with otherwise. Some might have storage issues and might instead donate the pieces (or sell them cheap) rather than just letting you borrow them.

Here are a few local theatre options that you can ask for donations:

Schools: Network and grow relationships with the other directors in your area. Make sure to let them know that they can borrow from you at any time as well. It should be a symbiotic relationship. Some of the big 5A and 6A schools have prop and costume storage that would make us blush. Ask the directors if you can come peruse their storage for an afternoon. With this and some of the other theatres and businesses, they might ask for a small borrowing fee, but it is likely much cheaper than buying outright.

Costume Shops: These businesses often have overstock or retired costumes they might be willing to donate.

Historical Societies and Museums: Some museums put on weekly, monthly, and yearly productions of their own. They might have period-specific clothing or props that fit your production.

Community Theatres: Your local community theatre and regional theatre will no doubt have an abundance of props, sets, and costumes. Even if you are just looking for a very specific piece (e.g., "I need a green leprechaun hat"), they might have just the thing. I can't tell you how many times community theatres have held garage sales to get rid of their excess supply or because they ran out of storage. Follow these theatres on social media. Look out for those opportunities.

Ballet Companies: Ballet companies are great organizations that often have very unique versions of costumes that they have been storing for years. When I directed *The Wizard of Oz*, I found out that the local ballet company had performed a ballet version of *Oz* a few years prior. At first, I was skeptical as to how a ballet costume would translate to the theatre stage, but when I saw what they had created for the munchkins, I couldn't pass it up. It was one of those things I would never have thought of, but once I saw it, I knew it was perfect.

Do-It-Yourself

After checking out your local theatres for donations, things to borrow, and things to rent, now it's time to explore things to make yourself. In most cases, making your own costumes, props, and sets is cheaper than buying them outright, but it takes significantly more labor to create. That is a cost-benefit analysis you need to figure out when you are determining what the production needs. Do you get more expensive costumes online with no labor, or do you make cheaper costumes by utilizing the skills of your production's families? Another consideration is which is going to look better. There is no hard-and-fast rule. I've seen handmade props that are far superior to the equivalent they could have gotten at a theatre shop. However, I've also seen handmade props that made me want to donate the real thing to the show.

If you have the money to hire for different things, do it. If you don't have the volunteers to make the things you need to make, there are professionals out there who can build a great set for you or sew a custom costume for you for a fee. If you have the money to go with a professional, do it. But if you have the labor at home, start there first.

When it comes to getting the props, sets, and costumes for the show ready, be less of a director and more of a facilitator. Find people you trust, good people. Make friends with the students' parents. Be nice, be an advocate for yourself, be kind to people, and get out of your introverted bubble. Talk with parents at games and school events. Make yourself accessible and friendly to the community so it doesn't seem like the only time they hear from you is when you are asking them for something.

Don't be afraid to ask parents for help, but make sure they aren't helping *too* much. Some parents will take a mile when given an inch. They sometimes disrespect the timeline given or the instructions given. Some try to take over the project and go over your head. Make sure to put your foot down and let them know you are still the director. Parents have so many ideas of what they think might work better and look better. Listen to the ideas, take the ones you agree with, but don't let them bully you into doing something they think works better. The director has the last say when it comes to these decisions. Stay strong.

Get your sewing team: "Does anyone have a sewing machine and know how to sew? We will cover the cost of the fabric."

Get your painting team: "Who knows how to paint well? Who wants to take a stab at our backdrop?"

Get your builders: "Who has tools? Where are my contractors out there?" Some parents work on building houses throughout the week. You'll have to convince them that the house only needs to exist for a week, but they will often make very high-quality stuff if you give them the room to.

Get your worker bees: These are parents who don't have specific skills like sewing or painting but are happy to help with any of the tasks you have.

Websites

If you didn't get what you needed donated or borrowed and can't or don't want to make it yourself, time to go buy it. Start online first before heading to the store. If you are in a small town, you might have to drive for over an hour to get to the big city to go shopping at stores you don't have in your town. Getting to places like Hobby Lobby or Michaels is good to get things quickly (same day), but these stores also have websites so you can shop from the comfort and convenience of your couch. Even if you end up buying it at the stores in person, you spend the time shopping online, so once you are in the store, you get in and out quickly.

Here are some primary websites to use when trying to acquire things for your production.

Amazon.com: Thank God for Amazon, where time-period costumes are sold for cheap. Hair, pants, paint, muslin, and more can be gotten there. Get a Prime account for yourself or your school and you can do all of your shopping in one place, and it'll be at your school's door in two days. Some companies on Amazon are based in China and make things to order, so some of those give a one month or longer delivery date. Make sure to do your shopping early on in your production just in case those perfect made-to-order costumes will be in on time. For better or worse, everyone has hopped onto the Amazon bandwagon, and nearly all costuming and prop stores sell their wares on there. You can also add what you need onto a wish list and send the wish list out to the school community. Some families may buy a thing or two off of there, knowing they bought something specifically needed for the next show.

Ebay.com: Don't forget about the OG online store. eBay is still around and still has great stuff on their platform. Also don't think of it as all used stuff. Although a lot of the things on there are used and resold by individuals, some companies sell shoes, clothes, and other items new straight off of eBay. If you are patient enough to wait for auctions to bid on, you can sometimes get a great deal lower than retail. There is also the buy now button if you want to have it then.

Mercari.com: This is a lesser-known and smaller version of an eBay-type site online. It is an app that people can just snap a picture of something they want to sell, put on a price, and get it sold. I've found some treasures on there, especially in the prop department. Check it out.

Facebook Marketplace: This marketplace will be great, especially for set pieces. Furniture is sold all over Facebook Marketplace, and a clever search can lead to you finding exactly the piece you need. Some of the sellers will also deliver it to you if need be.

Craigslist.org: Similar to Facebook Marketplace, you have people in your area selling all kinds of stuff; again, this is best for set pieces. With these types of sites, beware of scams. If you get a bad feeling about a transaction, don't be afraid to back out or pause.

TheCostumer.com: This is the largest theatre costuming company online. They have all kinds of props and costumes for theatre productions. They even have sections for specific shows where you can buy everything you need for specific trademarked shows.

Etsy.com: This site is great for unique, handmade costume pieces. There are also sewing artisans on there that will, if you contact them, make you a specific piece you need.

Here are a few honorable mentions for places to shop online for props, sets, and costumes:
Theatre House – https://theatrehouse.com
    Eastern Costume – https://easterncostume.com
    Discount Dance Supply – https://www.discountdance.com
    Halloween Costumes – https://www.halloweencostumes.com
    Costume Kingdom – https://costumekingdom.com
    Norcostco (Props) – https://norcostco.com
    Western Stage Props – https://westernstageprops.com
    Stage Sets – https://www.stageset.shop
    A to Z Theatrical Supply – https://atoztheatrical.com
    Act One Costumes – https://www.actonecostumes.net

Stores

Done with donations. Been there and done that with borrowing. Did the DIY. Went to websites. You have exhausted all other avenues of trying to find props, sets, and costumes cheaply and efficiently. Unfortunately, now it is time to head out to physical stores. In some cases, especially with building sets, this will be your only option. Also, in the case of same-day emergency last-minute purchases, stores are the only option.

Here are some of the key stores to visit to get everything else that you may need for your show:

Wal-Mart and Target: Basic general stores will be where you can find all kinds of things for your production. This includes real food that you might need your actors to eat onstage. These stores serve well when it comes to cheap fabric, normal modern-day props, and plain clothes and costume pieces like belts in bulk.

Department Stores: Dillard's, JCPenney, Macy's, and more. Be careful with these, because it can get rather expensive rather quickly if you are not careful. One of the first productions I directed, I didn't know any better, so I did all of my costume shopping at Macy's in town. Boy, that was rough. Looking back on that, I just laugh and shake my head at myself. Sure, you can find good, high-quality pieces at these places, especially when it comes to dresses and suits, but make sure you go when sales and deals are going on. And again, this is only after you have exhausted all other options.

Goodwill/Salvation Army: This will be your best bet when it comes to secondhand clothes and shoes. You can certainly also find all kinds of props and set pieces there, such as dishware, paintings, furniture, and more. These places also have great sales on certain days of the week or month.

Thrift Stores: Some thrift stores resell things at near-retail prices, so watch out for secondhand stores that are posing at firsthand prices. However, in some thrift stores, you can find some pretty perfect stuff if you look long enough. You might even find things you didn't have in mind, but once you see it you realize it is perfect for your purposes.

Garage Sales: This takes a lot of time and footwork, but you can't find better prices shopping out than at garage/yard/estate sales. These are usually held on Saturday mornings, so head out, roam the streets of your town, look out for the signs, and go to the sales. There is often a limited selection, but sometimes there are diamonds in the rough you can find.

Party City/Halloween Stores: These are your costume and prop stores in cities. Things can get rather pricey here too, but they also have things in bulk that can work well for your productions, including masks, wigs, props, colored hair spray, makeup, and more. The pop-up Halloween stores that start showing up around September sometimes stay open a week or two after Halloween, slashing their prices before they close up shop. Go capitalize on their deals when you can. This is also true when it comes to Halloween candy, Easter candy, and any holiday-specific things at stores around town.

Hobby Lobby: I have to admit that I've found the best stuff over the years at Hobby Lobby. Random props, baskets, boxes, canvas, set pieces, paintings, fabric, and more. Special shout out: I've found no place better when it comes to artificial flowers and plants. The key with Hobby Lobby is to wait on the sales. Each of their sections goes on a rotating schedule of sales every week. If you have the time, go when the things you are looking for are on sale, and you can get things at 30, 40, 50, and even 75% off.

Home Depot/Lowe's: These home improvement stores, in addition to your local hardware stores, will be your one-stop shop when it comes to set building materials. These stores will also offer unique solutions for building set pieces and props. They have great experts inside who will love the challenge of coming up with some ideas for a theatre set. One time, when directing *The Time Machine*, I was having trouble coming up with some ideas for the buttons and levers on the time machine in the play itself. While talking to my favorite store worker at Home Depot, he came up with some pretty useful solutions I would have never thought of without his help.

What to Do With It After?

So, you got all of the props, sets, and costumes, they were perfect, and the show is now over. What do you do with everything once the curtain closes for the final time?

Bottom line: DON'T GET RID OF ANYTHING. You have no idea what shows you'll be doing two years, five years, and ten years from now. These props, costumes, and set pieces you have donated, bought, and made can be used and adapted again in numerous productions in the future. Obviously, it's not feasible to keep full-built sets, but try to salvage as much as you can.

Inventory everything. If you do it as each show finishes, it's rather easy to update as you go. However, if you wait several years, inventorying several hundred pieces is a challenge perhaps too daunting. Inventory from the beginning so that you have a digital list you can reference before even making a trip to your storage.

Sort everything properly. All of the belts should be kept together, shoes should be kept in the same area, ties should have their drawer, as well as scarves and gloves too. Sort costumes based on what they are first (tops, bottoms, dresses, etc.), then by color. Put all of your similar set pieces together – chairs all together, tables and desks together, your foam pieces all stacked together. Sorting your theatre storage is key to saving precious time in finding things for your next shows.

Label everything. Once you have it all sorted, make big, legible labels denoting what is where. You might know where everything is since you sorted it yourself, but if you send students or families up to grab a pair of socks, they need to be able to easily see where the socks are.

"But David, we don't have enough storage!" Find storage. Anywhere and everywhere you can. Start in and around the theatre as close to the stage as possible to reduce travel time when transporting things for the show. Then try to acquire every closet, nook, and cranny that your school has. There are often attics, basements, equipment rooms, and unused classrooms that are great to store your theatre stuff. If you run out of room on campus, see if theatre families have an abundance of storage on their property. Then, yes, you as theatre director might have to sacrifice some of your own garage space. Lastly, there are storage locker companies everywhere nowadays. For a small monthly fee, you can store your excess props, sets, and costumes for years on end. Paying the fee is worth keeping all of the things you have used. It's certainly cheaper than having to re-buy everything. Don't let the lack of storage prevent you from keeping stuff after your show.

 Key Takeaways
1. However you get them, get props, sets, and costumes that are safe, efficient, cost-effective, useful, and re-useful, and that do not sacrifice any excellence or your vision for the show.
2. Acquire props, sets, and costumes by first asking for donations, then by asking local theatres, then by creating your own, then by shopping at numerous sites online, then finally by going to in-person stores.
3. Once you have props, sets, and costumes, don't get rid of them. Find storage space for everything, sort it all properly, label it all, and inventory it.

9
Lights, Sound, and Music

In the introduction of the "Props, Sets, and Costumes" chapter, I told a story about arriving at the private school and finding a meager number of props and costumes, and having to grow those items over the course of the next five years. For this chapter, the beginning of the story was the opposite of that one. When I arrived at the same school, the one with only 20 costumes in cardboard storage boxes, one would expect their lightboard, lights, soundboard, and sound system to be just as inadequate. On the contrary: just before I got there, they went through an upgrade and renovation of their performance space. They bought an abandoned building on campus, renovated it, and filled it with pretty darn good equipment. There was a dedicated lighting control laptop connected to a lightboard, which was in turn connected to 24 brand-new LED stage lights. There was also a 32-channel, top-of-the-line soundboard connected to two stage speakers and a massive subwoofer. There was also a sound stack backstage with wireless microphones, inputs for days, and just about anything one might need to get a show going right away.

Amazing, right? How lucky I was, right? Well . . . yes, and yes . . . however, when I got there, I knew next to nothing about how to run those systems, let alone what their pros and cons were. Why did I know next to nothing, you ask? Why don't we take a look at what light and sound equipment I had when I arrived at my first school, the charter school?

For sound, there was one speaker with one wired microphone that was plugged into the middle of the stage floor. For lights, get ready for it . . . it was a normal household two-switch light switch, which both controlled fluorescent lights directly above the stage. That's it.

So, at school 1, I have next to no real theatre sound and light equipment. And at school 2, I have more than enough equipment, but next to no experience to run it. How did I respond in both of those cases?

In this chapter, I will tell you. I'll help guide how to purchase and add proper theatre sound and light equipment if your space has none. I'll also help guide how to run proper equipment once you get it, or in my case, if it is already there. Sound good?

Getting What You Need

First, we will talk about some important points when considering what to get when acquiring lights and sound for your theatre program. This is of course assuming that an upgrade needs to be made. If you are all set, skip down to the next section, "Using What You Have." However, most theatre programs need to upgrade their lights and/or sound at some point in their director's tenure.

I may sound like a broken record at this point, but lights and sound are integral to an audience enjoying a theatrical production. They are less noticed by the layperson watching the show than, say, costumes or sets, but really good lights and sounds for a show go a long way toward turning an ordinary production into an extraordinary one.

When considering upgrading your lighting and sound systems in your theatre, it is important to think about the future. If you are upgrading and have the money to do so, get more than what you need for the next show. Get more, get bigger, get better. The hope and the goal is that your program will grow into needing even more equipment. Sometimes school administrators can stomach one large purchase in five years rather than five yearly purchases.

Next, you'll need to consider what level of equipment you want to work with. This decision is based on several factors, including whether students are running the equipment, the budget, the theatre space, and program needs. Although there are many variables in determining the different levels of equipment, I will separate them into three levels: beginner, moderate, and expert. They can also be called simple, medium, and difficult. They can likewise be called cheap, relatively Cheap, and expensive.

> **Beginner/Simple/Cheap:** This first tier involves having fewer lights, smaller boards, less powerful speakers, and non-mic'ed voices. Sure, it would be nice to have 24-plus lights for your stage, but you might only have the budget for four to eight. The good thing about lights,

especially the powerful LED ones of today, is that the farther back you put the light, the more stage space it covers. Another bonus to the LED lights of today is that they can shine any color in the spectrum. Having a small board to control those lights is also a must to keep it simple. You can find a very simple lightboard online for less than $100. It won't be smart, it's very analog, and all of the lighting cues will have to be done by hand, but it keeps costs down. Next will be less powerful speakers, but this will also include a smaller board. A two-speaker setup with a small four-input board can be bought at Guitar Center for about $200. They are loud enough to fill up a small to medium theatre space and can be used to hook up a few inputs. Lastly, no mics. Mics and mic systems are a very expensive part of theatre sound. It is good for our students to learn to project their voices anyway, so without the mics, they will have no choice. Now, if your students are projecting their voices great but the theatre space is still preventing the audience from hearing the dialogue or music, it might be time to consider moving to the next tier.

Moderate/Medium/Relatively Cheap: This next tier is an upgrade on the last one; getting a few more lights, getting smarter boards, getting some genuine speakers, and starting with beginning mic systems. This tier will allow you to get 8–16 lights for your stage, possibly including a spot. You might also be able to experiment with non-LED lights to get different looks and glows. You might be able to get a bottom-tier smart lightboard at this level. They will come with some software where you can program the lighting show without having to switch to each cue manually. Upgrading to smart with both lighting and soundboards presents a lot of possibilities for making a show run even better. Getting some large, genuine performance space speakers will be necessary at this tier. I'd start looking at other schools and pawn shops for some used equipment before buying new ones. Nowadays, they make rather small speakers that have a great sound and can fill up the space plenty. Lastly, with this tier, this is where you can get into some wireless mics. You likely won't be able to get enough wireless mics for all of your actors right away. At first, you get two to four of them, which go to your mains. Then every year you add one to two more, and before you know it you have a full 16-mic system. Quality in the receiver in the mic pack is important if your receiver will be far away/out of sight of the stage. Some of the cheaper ones don't reach the signal through walls or over a certain distance. My advice in this tier is to get fewer of the nicer ones rather than more of the less nice ones. However, it's the opposite when it comes to the wireless mics. When I arrived at the private school, a tech guy who had been advising them on all the equipment they got (and got a commission for the more he sold) sold the school $350 top-of-the-line Sennheiser wireless mics to plug into the pack. When I got there, I told him point blank, "You realize I have to hand these to 8-year-olds right??" Wireless mics are fragile and even the best ones break or tear. You can buy a $30 wireless mic for any of the pack inputs on Amazon. These work almost as well and are a fraction of the cost. So, if a student breaks it or it stops working through wear and tear, it is fine, you just get another $30 one. You can get 12 of those for the price of one too-expensive one.

Expert/Difficult/Expensive: This final tier is the pinnacle of theatre equipment. It's the best stuff, the biggest stuff, and the smartest stuff. The hope is that all of us are headed in this direction. Your program should be gaining money to put in the war chest, and the war chest purchases throughout the years usually go to equipment purchases like this. With this system, you can have a 16–32 light system controlled by a top-of-the-line smart software lighting board. You'll have multiple professional speakers with a proper subwoofer controlled by a soundboard with 16–32 inputs. You'll also be able to have a wireless microphone for every actor on the stage. This is especially important if you are performing big musicals with lots of ensemble singing. I still advocate that if you are having elementary and middle school students use wireless microphones to not yet get professional, super-expensive wireless mics. Stick to the ones you can replace easily and that work just about the same.

Using What You Have

Regardless of whether you arrive at a school with a perfect setup or one with next to nothing, you will have to learn what you have. Unfortunately, theatre directors are made to work with so much junk. However, whatever you have, familiarize yourself with it. Learn how to operate what you have available to you. Whether it is a $100 board or a $5,000 board, it will be useless if you don't know how to run it.

As time goes on, the newer equipment is becoming more user-friendly and intuitive, but you might not be inheriting the newest stuff. I've worked in theatres with equipment from the 1960s and 1970s in there! Have you ever run music off of a record player for a show before? 'Cause I have.

You as director are the resident expert. You need to know the equipment inside and out and how to troubleshoot problems when they come up. This is especially important if you are running the board(s) for the show. Even if you aren't running the board yourself, you are likely going to be the one to teach the volunteers/students running the boards how to work them. You have to do your homework, you have to work with it, you have to learn as much as you can so that the tech side of your show is as smooth as possible.

Here are some ideas on how to learn to use the equipment you have in your theatre program:

YouTube: YouTube is amazing when it comes to equipment tutorials. There are *so* many videos of people showing common issues with lighting and soundboards, troubleshooting errors, fixing breaks, unboxing, and more. Even if they don't have the exact model you are working with, the likelihood is that they have the same brand and a similar model that will work the same way.

The Manual: All of this equipment comes with manuals. Nowadays they are all online in PDF form. If you get new equipment in, *always* keep the manuals in a safe place. You never know when you'll need them. They are a great resource for setting up the equipment properly and troubleshooting issues.

Tech/Sound Person: Whether your school has a tech person familiar with the equipment or your town has a music/tech store that sells similar equipment, get that person to come teach you the ropes. Those expert sound (and light) people will often come in and help give you ideas about how to make your system better in the process. You can also reach out to local community or regional theatres. Those theatres usually have their number-one tech person who would be a great resource to help teach you how to work with your equipment.

Other Directors: Other directors in schools in the area (and not in your area) are a great resource for theatre equipment expertise. There are countless Facebook groups of theatre directors where you can post a question and you will get your answer in minutes. Have other local directors who know their stuff come by and help you figure out your equipment.

The Internet: Good to narrow it down, right? 'Just Google it' might be the most oft-heard phrase of the last 20 years. I am constantly amazed at how I can ask a very specific question about a very specific piece of equipment on the internet, and it will find someone who already asked that question. These pieces of equipment and others in the same brand as them are being used all over the world. Some people get on the internet and ask the questions you are likely having to troubleshoot or learn. Just Google it and see what you can find. If, in the worst-case scenario, you don't find your question answered, then you can go on one of those sites and be a person who asks the question to help out those who will come after you.

The Company: The company that made the equipment usually will have a telephone number (or email address) where you can contact them and chat with someone who can help you figure out the equipment.

Music

Lastly, in this chapter, I want to talk about music. This is always a consideration when you are directing a musical but is often one for straight plays as well. Intro, background, and outro music during straight plays, if used effectively, can really heighten the emotion of your show. But whether it is the backing soundtrack for your straight play or the music your musical actors are singing to in a musical, you can use different types of music. Some of those types of music and the pros and cons of each are discussed as follows.

Tracks

AKA Canned Music. Canned music – more than anything in musical theatre – gets a really bad rap. Here is my opinion on the matter that should become your opinion on the matter: "Canned is not Banned." The number-one complaint against music tracks is: "It doesn't sound as good." Really? Are you sure about that? Professionally recorded Broadway music tracks are played by professional musicians, a full orchestra (or band) playing all of the notes on the page. Are you honestly saying that sounds not as good as the high school orchestra attempting the music? The music tracks never speed up or slow down. The notes are never out of tune. Actors can rehearse with the tracks from day one. And it is, in most cases, much cheaper than hiring an orchestra or accompanists. "They do live music on Broadway! Live music is what theatre is all about." Yes, true, they do it on Broadway, but we are not Broadway. I am a huge proponent of getting the best sound out of your production. In most cases, tracks will give you that Broadway sound.

Now, there are tracks out there you should avoid. There are now MIDI tracks of full musical scores. Companies are selling these MIDI files because they are versatile. You can speed them up, slow them down, cut measures out, and most importantly, change keys. The problem with them is that they sound fake. They have that cringy MIDI sound that makes you feel like you are in an early 1990s videogame. If you are going with tracks, find a real orchestra recording. If all you can find is the MIDI, go with live performance.

Get acquainted with the computer application Audacity. It is a free, easy-to-use, accessible audio editing software. You can do all kinds of things to the audio files with Audacity to make some custom tracks for your shows.

You can cut sections, add sections, repeat sections, blend songs, fade in, fade out, speed up, slow down, change keys, and more.

Orchestra/Band

Here are a few reasons why you would opt for a live orchestra instead of recorded tracks:
- You want to or are made to collaborate with the instrumental music programs at your school.
- Your theatre doesn't have a good enough sound system to project the tracks properly.
- The tracks are cost-prohibitive or unavailable.

If one of these reasons is the case, then live music is where we should head.

Make sure the group that is performing the music is up to the task. Imagine having an absolutely perfect musical production: incredible acting, singing, dancing, costumes, sets, and props. But despite all of that being amazing, the middle school band is attempting to play music past their ability. It can very well ruin the whole show. Make sure that whatever group is playing for you has enough skills and rehearsal to pull off the music. No music is better than bad music.

Make sure all of the important instrument parts are covered. I was once in a production of *Fiddler on the Roof* and the live band didn't have a clarinet in it. Do you have any idea how much clarinet is in that show? A LOT. Certain parts can be doubled and tripled up, but cutting out important cues and melodic pieces in the sheet music can hamper the production.

Make sure there is room in your theatre space for the performers. Some shows have the instrumentalists onstage with the actors. Some theatre spaces have a pit below the stage. Some that do not have the ability to do the last two instead put the orchestra right in front between the audience and the stage. Be careful with this option as it may affect sight lines and be too loud for those in the front of the audience to hear anything happening onstage.

The more rehearsal, the better. The more you have the full orchestra or band playing with your actors, the better the actors will perform, the better the instrumentalists will perform, and the more knowledgeable the conductor will be in conducting the cues. Too often, orchestras come in for tech week or even just a day or two of tech week. This is not enough time for the actors, instrumentalists, or conductors to feel comfortable with performing for an audience. Get the instrumentalists in there early and often.

Piano

The last music type we will talk about is the solo instrumentalist performer. This is usually in the form of a pianist.

You would likely use a pianist instead of a full orchestra or tracks for one of the following reasons:

- The show is too small, minor, or short to warrant an orchestra.
- You don't have the money for tracks or an orchestra.
- The show calls for solo piano.

Piano backing up musical theatre is classic and has a charm all its own. The same warnings apply to a solo piano that did with an orchestra (more rehearsal, make sure they are up to the task, etc.).

Piano can be the most versatile option for live music. If you get a pianist who has a good ear for what is happening onstage, they can change *how* they are playing what they are playing to match the tempo, key, and volume of the singers.

Whichever type of music you use for your productions, whether it is pre-recorded tracks, live orchestra, or solo piano, make sure that it is the best version of what you have chosen. Don't settle for something mediocre when something better is just within your grasp.

 Key Takeaways

1. When upgrading the sound and lights for your theatre space, get an upgrade that will prepare you for the future, pick a tier of beginner/moderate/expert that matches your needs and skills, and advocate for yourself and your program, including the importance of upgrading this equipment to the administration.
2. Become the resident expert in the sound and light equipment at your school by watching YouTube tutorial videos, reading the manual, speaking with a tech person or other experienced theatre director, searching the internet for your answers, or calling the company that made the equipment.
3. Choose the best-sounding music for your production that fits within your budget, in your theatre space, considering your equipment and the pros and cons of track versus live orchestra versus solo piano backing.

10

Advertisements, Tickets, and Programs

Imagine both of the following scenarios:

First scenario: You are going to watch a school play. You arrive in the theatre's lobby in a long line. Once you finally get to the front of the line, there is just one person with a metal cashbox guarding the door. You have to pull out your wallet and give this person cash to get in because there was no way to get tickets beforehand. Lucky for you, you got a ticket, because eventually some of the people in line behind you were not able to get one because they had sold out. In that group of people turned away were some of the performers' families and friends. The person at the cashbox, having received your cash, tears off a tiny red raffle ticket as your means of entry. You walk into the theatre, most of the seats are filled already, and you are forced to take a corner seat near the back. As the play goes on, you realize that you want to match a student onstage with a name. However, you have no program. No one does. You want to know more about the production, or the director's vision. Sorry, no program. You want a souvenir to remember this play you went to because you are a scrapbooking person, but all you have to tape into your scrapbook is a tiny red raffle ticket that says "Admit One" on it. Alright, let's look at another scenario.

Second scenario: You are going to watch a school play. Although you arrive at the theatre later than you intended, about three minutes before the show starts, no worries, you bought your ticket weeks ago on the school's website. You get there and skip the line of people who are buying tickets last minute, say your name to the person with a clipboard guarding the door, and they check you off and hand you a colorful, thick, and detailed program with a nice 2-by-11-inch cardstock ticket, which says the show title, date, time, and more. Although you got there late, again no worries, your booked ticket was for a specific seat. You happily climb into the middle of the second row and wait for the show to begin. While you wait, you flip through the program and read bios about every student actor, you read the director's process and vision letter, and you see a calendar of dates for the upcoming productions. When you get home, you gladly and prominently display your ticket above your program in your scrapbook and can look back at it for years to come.

Some will see that first scenario and say, "What does it matter?" People don't need tickets, and most throw away programs. Some look at the second scenario and say, "Well, that all sounds really nice, but why bother at my school that has only 50 students?"

In this chapter, I will try to help you understand why legitimate-looking tickets and programs can go a long way toward growing the theatre program's legitimacy. I will also give you some techniques as to how technology can benefit your program by making ticket-buying and show-entering hassle-free. But first, before people buy tickets and way before they are handed programs, they need to know about the show in the first place. How do we make sure they know about the show and where to get tickets beforehand? Advertisements.

Advertisements

If you are at a small school of around 250 students, if every single student and parent doesn't know that your major theatrical production is happening this weekend, you are not advertising enough. It's harder in 5A and 6A schools to reach the thousands of students and families, but we at a small school have no excuse. Your goal should be that every single person on your campus is aware of your show. Does that mean that every single person will come? No. Some don't know anyone in the production, some don't like the play, and some don't like theatre in general. However, ensuring that every person knows about the production gives you no excuse for why any seats were empty. Remember this phrase: If a single one of your seats is empty in your theatre, you are not advertising enough. Do not underestimate the value of proper advertising. There is no such thing as too much advertising.

Some might say that it was too much, but what is the worst that could happen? They just see and hear about it a little too much? My argument is that there is no such thing as too much advertising but there *is* such a thing as not enough. Following are several types of advertisements you can produce for your show and some tips and things to avoid for each of them.

Poster

This is the classic, and likely the one you see the most. The poster. Just because it is done a lot doesn't mean you should avoid it. Posters are a great way to get eyes on your program. As we discussed in the "Getting Everyone Interested" chapter, the more posters, the better. Don't be frugal with the printing, don't be choosy with the placement. Get those posters *everywhere* on campus. Get them in the teachers' lounge, the cafeteria, the gym, your classroom, other classrooms, the hallway, and even the bathrooms for crying out loud. You should prevent the chance of any student or teacher saying, "I didn't see it!" Not only should you post them on campus, but if you want to attract community members outside of your school community, get them out into your town/city. Have your students take them to their churches. Get them into every coffee shop and café in town. Put them in other arts venues.

What should the poster look like?
- Bigger than a normal sheet of paper – 11 by 17 inches is the standard. Everyone else prints their stuff on normal paper, so why should we? If ours is bigger, it'll get noticed above the rest.
- In color, with a colorful, appealing, and good-looking picture. Stay away from black and white. Stay away from clip art or lame pics. Get a visually appealing painting or art piece or show a graphic that really draws the eye. Some use photographs of their students in costume in the show. This is alright if it is done well, but it can also easily look less appealing if the photo doesn't look right.
- Using a visually appealing, non-default, possibly a show-related font. If you use Times New Roman, Calibri, or Ariel in your advertisements, STOP IT. Using a default font in your ads shows that you didn't put in effort. It doesn't take that much effort, just highlight all of the text and pick a new font. It should be unique and different. It should draw the eye. It should be related to the show. When I directed *The Hobbit*, I wanted the poster font to be related to *Lord of the Rings*. After a quick Google search, there were *Lord of the Rings* and *Hobbit* fonts everywhere online. I picked one, downloaded it for free, and used it. There are thousands of handmade fonts online. Go look for one that relates to your show and use it.

- It should include all the information one would need for the show: (1) title of the show, (2) a short description of the show, (3) date(s) of the show (including day(s) of the week), (4) time(s) the show starts and the time(s) the doors open, (5) name and address of the show's venue (especially for posting them outside of school), (6) how and where to get tickets, including a website or QR code if you have that, and (7) any other information that you legally have to have on there via your show's contract.

School Announcement
Schools have different types of announcements. Some don't have them at all. But if your school does in some form, make sure that your show is in there.

It doesn't necessarily need to be you announcing it; however, if you choose a student, make sure they can give the announcement the gusto and legitimacy it needs to be fun and convincing.

Make sure it includes all the information for the show dates, times, tickets, etc., while also including a short blurb about the show and why people should come to it.

In-Person Announcement
This is where you as director will speak in front of various school gatherings, including lunch in the cafeteria, staff meetings, sports games, other fine arts events, other school-wide events, and more. Again, make sure all the important information is included while also adding fun, legitimate, and convincing rhetoric to get people to take an interest.

Social Media
It goes without saying, that social media is pervasive in today's society. Lean into it instead of away from it. Your show should be advertised on all versions of the school's social media using the poster file and other show photographs. Your program can even do a 'social media takeover' where your students can control the posts for a day or a week.

Email
Send a fun, informative, legitimate, convincing e-mail to the school staff, the parent e-mail list, the board, and any other e-mail list your school might have like a benefactor list or local school list.

Show Sneak Peek Performance
Have your show perform a scene or song at morning meetings, chapel, lunch, etc. Invite the parents of the performing students to come and enjoy the fruits of their students' labor.

Tickets

Think about all of the shows you've been to and what the tickets look like. I assume you've seen everything from those red raffle tickets to a professionally printed Broadway ticket, to no ticket at all. Nice, well-put-together, visually appealing tickets are important to building legitimacy in your program. Is it easier to go without them? Sure. Is it less work for you to not have to make them, print them, and cut them? Sure. But things like this separate the good programs from the great programs. However, tickets are not just physical, it is also how your audience gets into the show and where they sit when they get there. So let's talk about the three aspects of theatrical tickets: (1) what types/tiers/levels of tickets there should be, (2) how your audience members acquire them, and (3) what the tickets should look like when the audience has them.

What Types of Tickets to Provide

If your show only has 'general admission' tickets, where every person gets to choose wherever they want to sit, you are missing out on not only an opportunity for more revenue for your program but also having your audience members miss out on acquiring a good seat. The first-come, first-served model works to an extent. It gets people to show up early, stand in line, get excited, and race to their seats. However, you need to keep in mind people will *always* be late. They will be late getting tickets, late to arrive, and late to get to their seat. Some people buy their tickets very early but show up late on the night of. Some buy their tickets at the last minute, but show up early the night of.

If you have the capacity and ticket-selling software/site to be able to sell specific seats and provide tickets to those specific seats, do so. It is the best way to legitimize your program while being able to have people choose exactly where they want to sit when they buy the ticket. In programs like that, you can separate the seats at different prices. The front rows are the most expensive, the middle section is less expensive, and the sides and back are the least expensive.

A model I had for a while is two types of tickets: general and premium. Premium tickets guaranteed the ticketholder a seat in the first two rows. They were double the price, but some parents won't mind, they will just be happy to get a great seat. From the third row back was general admission. Some of your audience members won't care at all to sit near the front and will be happy being in the corner in the back.

However you split up the types of tickets, remember not to do just general; separate by price and location, and sell individual seats if you can.

How to Get Tickets

Using the introduction example: If the *only* way your audience members can get tickets to your show is at the door, you are doing them a disservice. I'm not saying *not* to sell them at the door. Selling at the door is important for last-minute buyers. However, if you get a good program going and plentiful and efficient ways for selling tickets, you might not need to sell at the door because you'll be sold out well before opening night!

Here are some of the ways to sell your tickets:

Online: There are so many great ticket-selling services online nowadays. Usually, it is associated with a fee either per ticket or upfront, but the fee is negligible compared to the convenience. Get a good site that works for your program. If you are selling individual seats, make sure you have a site that has that capacity. Post the website link and/or QR code on all advertisements.

At the Front Desk: On your campus, your wonderful front desk receptionist is the first line of defense for all visitors. Your community should know that as a show approaches, they can go to the front desk and buy tickets in person. Parents drop off their kids on campus anyway, so while they are already there, they can stop in and grab their tickets. When it is tech week, you should encourage the front desk person to ask every person (after they talk about whatever they came to talk about): "By the way, have you gotten your tickets for our show this weekend?"

Student Sold: The ol' Boy Scout and Girl Scout model. Some programs have been successful in giving, say, ten tickets to each of the performers, and they are responsible for selling their tickets by a certain date. They bring back the money for the ones sold and bring back the leftover tickets they didn't sell. You can give an incentive to students who sell all of their tickets. You can also give more tickets to those who sold all ten of theirs.

At Other Events: You should have a table/booth at other major school events as your event approaches. Sports games, school-wide events, other fine arts events, etc. Get a table, fill it with your show's advertisements, and sell there.

At the Door: If you still have tickets available by opening night, you sell the rest at the door. Make sure to have not just cash options; make sure there is a credit card reader as well for people to purchase conveniently. Some programs make at-the-door tickets cost more to incentivize buying beforehand.

What They Should Look Like

Tickets take many forms. I'll start with what they *shouldn't* look like. I've ragged on the little red raffle ticket enough, so, yeah, don't do that. Same with the posters: no plain fonts, no black and white, make them with good materials and make them big.

Some online ticket programs, especially for community and regional theatres, provide perforated tickets that are custom-printed for every show. Some programs, when tickets are bought online, e-mail the purchaser their ticket that is scanned at the door. If this is the case, I still say provide them with a souvenir ticket. It really is a nice touch for legitimizing your program.

What I went with was a thick piece of cardstock cut lengthwise four times creating four 2.25-inch by 11-inch tickets. Not normal paper, but nice, really thick cardstock. The color of the cardstock can vary based on what day the show is, what type/tier of ticket they have, or even just themed based on the show itself. On the ticket, it includes all of the show's information, including the exact date and time. They were printed in color, including a big colorful show title logo. Once you have your ticket file made for a show, the following shows will be easier to do as you just fill in different information for the different shows.

Programs

Programs! Get your programs here!

Programs should be provided to all audience members. They should be given at the door and should be well put together. But before we get to the free programs, let's talk about the ones that cost.

Commemorative programs are sold at sporting events and even at Broadway shows. These are usually $5 apiece and are nice magazine-type programs that include great photos of the event. You can include these commemorative programs in your show if you like. It is a nice little added revenue and can be a great keepsake for families. They are complicated and expensive to produce, but if your community is into it, go for it.

Anyways, back to our regularly scheduled *program*.

Programs are an excellent keepsake for the show, as they provide information to the audience about the show, the rules, the director's vision, the student actors, and future performing arts events. They can also be used to advertise certain businesses that donated to your program, to thank certain people who helped out with the production, and to let the audience know the plan/timeline for the evening. As stated earlier, programs should be provided at the door for everyone who enters the theatre, even the kiddos. Some parents will say "No, just one for us, thanks," which is fine. But some will allow it, and the kiddos get a kick out of having a program just like the adults. It gives them a sense of importance.

Before talking about what is inside the programs, here is a general rule of what they should look like (and not look like). Again, these rules are similar to the posters and tickets: no plain/default fonts – use unique and show-related fonts. No black and white, print in color. It's more expensive, but it's worth it for the legitimacy of your program. Use quality paper, if not thicker paper, then at least non-plain white copy paper. Get a nice tan/gold paper sometimes, or a pastel. White color is okay sometimes, but try exploring other paper colors. A generally good program size is a normal letter-sized paper folded in half to make an 8.5-by-5.5-inch folded booklet. If you have a lot of pages, you'll have to staple the middle, but if it's only two to four pages or so, you can go with just folding.

Alright, now let's break down what is inside them.

Cover

Use the best, most colorful, most unique show advertisement picture you can. This should be the show's logo or a painting thereof, or in some cases a student photo. It should cover the whole cover. You will need to include other legal text shown in your contract. Other than that, feel free to add the yellow "Playbill" top for a little added theatre flair. You can change "Playbill" to something that fits your program, if your school is called "Smith High School," then it can be "Smithbill" on the top. Keep the information on the front minimal, because you'll have plenty of room inside to include info.

Inside Front Cover

This is the credits page. Include the name of the show again, followed by all of the people on the production team and everyone else who helped with the production: Director, Writer, Composer, Lyricist, Music Director, Choreographer, Tech Director, Dance Captain, Production Assistants, "Special Thanks To:" Stage Managers/Techs, Hair/Makeup Captain, etc. etc.

Audience Notes

This is the rules and information page. It needs to be included. It goes a long way toward educating the audiences of today on how to properly act at a theatrical performance. Here is the information I included in one of my production programs for you to use if you'd like.

- No Flash Photography
- No Video Recording of Any Kind
- No "Screen Holding"
- No Cell Phone or Other Digital Noise
- No Talking
- No Singing
- Please avoid getting up in the middle of the performance.
- Please remove disruptive children.
- Keep the aisles completely clear of limbs, purses, etc., as students will be walking/dancing/running up and down the aisles several times during the production.
- Please do not disturb anyone else's enjoyment of this event in any way.
- This production will include one 15-minute intermission where you may use the restroom facilities, partake in concessions, and/or hang out on the patio outside. Lights dimming will indicate the end of intermission. Please be in your seat by the time the show begins and also when intermission ends as the room will go completely dark.

Company List

This should be a list of your actors in alphabetical order, including a nice photograph. Some programs will also include a brief biography of the performer as well, including what other shows they've done and what they think of the current show.

Show-Specific Information

This is where to include the show's information again, including who wrote it/composed it, etc. If there are different scenes, you can put those in if you wish. For a musical, include the songs performed in order per act. These show orders are important for audience members to reference to see where in the show they are at the moment, so they know how long it is until intermission/the end.

Director's Note

This is the privilege of the director to share their thoughts, dreams, visions, feelings, and experiences with this show. It gives the audience (and the students in the show) a deep, unique perspective as to why this show was chosen, an interpretation of its meaning, and how it has been going for this specific production.

Upcoming Events

This is a chance for you to include what is coming up in your program and the other fine arts programs at the school. Include next plays, musicals, productions, performances, summer camps, concerts, and more. Include the dates, times, locations, what group is performing, and how to get tickets if applicable.

Advertisements

If you had part of your revenue being donations from businesses in exchange for advertising in the program, they need to be included as well. I think it's important not to hide the advertisements, make them small, or diminish them in any way. They should be a featured part of the program with a nice, big, colorful ad. Ads that have taglines related to the show are a bonus.

Key Takeaways

1. Get people to know about your show and attend your show through various types of advertisements that are legitimate, colorful, plentiful, fun, informative, and convincing.
2. Tickets for your shows should be provided at different price points and should be available for purchase in multiple ways, including online, at the front desk, sold by students at other school events, and at the door.
3. Programs for your show should likewise be legitimate, colorful, well made, and filled with lots of information, including credits, audience notes, a company list with pictures and bio, show-specific information, a director's note, a calendar of upcoming events, and paid-for advertisements.

11

Picking Shows

How many musicals exist in the world? No, take a guess.

Now, how many plays? Take a guess.

Of course, there is no way of knowing the exact number of musicals and plays ever written, but I asked our friend Google, and here's what it had to say. The closest estimate for the number of musicals is 20,000. As for plays, that number jumps to 100,000. Those numbers could be way off, but let's just assume for visualization's sake that they are correct.

Now imagine it came time for you to pick your next production and all 20,000 musicals and 100,000 plays were stacked in a massive room in front of you. You cannot leave the room until you pick the perfect next production. Happy browsing!

For those of us who have had to pick productions, sometimes it feels as if this fictitious scenario is reality. The number of productions out there is astronomical. It can be beyond overwhelming to peruse, preview, and read potential productions, and then when you finally choose a show, it can be quite nerve-wracking worrying that you chose wrong.

In this chapter, I hope to give you the tools to narrow down that list of 120,000 productions so that your pool of potential productions is much, much smaller. We will analyze the process of picking shows based on present circumstances, history, and future hopes. I also hope to help you be confident in picking said production so that before a single student knows the title of it, you already know you made the right choice.

Picking Shows Based on the Present

What I mean by 'based on the present' is that you need to first consider who you have in your community now. Where is your program now? What are your current students' present strengths?

Pick for the cast you have, not the cast you want. A director colleague of mine found a show they were in love with, everything was beautiful, and they simply did not have the bodies. They tried to force it and it failed.

Don't pick too far ahead of time. Some directors are not one to pick ahead of time because they don't even know who they'd have and not have. Directors will have a good idea, and pick a show, but then the two to three people they thought they could count on decide not to audition. Don't pick too far ahead of time.

Pick a show that works with your community and cast. If you've got four boys and four girls and they are hilarious, don't do *Asylum*. If you've got some mopey dramatic kids, don't do *Into the Woods*. It is okay and encouraging to stretch performers, but not at the expense of your program's success.

Consider your students in seniority. We will talk about how seniority plays into casting in the "Auditions and Casting" chapter. However, if you are a high school director with a small group of dedicated and experienced seniors, or a middle school director with some really talented 8th graders, think about some options for them. That is where *The Hobbit* came from for me. That year I had three upperclass boys, all of whom were very talented and had been in multiple shows. Upon trying to search for shows with three male mains, I came across *The Hobbit* and knew it was a good fit for them. One became Gandalf, one became Bilbo, and one became Thorin Oakenshield.

Pick a show based on your students' present awareness, maturity, emotionality, and talent – especially for middle school content matters. The students have to be able to understand the content. They need to have characters they can portray.

Picking Shows Based on the Past

Unless your school's theatre program is brand new, you as a new director will be inheriting a program with a past. When you are hired into the job, your first priority is to get all the information you can about the program of the past, all the productions they've done in the last decade, what their schedule has been like, and more.

First, you need to think about scheduling more productions with fewer rehearsals. More Productions, Less Rehearsal. Figure out how many productions a year your school has done in the past. You might not even be a new director there, but now you are reading this and can change. Some programs only have two shows a year, and even worse yet some only perform one a year. That is not enough! How are students going to get invested and get better and get passionate about theatre if they only have one chance to perform a year? That's like joining the basketball team and practicing for a whole semester just to play one game. As mentioned in part one of this book, try to get at least four productions a year. This is between your extracurricular programs, curricular programs, clubs, and competition theatre. You schedule fewer rehearsals to keep the students' interest piqued. You want them to burst into opening night with excitement, not dragging their feet into opening night out of boredom. If you are directing a one-act play or short full-length, you do not need three to four months of rehearsal. The students will get complacent and bored, and it will show in their performance. Have enough rehearsal to learn the show and to get it ready for opening night, but not much more.

You need to look into the school's past and see if they have been performing one-acts or full-lengths, dramas or comedies, straight plays or musicals. If they have been doing only one-acts, it'll be your job to start out with a one-act, but to eventually build to a full-length. If they have been doing only full-lengths, you will want to avoid going back down to one-acts. With genres like dramas and comedies, you want to expand the school's horizon. Perhaps you find out they've always done a murder mystery every single year. Murder mysteries are fun, but show them that there is more out there. Perhaps they've only done silly modern comedies. Don't get rid of those entirely, but try to find shows that stretch their dramatic muscles as well. Picking a 'dramedy' is a good transitionary measure. As for whether they have been doing plays or musicals, if the school has been exclusively doing one or the other, it will be a shock to the school's system to right away introduce the other. If all they know is musicals, doing a straight play right away will have a lot of pushback and vice versa. There will be more information below in the "Future" section about building your first musical.

While looking into the school's past, it'll be important to avoid doing a production that was just recently done. The unofficial rule for repeating the same production is ten years. With a school, perhaps seven is the max since there is so much turnover. However, avoiding similar productions will spread the program's variety and avoid more complacency. I said in the intro there were 120,000 productions out there. Why in the world would you repeat one of those 120,000 so soon after your school has done it?

Now, a hitch to this is something I talked about in the Costume section in the last chapter. You may, like me, come across a stash of costumes from the program's past. Your budget may be minimal, and you can decide to save money on costumes and props to do that same play those costumes were from. This is a rare case, but it happens. In that case, they had done *Narnia: The Lion the Witch and the Wardrobe*, and I was urged by the administration to do that same one again as it had been seven years ago. However, if I could go back, I wouldn't have directed *The Lion The Witch and the Wardrobe*. I would have perhaps picked a *similar* production that could still use those costumes and save money. Perhaps *Prince Caspian*? Perhaps another fantastical story with animals?

When picking shows, you also need to consider *your* past as a director. If it is your first year and your first production, you don't need to be picking an incredibly difficult show to start with. Go easy your first year. You need to learn the ropes with training wheels before jumping on the motorcycle. If this isn't your first year and you've had some experience, it's important to know your strengths, know your weaknesses, and stay *near* your wheelhouse. Some directors say, "stay in your wheelhouse" or "do what you know." I think it's important for directors to try different things and to expand their skills and horizons. However, if you are a seasoned veteran and know exactly what you are great at and what you are passionate about, but most importantly exactly what you are *not* great at and what you hate, don't pick shows that you will not direct well.

I once knew a director who was about as seasoned a veteran as you can imagine. She was in her 70s and had been directing for nearly 50 years. Her resume, experience, and awards proved she was good at directing. However, her personality was very serious, very critical, very tough, very dramatic, and very competitive. Her strengths were in one-act competition shows, especially dramas, period pieces, true stories, and serious straight plays. She, however, volunteered to direct the theatre's next production, *A Play That Goes Wrong*. If you aren't aware of *A Play That Goes Wrong*, in short, it is the funniest production ever put onstage in the history of humankind. It is a slapstick, physical, farcical, play-within-a-play, murder mystery, British, ridiculous, silly, amazing production. This director knew nothing about slapstick. She openly admitted she hated farces, and it was immediately made clear that she did not understand the play-within-a-play genre. *A Play That Goes Wrong* was nowhere near her wheelhouse and so therefore the production suffered greatly.

Unfortunately, she nor the theatre didn't learn their lesson on that one, because the very next production was *SpongeBob SquarePants the Musical*. This seasoned director, who again had the respect of the theatre community, of the state and country, didn't understand the silly plot, characters, colorfulness, meaning, and ridiculousness that came with that cartoon-based show. Now, had they picked based on her strengths, they would have done a Chekhov play, or *Flowers for Algernon*, or a Holocaust-based play. She would have no doubt excelled at what she was good at. I use that example to urge you to be cautious. Develop your skills through the years, try things, experiment, but eventually sharpen and hone what you are good at and go with it. Know what you are good at and know what you aren't. Choose plays near your wheelhouse and your program will flourish because of it.

Picking Shows Based on the Future

Whether you are coming into a new program or an existing program, your eyes should always be on the future of that program and its growth. Picking shows based on the future of the program is an important factor you should keep in mind.

Picking shows that are 'hooks' are vitally important, especially if it is a new program with not a lot of participants yet. As mentioned in the "Getting Everyone Interested" chapter, you need to pick shows that will hook students into the program. Pick well-known projects versus unknown titles. Pick things that the students will like, love, be passionate about, and know beforehand. Pick one that has been a movie or a very popular play. Pick one that is overdone, it's okay right away. You can work your way to the obscure as the years go on. You need to focus on the growth of your program for the future, therefore, you need to get them hooked now. Pick shows with recognizable titles, recognizable characters, and recognizable songs that appeal to the students and will make them want to join to be a part of it.

Attached to hooking them, as the years go on, you want your students to commit to the program to help the future. So, it's important to know that if you want your kids to be committed, they have to want to do the play and they have to be invested in the story. If you choose unknown, unliked, obscure projects that the students don't relate with on a regular basis, you will hear these phrases on repeat: "I don't get it," "I don't like it," "This show is dumb," "I want to quit." You'll be fighting that fight for months. They can't grow for the future if they are fighting the whole time.

If your program has never done a musical or hasn't done one in years, you cannot just throw *In the Heights* at them and hope for a great production. It is important to plan for the future and build a musical. The same thing happened in one of my programs. They had never done a musical. I knew I wanted to get them to that point. So, during a play, I had three songs inserted into the play, one solo and two ensemble songs. They were simple, short, recognizable songs, but they stretched the actors' muscles in singing onstage. Not only was that for their benefit to get used to singing onstage, but it was also for my benefit to see if they had what it takes. Then the next play I did, I inserted a big, choreographed dance number during the dance within the plot. It was 2 minutes long and taught by a real choreographer. The students had a blast and did a great job. So now that I had been building up to it, the following production was their first musical. It had a solo and a few ensemble songs and a few choreographed dances. It was a comparatively easy musical, just to get their feet wet. I was glad that I used those other two plays to build up to it.

While I'm on the subject of musicals, let's briefly talk about "Jr." shows. If you feel like your program is only up to a Jr. show, that's fine. If you feel like the full Broadway version of the show would be too much for you or them to handle, that's fine. However, I encourage you to steer away from Jr. shows and to try to do the full-length Broadway versions of the show. Do *Annie*, not *Annie Jr.* Do *Shrek*, not *Shrek Jr.* Do *The Music Man*, not *The Music Man Jr.* Full Broadway productions of the shows are, for lack of a better term, fuller. They have more plot, more character, more songs, more dances, and are more enjoyable. Jr. shows take away a lot of plot, lines, characters, lyrics, and harmonies to try to squeeze a 2–2.5-hour production into 60 minutes. There are a few exceptions to this. Some shows are *only* available currently as a Jr. production, so if that show is the one you want to do, you have no choice. Also, Jr. shows are more for younger productions like elementary and in some cases middle school. I've seen far too many high schools perform Jr. shows and just thought to myself that those students could have done the whole thing. I know it's less work. I know it's shorter. I know it's easier. I know it's cheaper. But working less on shorter, easier, and cheaper projects is *not* how to grow your program. It is not how to direct a legitimate and excellent program.

Lastly, it's important to have your mind on the longevity of the program as well as your job in it. Nowadays, things are very touchy, personal, and controversial. Grey lines are moving all the time, and political correctness is sweeping across the country. Beware of selecting controversial projects. One of my colleagues said: "Anything remotely controversial and you'll be on the news." It's true. Don't be stubborn about it and push buttons just to push buttons. Be cautious. When in doubt, keep looking.

Key Takeaways
1. Pick shows based on the present status of your program now, including the cast you have, their skill level, their wheelhouse, their seniority, and their maturity.
2. Pick shows based on the past of the program at your school, including scheduling more productions with fewer rehearsals to grow the program, not picking shows that have been done recently, and not picking shows outside of your wheelhouse as an experienced director.
3. Pick shows based on the future of your program by hooking students in right away with shows they know and like, by building up to a musical slowly instead of slamming it on them, by avoiding Jr. shows in lieu of full Broadway productions, and by avoiding overly controversial topics that could jeopardize your program.

12

Traditions and Legacy

I was offered two jobs on the exact same day. Within the performing arts, you can't imagine two more dissimilar positions that I had to choose from.

Position 1: Head Theatre Director at a 4A public school. This school's theatre program was already successful. They consistently made 1's at contest. The school and program had been around since the early 1900s and had dozens of directors in that time. I would be coming in to maintain the program's already established success. I would be paid an average public school teacher's wage.

Position 2: Performing Arts Director at a small private Christian school. I was asked to come in to do three things: (1) direct, improve, and grow the established choir program; (2) rescue the small, failing theatre program; and (3) start a band program. The school had only been around for 20 years and had only two directors in that time. I would be paid 25% less than the first position.

So, I think you know at this point which job offer I ended up accepting – position 2. But go back, and look at the two choices. Would you have made the same choice? Everyone has different priorities and strengths, I know.

"But you would have gotten paid so much more at the other job!" Yes, I would have. But a simple fact remains about teaching in the performing arts: If you are doing it for the money, you are doing it for the wrong reasons.

Beyond the pay, what is the number-one reason that I chose position 2? Building traditions and legacy. If I took position 1, so far as contest excellence was concerned, all I could do was make things worse. They can't score higher than 1's after all. And they had been around since the Wilson administration – they had traditions already well established. With position 2, the growth potential was astronomical. I would be able to start a program, rescue another program, and grow yet another program. I would be able to create traditions. I could write their fight song that didn't exist yet, build to a tradition of excellence, and create the foundations of a legacy that could last for a century and a half.

As you are getting your program up and running, it is important to focus on creating traditions, continuing traditions, and solidifying traditions into legacy. Also, let's say that you took position 1 above – the already established program. Does that mean you can't add, change, or improve on traditions that are there? Of course not. It is easy in this profession to get caught up in the day-to-day short-term, but here it is time to think about the year-to-yearlong term.

In this chapter, we are focusing on the long-term. I'll talk about what traditions you and your students can start for your programs that can continue year after year, decade after decade. I hope to help you zoom out away from the minutiae of the day-to-day directing of a program so that you can build a legacy to last a lifetime and beyond.

Creating Traditions

Before we get to talking about all the kinds of traditions you and your students can start for your program, we need to first discuss how to properly introduce, change, or eliminate those traditions within a theatre program. We will break down three aspects of traditions within a theatre program: (1) traditions that are already in place, (2) traditions that the director creates, and (3) traditions that the students create.

Traditions That Are Already in Place

A new director coming into an existing program and getting rid of the traditions that are already in place there on day one is not going to be the director there for long. Coming into an existing program is hard enough, so don't make it harder on yourself by 'cleaning shop' in your first week. In most cases, you will be coming into a program that has already existed for years, sometimes decades. The students and school are used to some traditions that they have been doing perhaps from generation to generation. It is not the new director's job to sweep away years of tradition for the sake of their own vision.

Can you introduce your own traditions in addition to the traditions that are already there? Absolutely! (see next section) But don't replace their traditions with yours, at least not right away. If some traditions were in place before that you really don't like or think the school could do away with, you will need to eliminate them slowly over several years. Let's say you are the high school director. When you come in, the sophomores, juniors, and seniors will already know and have practiced the traditions left behind. The freshmen are your newbies. However, three years down the road, all of the classes will have never worked under the previous 'administration.' Does that mean at the beginning of year four you can nix everything? No. Because the original sophomores, juniors, and seniors will hold onto the traditions that were left behind and show the underclass students the ropes. It takes time. You will have to determine which hills you are willing to die on. Sometimes the students' happiness and content will trump your preference about what traditions they exercise.

There are exceptions to this rule, of course. If you get to the school and speak with the students and they are in overwhelming agreement that "Oh man, we hate that tradition," or "We never want to do that event again," then you getting rid of those unliked traditions will in turn fuel your own expansion.

In existing programs, overall, try to add things slowly and take things away even more slowly. When we are talking in this chapter about traditions and legacy, we aren't talking about just this school year. We are talking about building a program for decades. If you have decades, then you have a few years to make a slow transition.

Traditions That the Director Creates

If you are coming into an existing program or starting a new program, share your vision with your students. Make them feel as if they are on the board, on the decision team, and an integral part of the process.

Students will be reticent in a director's first years to the traditions they add if the director doesn't have any trust built up with the students. The students need to be invested in the director and the program and the director needs to likewise be invested in the students. Getting students to buy into theatre is investing in the student body outside of the stage. Being present in the students' athletic seasons, academic challenges, and fine arts events shows that you care more about them than the performance they put on. Go the extra mile, make them feel heard, welcome, and loved, and they will in return give you the dedication, loyalty, and excellence that a great program deserves.

It will become easier to add traditions if your theatre program feels like more than just a show. Your theatre program should exist outside of the current show they are performing. Your theatre students should become a club, a group, a family, and in the words of a colleague of mine: a cult. She says: "Students have to buy in to the cult. Theatre people speak their own language, the director has to sell that. Misfits who join theatre crave that sense of belonging. Embrace the tribe." If there is that close-knit tribe aspect to your program, the director will be able to steer the ship more effectively.

Be a change champion. A change champion is someone who is contagiously excited about the changes that are coming. If you as director are thrilled, excited, and bursting with energy about the changes that you're about to put in place, sometimes the students will catch that excitement and be thrilled with you. If you are hesitant and scared to introduce new things, they will likewise sense that and be wary of what is to come. With the new things you bring to the table, convince them of the pros, explain to them how it will help the program, and do so with bursting excitement.

Traditions That the Students Create

Let the students be a part of building traditions, with your guidance. Students can build traditions. Build with the kids. Ask them: "What do you think we ought to do?" Do it organically. It shouldn't seem like you are just throwing them a bone. They should sense that you really care what they think.

Remind them that they are a part of the legacy that you together are building that will last way past their time at the school.

Creating a student leadership group in your theatre program is a great avenue for student-led traditions and change. It is sometimes hard to get 30–40 students to agree on adding or changing something, but if they elect representatives, four to five students can get those things done.

Students sometimes come up with weird, wild, crazy, unusual stuff. A lot of directors out there don't tolerate anything they don't understand. Some directors don't like things that are too loud, too out of control, or too chaotic. Some directors try to get rid of the students' weirdness, wildness, and craziness. I say don't beat the crazy out of them – embrace your students' crazy. It's not out of control, it's not chaotic as long as you are controlling the chaos. They might come up with things you don't understand or would have never thought of in a thousand years, but if they are excited, having a great time, and growing closer as a program while doing it, more power to them! Don't stifle their creativity. Shepherd it.

Traditions to Create

Now that we have talked about the proper way to create traditions, it is time to list many examples of what traditions you can create. These ideas come from my experiences, other programs I've seen/heard of, and from several performing arts colleagues interviewed for this book.

Here are examples of traditions you can create in a theatre program. They are in no particular order.

Beginning of the Year Trip: A trip at the very beginning of the year. We had facilitators who would put together a program of leadership exercises and team-building activities. We all slept in sleeping bags in a yurt in the middle of the woods and had a full Saturday of programming. It was the *best* thing for the kids. The trip got them to bond right away and grow tight as an ensemble and a family.

Broadway Field Trip: A Broadway field trip in April for the freshmen classes each year. It doesn't have to be Broadway in NYC per se, any show in town will do, just taking them to see live theatre is excellent.

Alumni Chat: Invite alumni in to chat with kids. They're not going to come back on their own, but if they are asked to come back, they will. They can talk about their experiences and what they did.

Plaques: Keeping plaques and things that are important to people. Awards for most improved, most outstanding, performing arts student of the year, etc.

Invited Dress: If you want the cast to get the feel of an audience before opening night, hold an invited dress rehearsal, which is the final rehearsal before opening night, where your students can invite one or two family members or friends to come watch the show. This is especially important for comedy shows so that the students can get the laugh timing down.

Pigskin Revue: This is a revue of the previous year's shows in the next school year. So, say you performed *The Wedding Singer* and *The Lion King* during the previous school year. During the following school year, the remaining cast members perform a scene or song or two from those shows during the Fall sometime around Homecoming.

Costumes on Halloween Rehearsal: If you are rehearsing in the fall for a show, you will likely have a rehearsal either close to or on Halloween. This is a fun chance to tell your students that they can wear their Halloween costumes to rehearsal. Don't forget to take a picture of all those who participated.

Book Sign: On show weekend, have the cast and crew sign the script or a book of the show for you to be able to keep and display prominently.

Program Sign: Likewise, have the cast and crew sign a program to also be displayed.

Show Museum: In addition to the signed book and program, keep a few key props from the show and display them in your classroom or the theatre on a single shelf. It creates a little museum for the show for students down the years to look back on. In addition to the signed things and the props, you can also include pictures from the show and the official cast picture.

Awards Show: Hold an awards show at the end of the year to recognize student achievements in your program as well as relive inside jokes from memorable moments throughout the school year. Be careful with this one though; if there are 'nominees,' there is one winner and four losers. So, I'd stay away from nominees, and make sure that most if not all students receive something so that no one goes home empty-handed. Award shows can be fine if executed delicately.

Cake at Read-Through: At the read-through/first rehearsal, the first time the whole cast and crew is together after casting, have a custom-made cake there for them to munch on. Have your local bakery or grocery store write: "Welcome to _____" on the cake and fill in the blank with the location of the play (e.g., Welcome to N.Y.C., Welcome to Oz, Welcome to Narnia, etc.).

Tech Week Dinner: After the first rehearsal or last rehearsal of tech week, go out to a cast dinner to celebrate your achievements before opening night. It doesn't need to be mandatory, nor does it need to be paid by you/the program, just say, "after tonight's rehearsal, we are all meeting at _____, and hope to see you there."

Cast Photo: With all the things that are involved with putting a show together, it is easy to forget the legacy things. Make sure someone is set to take pictures of your cast in action onstage for posterity as well as a full cast and crew picture immediately following one of your shows while they are still in costume.

Show Reveals: Revealing what the next show is should be a spectacle, not just an afterthought. To reveal the name of the big spring musical, I would wait until mid-December at the school-wide Christmas concert. Every year I would go up and get everyone excited and say something along the lines of: "And now . . . without further ado, next semester's 3rd through 12th grade theatrical production will be. . . . *Seussical the Musical*!!!!" The crowd and students would go nuts because of the buildup of excitement. If it is just announced in class one day or put out on a social media post, the excitement will not be there.

Now that I'm on the subject of show reveals, let me steer you clear of an unwise trend I've seen on TikTok that some theatre directors have been doing to reveal their next show. Perhaps you've seen it too: At the beginning of the year, they put up the logos for 30 musicals. One of the musicals in the 30 is the musical they are going to do. The director takes one away every day for a month until they finally reveal the remaining show. I even saw one director do that whole process and then trick the students in the end. The musical they were doing was never on the board to begin with! But I hear you saying: "Doesn't that likewise build up excitement?" Yes. However, it also has students pick favorites, get passionate about picks that aren't picked, and increases a whole lot of disappointment that doesn't need to be there. When all 30 musicals are on there, they will undoubtedly have their favorites and ones they want to do. Each time they are ripped off the board is another strike of disappointment.

Your show reveal should not be a multiple choice; it should not leave the students wishing you had picked something else. It should be as if that is the only show in the world and, *of course*, we are doing it because it is the greatest show in the world for us at this moment and you are going to *love it*!

> **See the Show You're Doing:** It would be pretty rare, but if a local theatre or a theatre within driving distance is doing the same show as your program, go take them to see it. Some directors discourage this because they think it will taint their performance. I disagree. You can as a cast and crew watch someone else perform your show, and then you get to have an *in-depth* discussion about the show and what they did right, and more importantly what they did wrong. It gives your actors ideas of how to further develop their characters and performance. It also increases the passion towards the project for your students while they do it.

The following traditions are all a compilation of a few pre-show warm-ups that have proven fun and successful in the past:

> **Stretches:** There are hundreds of theatre stretches out there. Far too many to list here. But yes, it is important to stretch before shows. I would pose it as three different kinds of stretches: stretching the body, stretching the mind, and stretching the voice. Body: normal body stretches similar to ones they would do in P.E. Mind: relaxation, prayer, meditation, etc. Voice: vocal warm-ups, chanting show lines together, singing show songs together, tongue twisters, etc.
>
> **New Student Welcome:** During the warm-ups for your opening night, ask all students whose first show it is to step into the circle. Then

you can say a few encouraging words, other students can too, and then you go in for a big group hug of the newbies, and by the time the hug parts, the newbies have been brought back into the circle.

Circle Heartbeat: The whole cast and crew are in a circle holding hands silently. The director pumps his left hand squeezing the person's right hand to his left. The moment they feel a squeeze they squeeze the other hand, and so on and so on. It goes slow at first but eventually, the pump will go around the circle quickly similar to a heartbeat. Then you can talk about how the cast and crew need to have the same heartbeat out there, etc. etc.

Between Two-Show Day Nap: If you have a two-show day, you will likely have one to three hours between shows. It is unwise to let students leave and come back, so if you decide to keep them at the theatre, one of the activities you can do is to have everyone lay on the floor or in chairs (out of costume, of course). Then you cut the lights and say that we as a cast and crew are now going to have a silent time with our eyes closed. It is a time for quiet, reflection, meditation, and prayer. After a show the students are usually wired, so it's a way to recenter themselves and to get them ready to start the process of the next show.

Dance Party: Immediately after nap time, then you crank up the music and get the blood flowing again. It's like a day restart, and the cast and crew can enjoy cutting a rug with each other.

Circle Pinkies: Just before your show, gather in a circle and have everyone hold pinkies. Say a couple of things to them. Student-led prayer. Students say something. We've got a job to do, let's do our thing. After all that was done, we would flip out, get/give two hugs, and tell them to have a good show.

Senior Goodbyes: Before your last show of the spring semester, ask your seniors (or graduating 8th graders) to step into the middle of the circle. This is a chance for anyone in the circle to say anything they can. You can as well. Say encouraging things, memories, and how much of a difference those seniors have made on the program, whether it is their first show or tenth. CAUTION: One year I did this at the very end of warm-ups *right before* I called places. This was a very tearful exercise, so by the time everyone was done speaking, a lot of the cast members had cried so much that they ruined their show makeup. We had to delay the show by 15 minutes for everyone to pull themselves together. Make sure to do this exercise well before you call places.

Legacy

Once you have kept the traditions of the past, added student-created traditions, and started your own traditions, the legacy of your program will start to build. Day after day, show after show, year after year.

I can't help but ask Lin-Manuel Miranda to help me define what legacy means from his musical *Hamilton*: "Legacy. What is a legacy? It's planting seeds in a garden you never get to see."

Hamilton's image of legacy is planting seeds in a garden you never get to see. Alexander Hamilton was in his final moments thinking of his life and what he was leaving behind. Whether he died that day in Weehawken, New Jersey, or 50 years from then, at some point he would leave behind a legacy. We all will. All of the things we do in life for ourselves, for our family, and for others are all seeds planted in a garden we won't get to see grow. And like the pebble that creates a ripple effect in a pond, we will never know how big of an impact we had, how big the garden will be.

Next, when our time is up here on Earth, our life leads to our legacy. Legacy is what we pass down to future generations when we are gone. It is not our houses, cars, money, or possessions, it is our knowledge, our stories, our habits, and our personality.

High school theatre can be a transformative experience, fostering creativity, collaboration, and self-expression. But beyond the personal benefits, there's also the opportunity to leave a lasting mark on your program, inspiring future generations of actors, directors, and theatre enthusiasts.

Building a legacy is a marathon, not a sprint. It requires dedication, passion, and a collaborative spirit. By focusing on these aspects, you can leave a lasting impact on your high school theatre program, ensuring its success and inspiring future generations to embrace the magic of theatre.

Remember, a legacy is not just about individual achievements; it's about creating a vibrant and inclusive theatrical environment where everyone feels valued and empowered to explore their creative potential. So go forth, be a leader, and leave your mark on the stage!

In the context of a high school theatre program, "legacy" refers to the lasting positive impact you make that continues to influence the program even after you graduate. It's not just about personal achievements but about the contributions you make that elevate the program as a whole and inspire future generations of students.

Here are a few important pillars of building a good, decent, excellent, legitimate, lasting legacy for your theatre program:

Lead by Example: One of the most important things you can do as a director to solidify your legacy is to lead by example. Be prepared, punctual, and respectful during rehearsals and performances. Your dedication inspires others to strive for professionalism.

Mentorship: Volunteer your time to help younger actors during rehearsals or offer one-on-one coaching sessions. Passing on your knowledge and enthusiasm lays the foundation for future excellence.

Their Biggest Cheerleader: Celebrate your students' achievements. Be a positive cheerleader for your fellow performers and acknowledge crew members' contributions. Organize post-show gatherings or award ceremonies to celebrate successes.

Community Outreach: Reach out to the community past your school's borders. Volunteer your talents to perform at local events, senior centers, or elementary schools. This outreach fosters community engagement and showcases the program's talent.

Scholarship Fund: Create a theatre-based scholarship fund. Organize fundraisers or solicit donations to establish a scholarship that supports future theatre students.

Document Your Productions: Create photo collages, videography of performances, or detailed program archives. This documentation serves as a historical record for future generations.

Mentor Alumni: Stay connected with alumni who have gone on to pursue theatre careers. Their insights and aforementioned guest workshops can inspire current students and enrich the program.

 Key Takeaways

1. Traditions in a theatre program are a compilation of three things: (1) keeping existing traditions, (2) student-created traditions, and (3) director-created traditions. It is important to exercise all three of these to yield the most success.
2. Create traditions in your theatre program such as pre-show warm-ups, show museums, yearly trips, cast dinners, and more.
3. Leave a positive and lasting legacy in your theatre program by elevating the program's standards, reaching out to the community, leading by example, mentoring students and alumni, and fostering a spirit of excellence for future generations.

PART 3

Directing a Theatre Program

13

Auditions and Casting

What is the hardest thing about directing theatre? Is it the long hours? Working on multiple projects at once? Directing a show while also running the soundboard, lightboard, and iPad? No. The hardest thing about directing theatre is auditions and casting. I've always said that auditions and casting are the most difficult and yet the most necessary process in a successful theatre program.

You have to ask yourself: What is the alternative? If a director didn't hold auditions, what would be the outcome? This is not unheard of. Some programs across the country have an 'everyone gets in' policy when it comes to students who want to be in a production. That is fine in a few cases and sometimes unavoidable in others. Your school, especially a smaller school, may not have the luxury of having an excess of students wanting to be in a production. You might be struggling to just find enough to reach the minimum cast number. However, the goal for these programs is to grow so big and popular with the student population that you aren't even able to take as many students who show up because you might run out of stage space! I also argue, in the case of the schools struggling to find enough to meet the minimum number required, the ones that are forced to adopt an 'everyone gets in' policy, that it is important to still hold an audition. Even though you know you'll need to let everyone into the production, auditions are an important part of a young student's development through their education.

It might be cliché to say, but auditions build character. Once they go off into the real world, they will be facing all kinds of real, high-stakes auditions.

Getting into the college they want? That's an audition. Interviewing for a job? That's an audition. First date? That's an audition. Each of these real-life scenarios has a process, a vast number of people going after the same 'role,' and a potential for failure. In education, we should be preparing these students for the real world by giving them the experience of an audition.

But just because it is necessary doesn't make it any less difficult. Making tough decisions in casting can include: having three students who would be perfect for the main role but only being able to choose one, choosing to cast a sophomore in the lead role rather than the senior about to graduate because the sophomore earned the part, or running out of roles while casting and needing to cut the students who didn't make it in.

In this chapter, we will discuss these difficult scenarios and more as we dive into the process of the audition and the subsequent casting.

Audition Forms

Having a full detailed audition form will go a long way to helping a director cast the show. Sometimes the outcome of the audition leaves the director split on a few auditioners who did very well similarly. So how do you choose between them? That's where the audition form comes in. You need to be upfront with your students. Tell them that the casting is not *just* based on the audition. Sure, the audition is a major factor, but other factors come into play for a director's decision. Factors such as experience, seniority, schedule conflicts, training, history of behavior within the program, and more. The following section outlines what should be in an audition form and the flyer that comes before it.

The Audition Flyer

When I say 'flyer,' I don't just mean the paper that gets posted *all* around the school. This information also applies to any announcements you have in any form, including posts on social media. But from here on out, I'll just refer to it as a 'flyer.'

First, make sure to post the flyer around two weeks before the audition. Posting after that will not give the students enough time to figure out what they need to do, and posting too long before that will keep things too long outside of the news/attention cycle.

Your audition flyer needs to have all the basic information about the show, but as you'll see soon, it'll point to the production information form for more details.

Here is everything that should be included in your audition flyer:
- **"Theatre Audition":** Right at the top in big, bold letters. It will be the first thing they read; they need to know what they are looking at right off the bat.
- **Show Logo:** Keep it to a simple logo. If it is a show with a logo people will know, go with the recognizable one. The "Theatre Audition" and logo should take up the top one-third of the page.
- **"Who":** This is where you put who is eligible to audition (e.g., 3rd–12th grade, high school only, etc.).
- **"When":** The date(s) and time(s) of the audition(s). Do not include an end time to the audition as there is no way of knowing when a student will be released.
- **"Where":** Where the audition is taking place.
- **"What To Prepare/Bring":** This is the biggest information section. This is the section that if the student doesn't read the bigger and much more informed "Audition Information" or "Production Information," they will know the bare minimum of what is expected. First, you explain the audition form in one sentence, then you explain the audition process in one to two sentences. Audition form: "Bring the audition form filled out and signed by both the student and a parent." Audition process: "Prepare any song to sing a capella (without music); this song needs to be at least 30 seconds but no longer than 1 minute" or "A monologue, either dramatic or comedic, of your choice that is longer than 30 seconds and shorter than 60 seconds. This monologue does not need to be memorized."
- **Bottom Forwarding Information:** This is the information you'll put at the bottom of the flyer to point the students to the real big, full information about the audition and the show. *****See Audition Information and Production Information for full details. **** (The form and info are available at the front offices and the high school.)

Audition Information

The "Audition Information," "Production Information," "Audition Form," and "Casting and Attendance Agreement" should all be stapled together in one packet available to pick up at a common place on campus. This way all the information students and parents might need about the audition or show is all in one place.

If you have access to a color printer, color code the titles of these forms to help students and parents navigate the information. For me, I had Audition

Information in green, Production Information in blue, Audition Form in red, and Casting and Attendance Agreement in purple. These same colors should be used on the flyer and at the top of the packet.

This packet will have a *lot* of information. Some would say too much, but I say there is no such thing as too much information, and there is definitely such a thing as not enough information. Give them all the information they might need; if they don't read it, fine, it's on them. If you are thorough enough, there will be no questions and no need for an interest meeting because all the information will be there.

Here is what should be included in the first part, the audition information:
This information may vary based on your show, logistics, show type, and more.

- The (show title) audition will be held on (#) days: Wednesday, February 5th, and Thursday, February 6th, at 3:45 pm.
- An auditioner only needs to come on one of the days, and they do not need to stay for the whole audition. Once their portion is over, they are free to leave.
- The audition will start in the (audition location) promptly at 3:45 pm. After school lets out, get to the theatre as soon as you can. Once you are there, sign your name on the sign-in sheet to reserve your spot in line. Each auditioner will receive a number sticker to place on their shirt at that point as well. This process is first come, first served. Attendance and punctuality are extremely important.
- Auditions are open to (which grades can audition) currently enrolled (school name) students. (I put "currently enrolled" because at small schools sometimes homeschool students have asked to audition for our shows, or students that left ask if they can still be in shows. It's important to draw the line here if you wish.)
- Once the audition starts at 3:45 pm, the director (director name) will speak to all of those auditioning about the whole process in the lobby. Summary: Each student, in order of their number, will perform their audition song and then will be interviewed. Auditions are closed. Please bring homework/studying/or a book to work on while you wait.
- Because of the audition being first come, first served, each student's audition end time will vary. Students are encouraged to bring a cell phone to contact their rides once their audition is completed.
- (Following will be explanations of different types of auditions, including singing, dancing, and monologue. Again, these might vary based on your preferences.)

- Singing Audition: Students will do their singing audition one at a time based on the time they signed in/audition number. The singing portion will be in the theatre with the director. The rest of the auditioning group will wait in the lobby. Upon entering the theatre for your individual singing audition, you will give the director your filled-out and signed audition form, have your picture taken, go up onstage, and begin to sing your prepared song a capella (without music or accompaniment). Your song needs to be at least 30 seconds long but no longer than 1 minute. After completing your song, the director may have you sing one of the following songs *with* music accompaniment playing: "Happy Birthday," "Mary Had a Little Lamb," or "Twinkle Twinkle Little Star." Once both songs are completed, the director may ask you to read a few lines provided for you onstage. Then the director will interview you with questions about your schedule, audition form, and more. Once a student is done with their individual singing audition, they are free to go.
- Dancing Audition: A dance will be taught from the musical to the group as a whole. Then the group will be taken into the theatre to perform the dance. The dance will always be performed as a group. You are encouraged to have as much energy, character, charisma, grace, and confidence as possible while you are dancing, from start to finish. Your dancing audition will mostly be based on your performance in front of the director; however, it will also be based on how you learn your dance, your improvement, and your receptivity to critique during the learning process.
- Monologue Audition: Students will do their monologue audition one at a time based on the time they signed in/audition number. The rest of the auditioning group will wait in the lobby. Upon entering the theatre for your individual audition, you will give the director your filled-out and signed audition form, have your picture taken, go up onstage, and begin to perform your prepared 30-second to 1-minute dramatic or comedic monologue. After completing your monologue, the director may ask you to read a few lines provided for you onstage. Then the director will interview you with questions about your schedule, audition form, and more. Once a student is done with their individual audition, they are free to go.
- Callback: After both audition days, the director *might* hold a callback audition. The director will inform the students who are called back personally during school on Friday. Callbacks are a chance for the director to see actors another time to get a better idea of their acting ability, singing ability, and dancing abilities, or to gather more

information about their audition form. NOTE: JUST BECAUSE YOU ARE NOT ASKED TO COME TO A CALLBACK DOES NOT MEAN YOU WILL NOT BE CAST OR CAST IN A MAIN ROLE. ALSO, JUST BECAUSE YOU ARE CALLED BACK DOES NOT GUARANTEE YOU A ROLE OR A MAIN ROLE. The callback audition will be on Friday, February 7th at 3:45 in the theatre.
- If you have any questions about the audition process at all, please e-mail the director at (e-mail).

Production Information

The production information form is all of the information the students and parents would need to know for post-auditions. If they get into the show, this is what all of the expectations are.

Here are a few bits to include on your production information form:
- Is it a one-act or two-act show?
- Is it a "Jr." version or the full version?
- When will the cast list be posted, at what time, and where?
- Details about the first rehearsal/read-through
- General information about rehearsal days and times. Here is an example: "Rehearsals will (most likely) be on 3–4 weekdays from 3:45–6:00 with the exception of school holidays and events. The times and days will vary from week to week depending on the type of rehearsal and who is called. At read-through, a very thorough and detailed schedule will be given to the cast."
- "ATTENDANCE AT ALL SINGING REHEARSALS, DANCING REHEARSALS, AND BLOCKING REHEARSALS ARE ESSENTIAL BECAUSE WE HAVE LIMITED TIME TO LEARN EACH SONG, DANCE, AND SCENE. THEREFORE, ANY CONFLICTS YOU HAVE MAY AFFECT CASTING."
- What days and times are the shows?
- If a student just wants to be a tech, what is the process they have to go through for the audition that would be different than an acting audition?
- Informing the students that past production behavior affects their future productions. Here is an example: "If you have been in extracurricular productions at (school) before, as per policy, your behavior, responsibility, and talent during those productions will be a factor in your casting of this production. Note: Regardless of your performance at the audition and talent in previous productions, the other two pillars of Responsibility and Behavior are equally

important and equally taken into consideration; talent is not more important."
- Finally, an overall explanation that there will be a true casting. Here is an example: "Assumedly, there will be more students auditioning than there are roles in the production. Please know that the director will make casting decisions for the overall success of the production and the building and success of the theatre program as a whole. Casting is based on audition performances, conflicts, and behavior, responsibility, and talent in previous productions. If you are not cast in this production, know that it was done for one or more of the above reasons."

The Audition Form

This will be the form of the packet that you rip off and use for your casting deliberations. It will have the casting and attendance agreement signed on the back of it as well, so that you have all of the information you need in one place. The information on the audition form is not just for casting decisions. It'll help you as a director with different information once the show starts, including costume sizes and schedule conflicts.

Here are the many different pieces of information to ask for on your audition form:
- Name
- Age
- Grade
- Gender
- Height
- Hair Color
- Shirt Size
- Pants Size
- Shoe Size
- Dress Size
- Have you received any outside-of-school training in the performing arts (acting, voice, dance, other)? If yes, please list any training in the performing arts you received:
- Do you have theatre performance experience either at (school name) or elsewhere? If yes, please list:
- Will you accept any role or non-casting given to you without complaint and, if cast, will you also perform that role to the best of your ability with an open mind and open heart, and for the betterment of the production and program? (check yes or no)

- CONFLICTS: Please list *all* times and conflicts when you are *not* available for evenings from (earliest rehearsal can start) to (latest rehearsal will go) on weekdays until (opening night). This schedule must be accurate to the best of your knowledge. If it is not, you may be removed from the production.
- (This is where to include a comprehensive chart showing each day split up into 30-minute segments from the start of rehearsal time to the end of rehearsal time. The students will then fill out the sections with their regular weekly conflicts.)
- PLEASE LIST ALL ONE-TIME CONFLICTS (weddings, vacations, etc.) that might force you to miss rehearsals from now until ((opening night date)) (list date, time, and reason for conflict).
- PLEASE CHECK ALL OF THE SPORTS THAT YOU WILL PARTICIPATE IN AT (school name) THIS SEMESTER (ATTACH AND INCLUDE ALL SCHEDULES FOR PRACTICES, GAMES, MEETS, TOURNAMENTS, ETC.) ((then include a list of all of the sports for them to check off).
- BETWEEN NOW AND (opening night) WILL YOU BE AUDITIONING FOR, REHEARSING FOR, OR PERFORMING IN A THEATRICAL PRODUCTION OUTSIDE OF (school name)? (IF SO, EXPLAIN) (This is an important piece of information because although we want to encourage students to audition for community theatre and other productions, doubling and tripling up on productions might hamper their ability to be present at your production, so it is important to know that upfront.)
- Notes Section – For use by the Director *only*. (This is a big white box that takes up one-third of the page on the back of the audition form page. Everything above this all fits on the front page. This is the box in which you will write your immediate thoughts and impressions at their audition.)

Casting and Attendance Agreement

Getting people to join your theatre program is a huge priority and takes up most of your recruiting time. However, once they are in, high expectations need to be set about showing up:

1. On time
2. Every time
3. Staying the whole time. Right off the bat, before the audition, the students and parents should read this and understand these high

expectations you have for a student's attendance and how it affects the auditions, casting, and the show itself.

Here is the casting and attendance agreement that I used word for word. Feel free to tweak it to your own needs.
- Casting and Attendance Agreement: THIS PAGE MUST BE SIGNED BY BOTH THE STUDENT AND PARENT TO AUDITION!
  - I agree to play any role assigned to me without complaint. In doing so, I also agree to wear the costumes, wig, hairstyle, or makeup of the director's choosing.
  - I agree to abide by all theatre rules and its handbook while at rehearsals and performances.
  - I understand and agree that theatre is a collaborative, team effort, no part is too small and no person is unimportant, every single member of the production is a vital part of the success of a production and its theatre program, and absence from rehearsals by any member of the production hurts the production itself.
  - I understand and agree that in theatre all students are expected to be at all rehearsals they are called for and at all performances.
  - I understand and agree that in theatre all students are expected to be on time and to stay the whole time.
  - I understand and agree that in theatre if a student has a legitimate conflict with a called rehearsal, they need to let the director know as soon as they know about that conflict.
  - I understand and agree that legitimate conflicts include illness, family emergency, athletic games, or pre-approved conflicts given to the director on the audition form.
  - I understand and agree that absences from performances are absolutely unacceptable.
- I understand and agree that during the run of a production, if a student does not adhere to the above policies, they might be removed from the production by the director and/or their future with the theatre program and future productions may be at risk.
- By signing below, you agree to the above Casting and Attendance agreement, confirm that you have filled out fully and truthfully the Audition Form, and confirm that you have read and understood all of the Production Information and Audition Information provided.
- Student signature and date
- Parent signature and date

Auditions

Phew! Now that we got all those forms out of the way, it is finally time to start the audition. Here are several tips, tricks, and suggestions for successfully running auditions.

Open auditions to the whole school, not just the theatre classes.

If you are new to a program, it is helpful to have someone helping with your audition to give you some insider information on the students. This can either be a student who knows the other students who will be on your production team or a colleague who has been at the school for a while. They can help you cast at first because they know the students. They know whether they'll be reliable or not. "That kid gets in trouble too much." "Skips rehearsals too much." You might go against their advice, but be aware that it might backfire.

Auditions should be closed. Period. This is a controversial one because a lot of directors insist on open auditions. (Open auditions are where all of the auditioners are allowed to sit and watch all of the auditions, whereas in closed auditions the auditioners are in a separate room and not able to watch.) There is one exception to this, and that is the dancing part of an audition. I think it is important for them to learn the dance with the group and dance the dance with a group. However, for singing and monologue auditions, they should be solo onstage without the other auditioners watching. Why closed and not open? Well, as I've said before, casting is a tough call. Some decisions come down to the wire and could go either way. Some decisions are completely outside of the audition – for instance, a student might have had the absolute best audition in the world, but they have conflicts four days a week. If the audition is open, the people watching don't know that information. So, when the cast list comes out and they see that someone else got the part instead of that student, you'll be hit with all kinds of complaints. Everyone is a critic. Everyone sees things differently. An audition might have been technically better, but that student has something you want for a character that others can't see. A director shouldn't have to explain themselves to the masses. The director is the director, and the director has made a decision – end of story. You shouldn't have to hold a press conference and walk back an unpopular decision. I won't harp on this much longer, but just keep auditions closed and you'll save yourself so many headaches in the future.

For a musical audition, if you choose to hold both a singing and dancing audition, split the students auditioning in half. The first half goes with the choreographer and the second half starts with singing. Then they switch.

Have lines from the play on the stage ready for the students to read cold. They should be lines from all the main characters. Have them read from several you might consider them for to get their voice into those lines.

A capella singing and then singing with music. You read during the explanation of the singing audition that I expected students to come in to sing a song a capella and then with music. First, you have them sing a capella so that you can hear their voice unvarnished, pure, and raw. A capella singing also helps see if they have good relative pitch and a solid ear. But then, it is equally important that they sing with music. I usually just had a song that everyone would know, like "Happy Birthday" or "Twinkle Twinkle Little Star" pulled up on the iPad. Singing to music proves that the student can match pitch instantly. Some might have sung alright in their a capella song, but if they are completely tone deaf when singing with a track, this will present issues later and needs to be taken into consideration.

Write as much down as you can on their audition form. Believe me, after several dozen auditions, things will start to get lost and run together. Write down your immediate thoughts and impressions so that when you read it a few days later, you'll be able to trust your past self.

Post-audition interview. After the student was done with the monologue or song or whatever, I would have them come sit at the table I was at and chat with them for a bit. This is where I would go over their audition form with them. I would check to make sure everything was filled out fully, and if it was not, I'd ask them to be there on the spot. I would especially discuss their conflicts and get as much information on their availability as possible. This is also the time I would use to clarify their past experiences, their training, and their possibility of being in other productions besides this one.

Hold auditions in the performance space. Don't hold your auditions in a small classroom or alternate space. If you are going to be performing in the theatre or auditorium, that student needs to be on that stage facing the audience. That way you can hear their projection ability and see their stage presence.

Parents in auditions. This was always a tough one over the years. Some parents will insist on coming into their student's audition to sit and watch and support. This was especially true of my younger students in 3rd, 4th, and 5th grades. It was by no means the majority of students; I'd say it happened about 10% of the time. It's tough to just kick them out right there. However, insisting that it is a true closed audition might be the only way to make it work. Making sure that expectations are set, including with signs in the audition holding room saying something like "only the student auditioning will be allowed in" might help head it off at the pass. If when confronting a parent about it, they start to push back, you should retreat. It is not worth the fight at that moment. Just continue the audition. There is a factor that plays into that dynamic that might be worth looking into during the casting. If a student is insisting that their parents be in their audition for support, perhaps they are not ready to take the stage.

Say cheese! Take a picture of the student as they enter their audition. You can then print out those photos, cut them out, and staple them onto their audition form. This helps with casting as you will be able to visualize them in the moment much better if they are staring right back at you.

Take a number. In the lobby, there should be stickers with numbers on them from 1 to ??. It will help with your organization for casting and discussion with the production team if they have numbers on. It also helps to quickly write notes for a dancing audition. Make sure they write their number at the top of their audition form. The numbers also help with the order in which they will go for their audition. As the audition information form said, the process would be first come, first served.

Casting

Auditions are completed. Callbacks are done. Now the decision is up to you. Pretty much right away you will know whether you need to cut people or not based on the number of people who came to audition. If you have a show that has 16 roles and only 11 showed up, they all will likely make it in. On the other hand, you know that for this specific show, you can only take a max of 30 and 45 people show up. It's important to get in the headspace of having to cut students, as it is not an easy thing to do.

Your casting should be a real casting. The theatrical meaning of "casting" actually comes from a broader sense of the word. Originally, "casting" referred to the process of pouring something molten, like metal, into a mold to give it a specific shape. By the 1800s, the word was being used more generally to describe selecting something to fit a particular role or form. In theatre, actors are "cast" because they are chosen to embody the characters in the play, just like molten metal is cast to fill a mold. You are casting out the imperfections and creating something stronger and better overall. Just keeping everybody in, imperfections and all, will lead to an imperfect show. Even if you are only cutting one singular student. If that student being in the production will affect the production negatively, then you have to do what you have to do.

You're the director. You are the executive in charge. Casting is an executive decision. If you are deciding with your production team, remember you have the final say for the vision of the show.

The way that I would do casting would be to put all of the audition forms face up, with their pictures stapled to them onto a big conference table so that I could see them all. I would then sort them by who had a great audition (put at the front of the table) to those who didn't have a great audition (put near the back of the table). I would then sort them by age/grade, youngest on the left, oldest on the right. This is especially important with a show that has multiple levels in it (elementary/middle/high). You know that age will play a factor in what roles they get. For instance, for *Annie*, I told the students upfront that "The roles of Annie and the rest of the orphans will only be considered from 3rd–8th grade and the role of Daddy Warbucks, Miss Hannigan, and Grace Farrell will only be considered from 9th–12th grade."

Once everything is laid out and organized, it's time to make the decisions. The way I would do it is to write the role names on a yellow square sticky note and stick the roles on the front of the table. Once I decided that a certain student was cast in a certain role, I would place that sticky on the audition form and remove it from the table. For some shows, students will be cast in multiple roles, so make sure not to remove them from the table until that is the case.

Just like there will be some students you know for a fact that they will be in your show based on their audition and/or audition form, there will likewise be students you know right away that will be cut from the show based on their audition or audition form. If their weekly conflicts were too much, or they'd miss a show, or they bombed their audition, you might have a feeling right away that they won't make it in. However, don't throw them off of the table yet. You send them to the back of the table and keep casting. Who knows, you might change your mind. But once all the sticky notes have been given out and forms are remaining on the table, there's your answer.

Keep in mind that a casting decision is not necessarily final. Several factors may change a casting: a student drops out of a show, a student is kicked out of a show, you want to have a couple of students switch roles in the rehearsal process, you realize you need more people, you realize you need fewer people, etc.

Those you cut are not necessarily cut for good. That becomes your 'standby list.' If a student who was cast isn't able to continue in their role for whatever reason, in come the standbys. Also, for those you cut, if they indicated on their form that they are interested in teching, for sure make them a tech for your show (unless conflicts prevent it) so that they can still be invested in the show and not out of it entirely.

Seniority is a factor, but not a vital one. Seniority will always be a topic of discussion when it comes to casting a show. However, it is important to keep in mind the success of the show is more important in the long run. If a junior or sophomore earned the main role above a senior, then that's the way it goes. We should be rid of the culture of seniors expecting the top roles and freshmen expecting to just get ensemble.

Posting the Cast List and Reactions From Doing So

The final step in the process is posting your cast list. This is less simple than you think and needs to be handled delicately to protect feelings and avoid conflicts.

First, creating the cast list. If there is a list of students in the 'ensemble' or 'dance team' or 'company,' they should always be in alphabetical order to not show preference or undue ordering. If there are main and title roles, they go at the top, followed by medium and supporting roles, then small roles. If a student earned multiple roles, there's no need to put that student twice, just list all of the roles they earned by their name.

Post the cast list at a time when students are not in the building. I would normally do this after school once everyone was gone. It just creates an unnecessarily tense scene if you post it with students clamoring all around you. There is a famous "Saturday Night Live" skit on posting a cast list starring Will Ferrell that exaggerates this point hilariously and accurately.

Post the cast list in a place where students can easily find it, yet in a place where they can react without making a public scene. You want to teach your students humility in victory and humility in defeat, meaning that when they get a main role they shouldn't be yelling, screaming, cheering, and bragging. Likewise, if they don't get a role, they should not be yelling, screaming, or breaking down. However, teaching them those virtues and reality are two different things. Some students won't be able to help themselves. A student walking up to a cast list and seeing their name at the top is a big moment in their life. Likewise, a student walking up to a cast list and not seeing their name on it is also a big moment. These big moments should not be happening in the cafeteria in front of everyone, inside your classroom, or in the middle of the high school hallway. They should have a place that is accessible yet secluded enough for them to have their moment of joy or grief.

Reactions. Like stated earlier, although you want students to react appropriately to any kind of news from a casting, sometimes things get carried away. At best, the reaction will be regulated to when they see the cast list and nothing further. However, there are times that you need to prepare for the reactions to take over that whole day, week, or even month.

First, there are the reactions of students who got a good/big/main role but reacted inappropriately in a few ways. Perhaps they brag about it to others. Perhaps they make fun of those who didn't get a role or a big role. Perhaps their streak of haughtiness lasts past that day and into the production. Perhaps when they get started in the production, they think they can boss around other actors just because they are a main role. Depending on the severity of these reactions, it might be cause for immediate dismissal from the production. This is an important legacy-building point in showing your students that you will not tolerate anyone treating anyone else disrespectfully. Short of dismissing them from the production, make sure you have a very serious discussion with them and their parents to ensure the behavior stops immediately and never happens again.

Next, there are the reactions of students who got cast in the production but not in the role they wanted. Perhaps they complain to the administration. Perhaps they start spreading rumors about the person who is in the role they wanted. Perhaps they talk poorly about the director or the program. Perhaps once the production starts, they don't work hard or act well because they aren't in the role they want. Again, some of these could be calls for dismissal. However, it is a common human reaction – jealousy. It's important to know the difference between feeling jealousy and acting on jealousy. The best theatre programs build each other up, celebrate each other's successes, and cheer each other on. The worst theatre programs tear each other down, hope for someone's failure, and try to knock others off the ladder. You want to create a program where students are proud of where they are and happy for their peers no matter what the role.

Lastly, there are the reactions of students who were cut from the production. Perhaps they also complain to the administration. Perhaps they too spread rumors and talk negatively about the director, the production, the program, or other students. Perhaps due to their reaction to the news, other students might react on their behalf by either complaining to you directly or saying, "If you don't let them in, I quit!" If you have a program that has a true casting and that cuts students, you need to be fully prepared for these reactions. It will be very strong the first day and week. Your goal is to deal with it all as quickly, efficiently, kindly, and professionally as possible. A long-term effect of the reaction of a student being cut is that perhaps they choose to never audition again. It's important to keep up with these students. Talk to them. Encourage them to get trained up, or to clear up their schedule. Let them know that it wasn't personal and that they should try, try, and try again.

Key Takeaways
1. Create a full, detailed, and comprehensive audition form, which includes Audition Information, Production Information, an Audition Form, and a Casting and Attendance Agreement. This form should have the goal of answering every question that parents, students, and you as the director might have.
2. Have your auditions be closed, parent-free, and open to the whole school, and include an auditioner number, a picture taken, and as much initial impression information written down by you as possible.
3. Although casting is hard, it is necessary. Have a true 'casting' for your show where you don't just focus on seniority, where you create a standby list, and where you understand that you as the executive director are in charge of the final say for the vision and success of the production.
4. Post the cast list after hours, in an appropriate order, and in a place that prevents a possible public scene. Then, prepare to handle reactions and backlash from the casting that may arise.

14

The Schedule

I had a director of mine in a community theatre production who set the production's schedule before auditions. Sounds okay so far, right? I went into the audition and there was a full calendar from read-through to closing night, including specific rehearsal pages and start/end times. It was nice because it gave everyone at the audition a good idea of the commitment to the production and the ability to write in their conflicts for the run of the production. However, when I was cast and arrived at a read-through, the calendar didn't change at all. I thought that strange because I thought that the audition calendar was just a placeholder until they were able to sort out the conflicts of those cast members. Perhaps they hadn't had a chance to change it yet, right? Well, the production's rehearsals began, and I quickly began to realize that the helpful schedule that was set before auditions was actually set in *concrete*. The director did not change any of the rehearsal times, rehearsal plans, or rehearsal days, not once for the entire production. What if we had a scene with three people in it that we were scheduled to rehearse that night and one of them had a prior conflict? The rehearsal still happened, the two people rehearsing struggled the whole night without their scene partner, and once the third person did return a few days later, they had to re-do all of the blocking and rehearsal anyway (at the expense of the rehearsal time that evening, I might add). The first rehearsal without everyone there was a waste of time for the actors who showed up. The second rehearsal where they eventually did do the scene all together was a waste of time for the rest of the cast who were called for something else that evening.

The issues didn't stop there. Most of the cast was going to be an hour late? Too bad, the rehearsal still starts at 6:30 – and those who are made to show up at 6:30 just have to wait around until the rest of the cast arrives anyway, wasting their time. Actors A and B have a duet rehearsal on Monday and actors B & C have a duet rehearsal on Tuesday. Actor A has a conflict and cannot make it on Monday but is free on Tuesday. Does the director ask Actor C to come in on Monday and switch the two rehearsals? No, they don't. Actor J has a smaller role and is called to come in for an all-cast blocking rehearsal. The rehearsal lasted three hours, and Actor J wasn't onstage until the last ten minutes of those three hours. With proper rehearsal planning, could Actor J have been asked to come 30 minutes before the end of rehearsal rather than wasting two-and-a-half hours of their time? Yes, but that is not what happened because the director did not plan the schedule well.

The best schedule in a theatrical production wastes the least amount of time for those in the production. The best schedule is flexible and ever-changing, adapting to unexpected absences and prior-known conflicts alike. The best schedule gives the actors and crew the maximum amount of time to properly and fully rehearse the production.

In this chapter, I will discuss how to craft the perfect schedule. We will continue to discuss the vast importance of flexibility while also setting the director up for success in crafting a well-thought-out and organized schedule from day one. We will also dive into the various production workdays you can add and how they can make your production run more smoothly and efficiently than you could ever imagine.

The Pre-Audition Schedule

Some programs provide a full detailed day-by-day schedule at the audition. They feel that it shows organization and gives the actors an idea of when they would be called. However, no one is cast yet, so they don't know if they should expect the main role's schedule or the ensemble's schedule. Also, once you get everyone's conflicts at auditions, you are going to have to completely redo the schedule anyway, so why give yourself double the work?

I am advocating for you to give a vague generalized schedule to those auditioning and then a full detailed schedule at the first rehearsal. A vague generalized schedule is what was seen in the prior chapter, "Auditions and Casting." All I told my students about the schedule were three things:

1. What days of the week rehearsal will be held
2. What time rehearsal will start and end

3. What days are absolutely mandatory with no excuses (tech week and shows)

Students at the audition should get information similar to this example: Rehearsals are generally Tuesdays through Fridays. Rehearsals start promptly at 3:45 and end at 6:00. Days you CANNOT miss: Monday, April 20th through Thursday, April 23rd (tech week) and April 24th/25th (shows).

That is all they need to know at this point. Any other information is just fluff until everyone is cast and you know of all the conflicts.

The First Rehearsal/Read-Through Schedule

Now that auditions are over and the cast list is set, this is the time to create the full production schedule. Now, this doesn't mean that you can't prepare the schedule before auditions: selecting what each rehearsal will be, how much you need to block each scene, what songs will be rehearsed together, etc. However, although you can put these rehearsals in order, resist setting them to the calendar until you get your students' conflicts. The more you have set before you see the conflicts, the less flexible you will be.

Feel free to craft your schedule to look like whatever you think is best. I'll tell you what has worked for me in the past, take it or leave it. I used a simple Microsoft Excel spreadsheet. Four columns: Date, Time, What, Who. For example, Date: Thursday, March 12th. Time: 3:45–6:00. What: Blocking Rehearsal – Act 1, Scene 5 Part 1 – CHILDREN MEET MARIA. Who: Franz, Captain, Frau Schmidt, Maria, Children.

On this schedule, I would include every single day, even weekends, from the first rehearsal to the post-production workday. I would include all holidays, production workdays, other performing arts events, school event conflicts, and completely blank days. Including the days that are not rehearsal gives the students and families a good idea of the big picture of the production and how many exact days until X.

Other than what it should look like, here is a hodgepodge of advice for building the perfect schedule.

Do Not Waste People's Time: Read the story from the intro, then read it again. It is bad to waste people's time. If someone is only going to be used in rehearsal for 30 minutes, don't call them for all three hours. If there is a conflict that comes up, don't hold a wasted rehearsal followed by a doubled-up catch-up rehearsal. I even saw that director call someone and forget they had called them and they came to a three-hour rehearsal and did absolutely nothing.

I know that building the perfect schedule takes a lot of work. Compiling 40 audition forms worth of conflicts times the 30 rehearsals you are going to have, divided by who got cast as what, plus all of the other school/holiday/family conflicts that are present equals a complicated mess. But it is worth the time, I assure you. Take the time, figure it out, make it work.

Build some extra room into your schedule for emergency catch-up/makeup rehearsals. Conflicts will arise, and rehearsals might be cut short. You might just run out of time, and therefore you aren't ready for opening night. Never fear, your makeup days are there! For school holidays such as spring break or a three-day weekend, I would put something along the lines of (Winter Break – Possible Rehearsal(s) TBD). For the two weekends before tech week, I would put the same thing. These are only to be used as needed. Don't hold the rehearsal just to polish. Hold the rehearsal to make up for lost time or a lost rehearsal.

As opening night approaches, the end time for rehearsal will go later. If rehearsal usually ends at 6, once you get to act run-throughs it might go to 6:30. Then full run-throughs will be at 7:00. Lastly, final dress rehearsal will go until 7:30. These are the expectations that come with an excellent theatre program. These extra-long rehearsals are especially needed for a long two-to-two-and-a-half-hour musical. By the time everyone gets there, you have your beginning speech, and everyone gets ready, certain delays during the show, and once the show ends it'll be well past 6. And that doesn't leave time for notes at the end.

Non-Linear Rehearsals: There is absolutely no reason that rehearsals need to be linear (following the play's order). The order of rehearsals should be based on the conflicts and what needs to be worked on first/most.

Consider the experience level of your students. Experienced students will be able to pick up a song, dance, or blocking quicker than newbies. If you have a majority of newbies in your cast, you might have to schedule more rehearsal time for them.

Short rehearsals are better for focused work, while longer sessions allow for building stamina and running scenes in sequence.

Schedule Flexibility: Flexibility is the key to a great schedule. You need to not only be flexible to the conflicts that are on the audition forms at the beginning of the production, but you also need to work in flexibility for the last-minute emergency conflicts. Things happen: family deaths, medical emergencies, school/grade/test conflict, etc. Be prepared to change rehearsal even that same day, even in the moment. Call fewer people, call different people, and work different songs/scenes. Do whatever you can to have a productive rehearsal. If all else fails, you can cancel the rehearsal, but know you will need to make it up during one of your built-in makeup days.

Rehearsal Schedule Second Draft: Midway through the production, say, a month in, things might have changed drastically since the first rehearsal. You might have different students in different roles, you might have gotten things done quicker than expected, or not as quickly as expected, in your first month of rehearsals, and dates/times might have changed for production workdays, tech week, and school events. In this case, it is good to edit and reprint a new schedule for your cast and crew. It'll be fresh and up to date and shorter. It'll reinvigorate their knowledge that opening night is upon us, and it'll help build in that flexibility that is sorely needed.

Musical Production Rehearsal Order

Imagine that you are a young first-time actor in the musical *Annie*. You have been cast as an orphan in Miss Hannigan's infamous orphanage. What is the big musical dance number for the first scene? "It's the Hard-Knock Life." That's 2 minutes and 20 seconds of singing and precise choreography to kick off the show in a big way. However, it is your director's first time directing a musical, and that director didn't read this amazingly helpful book! So, that director scheduled the blocking rehearsal for the "It's the Hard-Knock Life" scene on day 2 of rehearsals, then they scheduled the choreography rehearsal for that number on day 15, and scheduled the music rehearsal for the iconic song last, on day 29.

You go into the blocking rehearsal, your first rehearsal ever, and learn the basics of the blocking of the scene. How to get onstage, what to do onstage, how to get offstage. However, there is this huge gap in the scene where the director says, "This is where y'all will sing 'It's the Hard-Knock Life'." So, as you run the scene that day a couple of times, you have to stop whenever Miss Hannigan says: "Why any kid would want to be an orphan, I'll never know." Then, the cast rearranges themselves center stage where the unknown ending pose of this song you don't know is and continues the scene with you and the rest of the orphans saying through clenched teeth, "I love you, Miss Hannigan." The blocking is fine, but that big gap makes the scene choppy and stumble a bit.

Fast forward to day 15, time to learn some choreography. The choreographer teaches the steps to the lyrics of the song. Remember, you don't know this song and haven't learned it yet. So, when the dance is run with the song blaring on the speakers, none of the actors, including yourself, are singing. Some pick up a few of the words, especially the repeated line "It's the hard-knock life for us!" Everyone learns the dance steps relatively well, but no one has the muscle memory of having sung the song at the same time because they haven't learned it yet.

Fast forward again to day 29. At last, music rehearsal, time to learn this song. Although you heard the song many times in your choreography rehearsal, it still takes some learning, especially some of the interesting harmonies throughout the song. There are also a lot of lyrics to learn and memorize. Uh-oh! Guess what, rehearsal is on day 30? First run-through of Act 1!

So, the next day comes, and the director is expecting the young actors to execute the first scene well. However, when the run-through comes, most of the actors have forgotten the blocking as it was over a month since they did it, half of the actors forgot the choreography steps since they last did it two weeks prior, and just a few actors sang the song because, although they learned it the day before, they were so focused on trying to remember the choreography that they couldn't yet sing at the same time. Your director has done you a disservice, and the production will suffer because of this. Blocking will be choppy, choreography will be less practiced, and songs will be softer because fewer of the actors will be singing constantly.

Now, let's imagine that when you were cast as an orphan in *Annie*, your first production, that your director *did* read this book and knows the proper structure of musical rehearsals. The first rehearsals are all music rehearsals. You learn "It's the Hard-Knock Life" on day 2 and then continue to review it and memorize it in the following music rehearsals. The second grouping of rehearsals are dancing rehearsals, so day 15 rolls around and you learn the steps to the song while also singing the song every step of the way. That way, by the end of learning the dance, your body has connected the muscle memory of the steps to the movement of your lips and voice singing the song. Finally, the blocking rehearsals are the last thing prior to run-throughs. Day 29 comes, you and your fellow actors learn the blocking for the scene, and this time, when you run the scene, you don't stop, the blocking blends right into the song, and the company gets to rehearse the song and dance another five times that day. So, the first Act 1 run-through comes the following day – how confident are you as a young first-time actor in that song? Way more than in the first scenario, yes? You have now sung the song dozens of times, danced the dance with the song a dozen times, and rehearsed the full scene with the song and dance five times. During the Act 1 run-through, the performance is already close to opening-night standard. Just throw on an apron, grab a bucket, and bring the audience in, we are ready!

Structure the schedule for a musical production by holding the music rehearsals first, the dancing rehearsals second, and then the blocking rehearsals last.

Production Workdays

The biggest production of my career thus far, *The Broadway Revue*, is done. Two-and-a-half months of rehearsal are over, three sold-out shows have been performed, and I walk into the dressing room on Monday morning after the performance weekend. Four hundred and fifteen costumes remain hung up in each actor's place. I go backstage – 14 massive set pieces and over a hundred props remain. The stage needs to be reassembled into its default form, technology and tools remain out of storage, and all manner of trash, loose hangers, and student-left-behind garments are littering the backstage, dressing room, and bathroom areas.

How long do you think it would take me to clean, sort, wash, organize, disassemble, transport, and store everything mentioned if I did it alone? Days? Weeks? Oh, don't forget, I have a full schedule of classes throughout the week and another production for the high school theatre class that opens in 10 days. Even if I am not stubborn enough to do all of that on my own, it would be impossible. Although would you believe, that once I asked for help, the whole process took only two hours? Such was the magic of the post-production workday.

Every Monday after the final show performance weekend, every member of the cast, crew, and production team was required to return one last time. They were also highly encouraged to invite parents and siblings as well. After school on that Monday, I walked into the dressing room and 75 people were waiting there for me, ready to get to work. I had all of the tasks already taped up onto the wall, so after a brief explanation of how it would all work, my 'army' of parents and students got to work. After two hours, the dressing room, backstage areas, and the stage were spotlessly clean and empty. Every costume, prop, and set piece was sorted, inventoried, and put in its labeled proper place on the third-floor theatre storage area. A massive production that took months to create was reset in an afternoon.

In this part of the chapter, I will discuss the different workdays you can hold within your production and the benefits of each of them.

Movie-Watching and Costume Fitting Day

Movie-watching and costume fitting day happens around a month or month and a half before opening night. It is the chance for students to try on their costumes, for you to plan any alterations or additions that need to be made, and for the production company to enjoy their time together watching a movie of the production.

Movie Watching: While students are getting fitted for their costumes in the other room, in the main room (usually the theatre with a big screen) the students will watch a full-length movie of the production they are working on, or something inspiring if there is not a movie of it. In some cases, for PG-13 and R movies, you will need to get your students' parents' permission to screen the film. For some well-known productions, it'll be easy to find any number of movie adaptations: *Peter Pan*, *A Christmas Carol*, *The Time Machine*, *The Wizard of Oz*. However, if your production does not have an adaptation of it, pick something in the same genre, by the same writer, or even a stage recording of it. Provide snacks and food by asking parents to bring stuff by for this chill, yet very important day. Make sure to speak with the students before and after the event. Make sure they know they are not free to go once they are done with their fitting.

Costume Fitting: All hands on deck, so far as your costume crew is concerned. Have your sewers on hand, your pinners, and also your measurers. You need to get lots of eyes on the costume to quickly assess what works, what doesn't, and what needs work. It is good to have multiple options for a costume so that you don't feel stuck with a costume that doesn't work. It goes without saying, but don't hold your costume fitting until all of your costumes are in. This requires preparation on your part to get your costumes in the first month of the production. Depending on how many students were in the production, I would usually have two students doing fittings at once. One is in the bathroom changing while the other is getting looked at and pinned. The fitting usually lasts the length of a rehearsal, and that two-and-a-half hours will be gone before you know it.

Pre-Production Workday
AKA "production workday," this is the big workday before the show opening. This is the time to build sets, props, paint, sew, etc. All hands on deck day! All cast, crew, and families are invited. This is usually held on a Saturday, so it is tough to make it mandatory. I would start mine at noon and we would usually be done by 5 or 6 pm. I would be sure to have donuts, snacks, drinks, and pizza on hand for anyone who wants some. Just saying that you will provide food will get half of your workforce there. Even with food, most people don't stay for the full five to six hours. Some do, especially those without conflicts that day, but inevitably the work runs out and all that is left is the painting, which few can do well (see below).

I would have sheets of paper printed out, one for each job that needed doing. There are fully detailed instructions on the sheet. Then I would line up the sheets in seats in the auditorium. If some certain props or sets have to do with that job, they would be placed near the sheet.

The jobs range from a five-minute job to a three-hour job. They also range from building things to cleaning things, to prepping things, to painting things.

Here are just a few summarized examples of things that can be done for the production workday:
- Organize costume storage
- Clean backstage areas
- Carry furniture to the theatre
- Repair or paint furniture
- Sort/organize makeup and supplies
- Build props
- Set up prop tables

I would separate the tasks into six categories so that people who want to work on certain things can find the tasks they'll be good at. This doesn't mean they can't change categories as the day goes on, but some parents will be there just to build, and some others might only be there to sew.

The six categories are:
- Movers
- Builders
- Painters
- Sewers
- Propers
- Organizers

A note about the painting. Depending on your production, painting is going to be the biggest task that takes the longest on the workday. Some sewers will take their stuff home for a few weeks, and some builders might too, but the painting is usually done in-house. First things first, get your paint expert/captain on hand. I was fortunate to have the art teacher at the school volunteer every time to help out. In your painter's crew, there will be two kinds of painters: experienced/talented painters and 'broad' painters. 'Broad' painters can paint big things quickly. Use them for the backgrounds and walls. "Paint this wall brown." Got it. The experienced and talented painters will be used for the intricate background, artistic props, set pieces, and more.

Here's the biggest piece of advice I can give you regarding painting. You will *always* run out of time for painting. No matter how much there is, no matter if you think it will for *sure* be done within the workday this time, it won't. Painting is a long, tedious process that involves planning, drying, background, drying, main work, drying, details, drying, and second coat. Did I mention drying? Be patient with it. Have a contingency plan for a second smaller workday or for the painters to come in the following week to finish up outside of the workday.

Sitzprobe and Standzprobe

Sitzprobe: A sitzprobe is the bringing together of the singers and the accompaniment for the first time to focus solely on the musical aspects of the production. It is a chance to, after all music rehearsals have taken place, run through all of the music, melodies, harmonies, and accompaniments. The main purpose of a sitzprobe is to ensure the singers and accompaniment orchestra are perfectly in sync. It's a chance to iron out any kinks in timing, balance the sound, and establish a cohesive musical foundation before adding other layers of performance. It is called 'sitz,' meaning 'sit' – so no blocking or choreo, just focus on the music. It's also a great opportunity for the cast to hear some of their castmates perform those songs for the first time. Even if you don't have a live accompaniment (orchestra or piano), still hold a sitzprobe with the tracks as a review of all the music. Most likely, the only time you rehearsed the songs so far was in music rehearsal. It is a great refresher.

Standzprobe: I claim to have made up this term . . . but surely someone else did. I just took the word 'sitz'probe and put it in 'standz'probe to mean a standing rehearsal, in other words, all the dances! Once all your choreography is done, now is the time to review everything with the whole cast. You'll be able to do several run-throughs of the dances, help catch up people who were missing, and get a good refresher on everything, usually close to full run-throughs of the show. Make sure that if there is singing in the dances that they are singing every time.

Post-Production Workday

Post-production workday is just like a pre-production workday but in reverse. Instead of putting things together, they are taking them apart. Instead of setting it up, they are tearing it down. Instead of carrying stuff from storage to the theatre, they are carrying it from the theatre to the storage. You get the idea. The intro story about the post-production workday after the *Broadway Revue* is a post-production workday at its finest. If you have all hands on deck again, one last call for your students and families, the Monday after your show, you'll all get it done in a matter of hours.

It's key not to do this immediately after the show that night or even the next day. Wait until the following week.

Set up the work tasks just like the pre-production workday with categories for types of work, papers with detailed instructions, and food provided. By the time you are done, the theatre, storage areas, backstage areas, green rooms, bathrooms, and dressing rooms should be completely cleaned, reset, and ready for the next thing.

Post-Production Review Day

This is an event I would hold one to five months after the production was over. Why such a wide array of time? Well, sometimes we were all busy with other productions and it's easier to do these events as the year comes to a close. But it is important to make it at least one month after the production to give students a chance to come down off of the high of performance, get some space between them and the production team, and then come back with fresh eyes and ears.

The main aspect of this review day is to watch the recorded video of your production. Always record your productions for posterity and review. It is integral to an actor's growth to watch themselves onstage and see how they can improve.

Other things you can do at this event include take surveys about the program/show, discuss future shows and the future of the program, and do a Q&A debrief session about the show. Yet again, as always, provide food for them.

 Key Takeaways

1. Provide a schedule to auditioners at the audition that is vague and generalized and only has what days of the week rehearsals usually will be, what time rehearsals will usually start and end, and what days are mandatory.
2. Craft a perfect, efficient, and flexible schedule to provide for the company at the first rehearsal. This schedule needs to be non-linear, flexible, that doesn't waste people's time, and has built-in makeup rehearsals. Then come out with a second updated draft midway through the production.
3. Musical rehearsals in order should be: music rehearsals, then choreography rehearsals, then blocking rehearsals.
4. Hold production workdays to increase the efficiency of your production as well as the enthusiastic buy-in of the students and families who are participating. This includes a costume fitting, pre-production workday, sitzprobe, standzprobe, post-production workday, and production review day.

15

Rehearsal

A director of mine in college didn't believe the production needed to be fully ready and done until opening night. Some actors didn't get some key props until tech week, the real sound effects and special effects weren't being used until two days before opening, mics weren't used until final dress rehearsal, and the actual production lights were first used on opening night. So, when we got out there and performed onstage on opening night, do you think that it was as good of a performance as it could be? Of course not. It took us until the second weekend of shows to really feel comfortable. That is because we weren't really rehearsing the full show.

I used that experience in college to better myself as a director. I vowed to have the entire production completely ready by the *first* day of tech week. That's right: All costumes, props, lights, sounds, effects, mics, lines, songs, and everything else was ready and used as it would be on opening night. That way, my actors would have an entire week of being able to properly rehearse the full show with everything involved four times before an audience was brought in. By the time opening night rolled around, the cast was very comfortable and felt ready, even eager to show off the play, rather than terrified.

Most of what we do in theatre is rehearsal. If you take a 60-day-long production that only has one weekend of three shows: rehearsal is 57 days and the actual show itself is only 3 days, that's 5% of the production. So, if rehearsal is an overwhelming majority of what we do in theatre, we need to do it right.

In this chapter, we'll talk about not only getting your production ready by the *beginning* of tech week, but also holding productive, efficient, worthwhile, and useful rehearsals.

Read-Through

We will go through this chapter by breaking down the different types of theatre rehearsals you can hold and a few tips and tricks for each, starting with the first rehearsal/read-through.

Although the schedule sometimes doesn't allow it, try to have your first post-casting rehearsal be an all-cast and crew called read-through. It is a great chance for everyone to meet, get to know each other, get to understand the show, and get things kicked off right. Anyone involved with your show should be there, even if they won't be coming in until tech week. It brings everyone together to start to strive towards that common goal. It also gives everyone involved with the production a perspective on just how far the show has come from read-through to closing night.

Try to have the room set up as nicely, neatly, and professionally as possible. This is one of those 'it's just the little things' things, but putting in that little extra effort to make sure the pens and highlighters are lined up exactly the same on each chair can go a long way toward making it seem legit. I held my read-throughs in the audience section of our performance space (the chairs were movable). If you can, try to hold the read-through in the performance space, even onstage if you want, but this isn't necessary, just as long as you have enough room for everyone and everyone in the circle can see everyone else.

I would put the chairs in a sort of egg shape, all facing inward so that everyone can see everyone. In the middle of the chairs would be a table with a show opening cake that would have "Welcome to _____" written on it, with the blank being filled with the location of the show. I would also provide water as well. More food is fine too, but if you have a limited food budget for things like this, I would keep it small, or perhaps ask them to bring a potluck dish. With this being the first rehearsal, the students and parents will have a bit less buy-in than they will later on, so if you were to only ask people to bring food once, I wouldn't ask for this one.

On each student's chair, I would put one mechanical pencil with an eraser, one skinny highlighter, and a binder that contained: the show script, the schedule, any unsigned paperwork, and the theatre program handbook. The theatre program handbook was a 22-page document that went more in-depth about the policies, expectations, and rules of the program to be signed by every cast and crew member as well as their parents.

At the read-through, here is the order in which we would do everything:

Rules/Procedures
Go over the casting and attendance agreement again. Cover key parts of the handbook and assign a date to have the signed handbook page returned.

Introductions
We would go around the circle and every cast and crew member would introduce themselves with their name, what grade they are in, the role(s) they are playing, and something like a fun theatre story or fact. This is a great opportunity to introduce your production team, especially if they are someone the students haven't worked with before.

Food/Drink
After introductions, we would break for a few minutes to grab a slice of cake and whatever food was there, then it was back to the seats to continue.

Schedule
We would go in-depth about the schedule as a whole. I would have the students highlight the rehearsals they were called for. I would also provide two copies of the schedule: one for their backpack/organizer and one for the fridge at home for their parents.

Script and Scenes Overview
We would then do a general overview of the show from start to finish. Mostly just an explanation of the script, what it looks like, how to read it, etc. I would then explain the general plot, action, and scenes of the show.

Character Development Explanations (Individually)
Then I would pull each actor aside one by one and explain their character to them briefly. These are character development explanations where it gives the student a good idea of how to kick off their character, especially for the read-through they are about to do. This isn't your chance to do a full acting coach job, but just enough to get them going. While the students were coming up one by one to meet with me, I would have the rest of the students doing several things, including highlighting their scripts, highlighting their schedules, reading the handbook, etc.

Full Read-Through/Sing-Through of the Production

Finally, we would get to the read-through portion of the read-through. Given everything that we did before, we likely have an hour left in the rehearsal. Unless it is one-act, there is no *way* we are finishing that read-through word for word. In fact, I don't believe I've ever done a full word-for-word read-through in my life. There just is never enough time. That's okay! Just make sure to cover a few of these key things during your read-through portion: (1) read key scenes; (2) make sure every student says at least one line (if they have one); and (3) play at least a bit of every song (if it is a musical).

Music Rehearsals

This part of the chapter on music rehearsals will be geared towards your production's music director. If you (as the director) are also the music director, read on. If you have someone else as your music director, hand the book to them.

Before the first music rehearsal even happens, the students need to be armed with a lot of resources to help with their success. It is your job as music director to get these resources ready for them. It might be a bit of work on the front end before the read-through, but I assure you, if you provide them with the resources and they actually use them, it'll make your job easier as the production goes on. The goal should be to have these resources ready to provide to them at the read-through/first rehearsal. If the director is following the musical rehearsal order I suggested earlier (musical then choreo then blocking), then your music rehearsals will be right up next. The resources I am talking about come in three forms: learning tracks, real song tracks, and rehearsal tracks.

Learning tracks are their singing notes played on a piano with no accompaniment behind it. I usually separate my rehearsal tracks into song section segments, never getting longer than 12–16 measures. This is especially important when it comes to ensemble songs and harmonies. For students, harmonies can be tough sometimes, but these tracks help solidify it as their own melody. I usually posted one big folder full of little folders in a Google Drive that the students can access. The little folders were each song, then within the little folders, it had even more folders separated by parts. To record each file, I would put my phone with the voice recorder on the piano, press record, say "Red and Black, Measure 42, Tenor 1 Part," then plunk out the notes in that section of the song, then press stop. I would then immediately label the track

I recorded with "R/B 42 T1" and move on to the next one. This takes a lot of work on the music director's part on the front end, but some learning tracks are available online, so be sure to look first before you record.

Real song tracks are the actual recorded Broadway cast soundtrack versions of the songs in the show. If the show you are doing is popular with the kiddos, they'll be more familiar with the songs, but if it is unknown to them, they need to quickly become familiar with them. They should not be hearing these songs for the first time at their music rehearsal for that song. Provide another Google Drive folder with the real song from the show for them to learn and practice with. Some versions have different lyrics or different musical sections than the songs that you will be doing for the show, so make sure to take note of those changes, and either cut them from the track or just inform the students that it'll be different.

Rehearsal tracks are the tracks that your company will be performing with on opening night. If you are having live accompaniment for your show, get your pianist/band/orchestra in ASAP to rehearse the music and record it for this purpose. However, if you are sticking with tracks, the companies nowadays provide these to shows from day one of the production. Make sure the students have access to the app to access the tracks and make sure they are practicing with them.

For main characters with solos, I expect my students to learn their songs *before* their music rehearsal for that solo. It wastes everyone's time if, again, they are hearing the song for the first time in the music rehearsal. You should set the expectation that the students know their song by the time they step into the music rehearsal. You will likely only have one rehearsal for each song, so do you want to spend it plunking out the song note by note? If they learn their song beforehand, then you can work on dynamics, tone, acting, and tweaking the little things.

It goes without saying, but students should be expected to have their script and music with them with a pencil. They should be writing down the changes and updates you have for the music and should be adhering to those notes until they are off-book.

Try to have the goal of getting off-book by the end of the rehearsal. If you dedicate a single two-and-a-half-hour rehearsal to just one song, they will have heard that song dozens of times by the end of it. Challenge them to try to put their lyrics and music down by the end of it.

When rehearsing for each song rehearsal, I would do the following in order: (1) Listen to the real song track, (2) Have them sightread along to the real song track, (3) Learn parts for a 12–16 measure section on the piano, (4) Sing to the real track for that section, (5) Sing to the instrumental track for that section, (6) Repeat steps 3–5 until the song is learned, (7) Sing the whole song to the real track, (8) Sing the whole song with the rehearsal track, and (9) Try to sing and memorize the whole song.

Once music rehearsals are over, the music director should not disappear. Hopefully, they will be able to be in choreography rehearsals to make sure students are singing, run through rehearsals to keep up with the melodies and harmonies, and tech week to make sure everything is balanced with the music. A music director should always be around giving notes and improving the performance. The director is focused on the blocking, the choreographer on the dancing, and the music director needs to stick around so that someone can be focused on the singing. It's called a 'music'al after all, not a 'block'ical or a 'dance'ical.

Dancing Rehearsals

This part of the chapter on dancing rehearsals will be geared towards your production's choreographer. If you (as the director) are also the choreographer, read on. If you have someone else as your choreographer, hand the book to them.

If the director followed the suggested order of musical rehearsals (music, then choreo, then blocking), then the students should come to the dance rehearsals already knowing the songs they will be dancing to. It is *vitally* important that the students sing every single time they dance to the song. Learning dance steps is hard, but it is even harder to RE-learn those dance steps while singing. The body is going through a muscle memory exercise. If the body connects that the mouth and voice have been singing these words while they kick their leg up high at that part, then it'll become second nature. However, if the student was practicing the dance moves without singing, once they get onstage, they will be learning to dance again while struggling to sing for the first time while doing that kick. It is difficult for the choreographer to keep up with this aspect of the rehearsal while teaching everything, so make sure to have someone else in the rehearsal, preferably the music director, to keep an eye on the students who are not singing and stay on them until they do.

Whether the student dancers are singing or not throughout the song, it is also important to keep an eye on their facial expressions as they dance. A lot of people learning dancing will have intense thinking-focused facial expressions while learning. However, it is important to again keep their muscle memory to remind them to have the facial expression needed for that particular song (happiness, joy, anger, etc.).

Emphasize the importance of wearing dance-appropriate clothes and shoes. In most cases, students will be strolling into rehearsal after a long day of school. Dancing in the same blue jeans, boots, and collared shirt that they have been wearing all day will not be conducive to their success. Make sure they bring dancing clothes and shoes. If you have the resources for it, provide lockers where they can store that stuff every week so that once they get there, they can change and get ready.

Just like with the music director, the choreographer should record 'learning tracks' for the students. But instead of an audio recording, these will be video recordings of each dance or all the sections of each dance. This can be either by the choreographer alone or recorded at the dance rehearsal and posted immediately afterward. These learning tracks are great for students remembering the steps, even as they are walking into another rehearsal one day down the road.

Once the dance is completely learned, if you have access to it, go to the real performance stage and get the students to do it again a couple of times there. If you are rehearsing in a dance studio gym or some other non-stage area, dancing on the stage will get their cognitive processes working to transfer their dance more easily to the stage.

Dance rehearsals in order would usually be: (1) stretches; (2) the choreographer teaches the moves slowly for a 16–32-measure section; (3) run through that section without music; (4) run through that section with the real tracks; (5) run through that section with the rehearsal tracks; (6) combine that combo to the previous section of the dance; (7) repeat steps 2–6 for the rest of the sections of the song; (8) full run-throughs without music; (9) full run-throughs with the real track; (10) full run-throughs with the rehearsal track; and (11) full run-throughs onstage.

If a dance is particularly fast and/or complicated, the choreographer can slow down the track to 75%, 50%, or even 25% speed. YouTube has this feature on some songs, or you can create slow tracks using the app Audacity.

Just like with the music director sticking around, the choreographer needs to continue to be present and give notes, fixes, and reminders in every rehearsal that will contain one of their dances.

Blocking Rehearsals

The music is learned, the dances are on their feet, and now it is time to get onstage. The director takes the reins and helps teach the actors how to get onstage, what they do onstage, and how they get offstage.

Usually during blocking rehearsals, the director will get the scene up to the moment the dance starts and then stop. For the most part, the dances will have already been rehearsed in full, so focus on the blocking and acting for now. Combine it with the dances if you have time in that rehearsal, but it is more important during these specific blocking rehearsals to stick to the non-music scenes.

If you are not directing a musical, then all of your rehearsals will be blocking rehearsals!

The speed at which you block the scenes is determined by a number of factors: (1) How much rehearsal time do you have? (2) How many rehearsal days do you have? (3) How experienced is the director in relaying the blocking information? (4) How experienced and receptive are the students in getting and executing the information? (5) How complicated is the blocking? (6) How many people are onstage at once? (7) How long is a 'scene' in the script? and more. In some blocking rehearsals, you can knock out two to four scenes, but in others, you'll only be able to dedicate time to half of a scene – it depends on a lot.

Regardless of how much you rehearse, repetition is key with blocking. I've had a few directors who taught the blocking for the whole rehearsal and never went through it at the end. After a blocking rehearsal, there might be many weeks between the time we did that scene and the next time we did it.

You better believe by the time we did a run-through of those scenes a few weeks later, nobody remembered what they were supposed to do because they had never done it in sequence before. Teach the blocking, make sure it's right, then run it, run it, run it. The repetition can also help with line memorization as well. Your goal should be to run each scene at least three to four times per rehearsal. Done blocking, done with four run-throughs, and still have 30 minutes left in rehearsal? You can let them go early, right? WRONG. If you have the dedicated rehearsal time, USE IT. Make your show and the students better. Work on other things. Run dances. Rehearse songs. Then when the end of rehearsal finally comes, run the blocking scene one more time.

Students should have scripts onstage with them as well as a pencil. They should be writing down the director's notes, drawing little stage maps of their paths, and remembering notes from the music director and choreographer about the scenes as well.

At the beginning of blocking rehearsals, if you have the time to do so, it's helpful to do what's called a 'mini-read-through.' This is a full read-through of all the scenes you are blocking that day. This is a chance for the director to correct diction, volume, acting choices, accents, and more about the way the students say the lines. It's important to make sure they are saying the right things in the way the director wants them said before they run through it several times and get the wrong way stuck in their brains.

Run-Through Rehearsals

Once all the singing, dancing, and blocking have been learned in a production, the cast will now do run-throughs of the show.

Depending on the number of rehearsal days you have left after everything is learned determines how you can split your run-through rehearsals. Let's imagine you have plenty of days remaining before opening night. Start with fourths: Run through the first fourth of the play only. During that fourth, you review the music, dances, and blocking in that section of the play, then keep running that same section. Then the next rehearsal, you do the second fourth, then the third fourth, then finally the last fourth. This would be four full rehearsals working on transitioning from scene to scene within a split-up way. The next run-through split up would be thirds. Do the first third, then the second third, then the third third. Three full rehearsals this time. Next, of course, would be halves. First half and second half. Two rehearsals. If your production is a two-act play, it's already split in half for you: first act and second act. If you don't have a copious amount of rehearsal days left, start with the thirds or the halves instead of the fourths.

Once you are done with the split-up run-through rehearsals, it's time to put it all together. I think it is important for the first full run-through to be what I call a 'trainwreck run-through,' where the director is not able to stop the run-through. The students just do the whole production with all the lines, songs, and dances from start to finish. It gives the director and especially the students an idea of where the production is at (if it were performed that night) and how much work there is left to do. Sometimes the trainwreck run-through isn't too bad, and it'll increase confidence within the production that will lead to students being more proud and excited for the production, and they'll try to get more people to come to it. A good first full run-through will also allow you and the students to work on even more intense, detail-oriented things about the show to make it even better. However, sometimes the trainwreck rehearsal lives up to its name. It's a disaster from start to finish. Well, that's okay too. It will kick the students into gear and have them work even harder to make sure they catch up by opening night. Students don't want the show to go badly, and they don't want to be embarrassed onstage. If they are scared by a run-through of theirs enough, they'll put in the extra time to make it better. If the first full run-through is truly bad, it might be time to call extra rehearsals if you feel like the production will not be ready in time.

Have you ever watched a theatrical production where the beginning is excellent, the middle is alright, and the end is not good? This is because directors tend to always start rehearsals from the beginning. The beginning of the production then becomes the most-rehearsed part of the production and therefore is the best. Don't keep running something if it's solid. Start with the stuff that is not solid. Focus your energies on things that need fixing before you 'start it from the top' yet again. The same goes for dances and songs. Usually, the thing most danced or sung in the song is the beginning. Make sure the students focus on the end just as much as the beginning.

Usually, during full run-throughs, you will not have enough time to re-teach scenes/songs/dances. That is why students must take copious notes during the individual rehearsals and practice before the run-through rehearsals. Harping on them to keep up with their learning tracks, learning choreography videos, and studying their lines is imperative to avoid having to re-teach at these limited-extra-time rehearsals.

At a certain point in the schedule, one of the first full run-throughs will be "Line Memorization Day" where students will be 'off-book' and will not be allowed to have a script onstage. Depending on how extensive your rehearsal schedule is and how intense the line load is for the show determines when this cut-off happens. At a minimum, I would call them off the book two weeks before opening night. That gives them a full week of non-tech-week run-throughs to work out the kinks, and then a whole other week to focus on the rest of the show and tech. At maximum, I would call off-book three-and-a-half to four weeks before opening night. This is also dependent on whether there is a school holiday in the middle of your rehearsal schedule. Especially during the spring productions, we would always have an entire week off for spring break. You wouldn't want to call off the book right before that break because they'll forget everything over the break. Call it after the break and encourage them to keep on their lines during the break. You can't call off the book and then not have them rehearse for a while. Just because you have an official off-book call doesn't mean that they can't try to go off-book beforehand. If a character only has one or two lines in that scene, why are they holding their script for that run-through? Different actors have different line loads. A main character might have 100 lines while a minor character has 10 lines. If the main character forgets or calls "line" on five of his 100 lines, he is at 95% memorization, which is excellent. However, if the minor character forgets or calls "line" on five of his ten lines, he is at 50% memorization, which is terrible. I know it's easy to focus on your main characters in the show, but the minor characters with fewer lines should not be forgotten. Keep on them and hold them to a high standard if they have much fewer lines to memorize.

Tech Week

Tech Week. AKA "Hell Week," "Focus Week," "Gremlins Week," and "Magic Week."

The importance of tech week should never be understated. Your students, parents, colleagues, and the whole school community should understand that tech week is of the utmost importance. Throughout the rehearsal process, you are encouraged to be flexible, accommodating, and compromising so long as students are gone from rehearsal or coming late or leaving early. However, when tech week rolls around, everyone should know that the flexibility, accommodations, and compromise are over. It's the week for theatre, and everyone else gets out of the way. These expectations should be set early and reminded often. I had the mantra for tech week: "No absences, no latecomers, no early-leavers, no excuses." (Of course, family and medical emergencies still apply here, so be sure to be prepared for any eventuality.)

Tech week is the make-or-break time for a production. Usually, it is the four rehearsals preceding opening night. If opening night is on a Friday, then tech week is the Monday through Thursday of that week. As I said in the schedule chapter, these rehearsals will be scheduled to go longer than regular rehearsals just because of all that is involved with getting it ready, running the show, and debriefing after.

The introduction for this chapter tells the story of those directors who wait to get everything finally ready until opening night. Another story: I was the music director for a community theatre production. I came to opening night and sat in the audience. The show was supposed to start at 7:30, but 7:40, 7:45, and 7:50 rolled around, and no curtain. I was about to text someone to find out what was going on, but then I heard a noise from behind the curtain on the stage. It was the sound of a drill. Yep, the stagehand was *still* putting the set together even after the show was supposed to open. That is totally unacceptable. All of the people in your cast, crew, production team, and any other helpers should know that everything is due the first day of tech weeks, no ifs, ands, or buts. Are costumes being altered and sewn? Then they have to be in the dressing room for all of tech week. Are sets being painted and built? Then once tech week starts, they need to be done and dried. Is the backdrop still being worked on? Make sure your artist has it done and hung by Monday.

Any costumes/props/makeup/hair products that students are providing must be brought on the Monday of tech week and left in the dressing room. Usually, this mostly will apply to makeup and hair products, as students will use their stuff most of the time. However, if you are expecting them to provide costume pieces, shoes, or props as well, they expect to have it in by tech week as well. Make sure to have a place where they can bring that stuff and leave it early before tech week so that they don't forget the day of the show.

Having everything ready at the beginning of tech week helps the production become even better. If everything is ready, then the actors and directors can work on fixing the little things and big things that pop up with their performance instead of focusing on things like lights, mics, set pieces, props, and more. It also gives those running the lights, sounds, mics, and set transitions an entire week to practice run-throughs of the show. Everything is there, everything is ready, and everything is used, including mics, techs, walkie-talkies, sets, props, costumes, makeup, hair, music, sounds, lights, and full audience set-up.

Now, here is the secret caveat to this. If your expectation and rule is that everything *must* be in by the first day of tech week, if something goes wrong and something is a day or two late, guess what? It's alright because the show hasn't opened yet! However, if the expectation is that everything needs to be ready by opening night and then something goes wrong and is a day or two late, guess what? The show doesn't have whatever is missing or went wrong. Expecting to have everything there and ready at the beginning of tech week gives you four days of buffer for things to go wrong. You would much rather have things late and go wrong during rehearsal than for the actual shows.

During tech week, make sure that no student may watch out in the audience; he/she needs to use the dressing room/backstage areas just like a show. Sometimes during your blocking and full run-through rehearsals, students want to come out into the audience and watch the scenes they are not in. That is fine and encouraged for cast comradery and show excitement, but when tech week rolls around, they need to be in the dressing room, green room, backstage, or onstage. Nowhere else. They need to be practicing their transitions and paths to get from their dressing room to their spot onstage.

The final dress rehearsal on Thursday, the day before opening night, will be "Show Conditions," which means there will be no lines called, the director will not interrupt for any reason, and whatever happens, will be acted like it is an actual show performance. During tech week, a few things go wrong, such as missed sound cues, technical issues, costume issues, and more. So, it's understandable sometimes to stop the tech week run-through to fix the issue before continuing. However, you and your cast and crew need at least one full show condition run-through to practice what to do if something goes wrong during the show. Unless there is some kind of emergency, when the audience is there during the show, problems need to be fixed on the spot and on the fly. A show conditions run-through in tech week will prepare everyone's minds for 'showtime.'

Overall Rehearsal Tips and Tricks

Here is a collection of tips, tricks, and advice about rehearsals in general to keep in mind for your program.

Snack Stash
For every rehearsal, have a big tote called the 'snack stash': This would be filled with individually packaged, non-perishable snacks such as chips, granola bars, and fruit snacks that students can munch on during (appropriate times in) rehearsal. I had my parents donate to the snack stash from time to time, and it would usually be full throughout the rehearsals. Make sure you cap a limit on the number of snacks they can take during rehearsals, or you'll have your senior boys grab 15 snacks without a second thought.

Water
You must provide water for your students for every rehearsal, but especially for music and dancing rehearsals. Students nowadays are dehydrated enough as it is, and going up onstage and doing everything we are asking them to do will further dehydrate them. And the little water fountain out in the hall isn't going to cut it. Have parents provide water bottles, water jugs, and cups, or at the very least, make sure your students bring their water bottles and fill them up before rehearsal. Encourage them to take water breaks, especially during dance rehearsals.

Map Out the Time
Schedule your rehearsal as much as possible ahead of time. Plan to accomplish these goals, then review. A director should know exactly what is planned for rehearsal from start to finish, minute by minute. Don't fly by the seat of your pants, because it'll lead to wasted rehearsal time. Have a plan, make the plan consistent, and do that from the moment they hit the door. Be organized. Have a plan. Get a planner, get organized.

Getting There
Everyone has a job to do right when they arrive at rehearsal. What is it? Change? Set up the stage? Study lines? Run music? The students should know what their job is right when they arrive, and they should be doing that job. Distractions and downtime take away from precious rehearsal time. They have to do something when they get there: Have them help research a prop on Amazon, have them help you take notes, or call lines, and understudies have their jobs as well. Nobody should be sitting doing nothing, because that's when people get bored and things go wrong.

Homework and Studying

In the school setting, it is important to provide time for students to study and do homework during rehearsals. During the schedule chapter, I encouraged you not to waste students' time in rehearsals, but sometimes it is unavoidable that some students will be out in the audience waiting for their scene to come up. Besides learning their lines for the show, what else should they be doing? Homework and studying. Their parents and teachers will appreciate this extra time given during your activity.

Not Called? Don't Come

If a student is not called for a rehearsal, make sure they aren't allowed to come. These are for the specific music, dancing, and blocking rehearsals. We need to cut down on distractions as much as possible. A student who is not called but hanging out at rehearsal can only provide a distraction to the students who are called.

Be Predictable

Model good behavior. Be predictable. Be consistent. Be predictable and consistent when it comes to how and when you start rehearsal, what you do during rehearsal, and how and when you end rehearsal. Don't end rehearsals some nights right on time and some nights 25 minutes late. The parents and students won't appreciate that inconsistency.

Picking a Musical

This is a quote from a colleague of mine: "For musicals, if you are not a formally trained musician and do not have access to a formally trained person, DON'T DO ONE. You're not creating opportunities for students; you're creating opportunities for them to be embarrassed. Nothing kills a program faster than bad shows." She's right. If you, for whatever reason, don't have access to a proper music director and choreographer, do *not* pick a musical just because you want to do it. It'll lead to a bad show, embarrassment for the students, and a decline in the program, all of which are unacceptable.

No Phones

I know, in this day and age, easier said than done, right? Having a no-phone policy at rehearsal is easy or hard depending on what type of phone policy your school has. If the school is particularly strict when it comes to phones, it'll be easier. However, if your school is lax on the phones, you will have to put down your foot harder. In either case, if your rehearsal is after school, students will think that "school's over, so it's phone time." Keep the policy in place and stay consistent. There are exceptions sometimes for having scripts on phones or using the phones for homework in the audience, but be careful with those exceptions because students might take advantage of those limitations. Within your theatre phone policy should be a stern punishment if you catch a student on their phone onstage. You can have a basket to turn in phones at the beginning, a policy to keep phones in bags or out in the audience, phones off or on silent always, etc. Keep these expectations high and it'll lead to a program culture of legitimacy and excellence.

Key Takeaways

1. Your first rehearsal/read-through rehearsal should not just be reading/singing through the script. You should include policies, handbook discussions, schedule details, introductions, food, and more.
2. Music, dancing, and blocking rehearsals should all have a plan, should involve students using their scripts/music and a pencil, should involve a lot of repetition, and should strive for memorization by the end.
3. Run-through rehearsals should first split up the show into fourths, thirds, and/or halves, before doing full run-throughs. At these run-through rehearsals, the students should know their songs, dances, and blocking enough so that it doesn't need to be retaught, and the end should be rehearsed just as much as the beginning and should contain before tech week a line memorization off-book call.
4. Tech week is the end-all-be-all week for a theatrical production where everyone involved with the production is ready by the first day, understands the importance of the week, is running at show conditions all week, and is fully prepared for any eventuality that might happen during a real show.

16

The Performance

It's opening night of the big spring musical, with a sold-out audience. Principals, parents, the board, the mayor, *everyone* is in attendance waiting to see this show. The show is supposed to start at 7 pm.

You, as director, are not able to start the show until 7:25 because this was the first night that the whole cast had their hair and makeup done and there weren't enough hands to help with it all. (Truth be told, not everyone has their hair and makeup done yet, but you could not make the audience wait any longer, so you just apologized to the students who didn't have theirs done.)

While the audience was waiting the extra 25 minutes, they had no snacks or drinks because no concessions were provided. They had nothing to do or watch or listen to because you didn't put together any music pictures or videos to keep them entertained before the show.

You get the show started. However, midway through Act 1, your lead actor, who is supposed to be wearing their costume pants, instead comes out in athletic shorts. It turns out that they, in a hurry to get dressed, ripped their costume pants in a not-so-flattering place. You didn't have an emergency costumer or emergency costume on hand, so they had to go without.

Close to the end of Act 1, your lead actress, who is supposed to walk out with a sword to knight another character, walks out empty-handed and has to mime the sword the whole rest of the act. She couldn't find her prop because there were no 'prop-er' places for the props to go: no prop tables, no prop shelves, nothing. Actors were just in control of their own props, and one of the other actor's little brothers found the sword and played with it a bit before putting it someplace where the actress couldn't find it.

Intermission is similar to before the show. The audience has nothing to munch on, nothing to drink, nothing to watch, nothing to listen to. Besides going to the restroom, they just sit in an awkwardly quiet performance room waiting for the show to continue. Intermission of course takes twice as long as it was supposed to because you, as director, were handling the hair/makeup, pants, and sword crises. Nevertheless, the show must go on. Surely nothing else can go wrong, right?

Think again. Midway through Act 2, three actors who are close friends who are all in a key scene with the main character who is supposed to come on at the same time don't. The main character stands awkwardly onstage, waiting for them to enter but they don't. An excruciatingly long 45 seconds go by before the three tardy actors burst onto the stage out of breath. The three actors didn't miss their cue on purpose. The beginning of Act 2 was quicker than normal, and they got caught up watching TikToks together in the dressing room. The main issue? There was no video or audio feed from the stage to the dressing room, so anyone not onstage or backstage could not see or hear what was going on onstage.

Surely, I'll stop stressing you out now, right? Think again, again. The end of the show comes, and you, as director, come onstage to make some remarks. It has been a uniquely stressful night, and you are a bit flustered. You speak to the audience and start thanking a few people, but because of your stress and because you don't have any notes or a script, you forget to thank your stage manager and actually forget to acknowledge the seniors in the show, as it is their final show. Every senior in the years prior got this moment, but they didn't. They are devastated.

Okay okay, enough stress. I'm sorry. Performances can be stressful. Things can and will go wrong. Something that you planned for half a year, rehearsed for two months, and spent thousands of dollars on gets ruined right at the finish line.

In this chapter, I hope to alleviate these stresses for you and try to prepare you for several eventualities that might occur at the performance. First, I will list some ways to make the performances of your productions as smooth, stress-free, and enjoyable as possible, then I will present you with a minute-to-minute timeline of your performance night.

Performance Things to Note

I will have an extensive list of things to note for your performance days here, but I will start by addressing all of the 'stresses' from the intro in order:
    Makeup and Hair Helpers: Depending on how skilled your students are at makeup and hair themselves will determine how many helpers you

might need on hand to get makeup and hair done on time. If you have a rather skilled bunch of high schoolers, they will get theirs done and will be able to help the younger ones. If you have a designated makeup and hair tech who is not in the show, they'll be able to help throughout the night, but only one student at a time. For the most part, makeup and hair are done before the show starts. There are, of course, exceptions with character changes, quick changes, etc., but mostly everything is prepped before the show. If you find out you don't have enough people on hand to help with makeup, that's when you can call in reinforcements. Certain moms would love to help with this, and they do a great job. They'll prefer to start with their daughter or son, of course, but then they are skilled enough to help many others. Make sure you have enough people on hand to get it done on time. Makeup and hair not being done is not an excuse to delay the show.

Concessions: We talked about this at length in the "Money" chapter, but concessions should be an important part of your program. It not only brings in revenue, but as you saw from the intro situation, it gives the audience something to do while they wait. What would you rather do, just sit in a chair waiting for a play to start? Or sit in a chair waiting for a play to start . . . *while eating M&M's??*

Pre-Show Entertainment: At a minimum, there should be music playing in the background. That is the absolute minimum. It shouldn't be random music either; it should be music related to the show somehow. For *Annie*, 1930s music. For *Broadway Revue*, musical theatre hits (ones not performed in the show.) For *Oklahoma*, country music, etc. However, getting creative with your pre-show entertainment can give the audience something better to do than just sitting there with M&M's. If your entertainment is entertaining enough, then the time they have to wait flies by, and they'll be surprised when the show starts sooner than they imagine.

Here are some things you can do for pre-show entertainment that can bridge the gap from when the doors open to when the curtain opens:
- **Performances by students** – Solos, duets, trios, small groups, performing songs, scenes, monologues, or short plays.
- **Picture slideshow** – This can be of pictures of this production through the rehearsal process as a behind-the-scenes look, or pictures from previous shows to see how your program has developed over the years
- **Videos From the Past** – Video clips from shows your program has done in the past. This also shows the development of the program

while showing families photos of their little ones when they were much smaller.
- **Interactive Displays** – Set up displays with props, costumes, or historical information related to the show. Encourage audience members to mingle and discuss.
- **Trivia or Games** – Host a short trivia game related to the play or theatre in general. Offer small prizes to keep it fun.

Costume Emergencies: They happen all the time. These kids grow faster than we think! First contingency, have backup costumes on hand just in case. The costumes in the dressing room shouldn't just be the costumes for the actors, but there should be a rack or two of backup costumes for this very reason. It is not just malfunctions that happen, but sometimes clothing articles get lost or forgotten. It is good to have backups. However, if that fails, and a student has a costume malfunction, you need someone on hand who can fix it on the fly (no pun intended). They don't necessarily need to be waiting in the dressing room the whole time for an emergency. However, if they come to every show, and then something happens, tech can come out to the audience, get them, and bring them back to help with the costume crisis.

Props in Their 'Prop'er Place: A prop table needs to be set up with painters' tape or something similar denoting what props go where. So, before the show, the techs can look and see what props are missing and go find them before the show starts so that an actor doesn't have to mime a sword onstage. Sometimes students use props and then exit the other side of the stage, or absentmindedly take the prop to the dressing room. You need your stagehands on hand to keep an eye out for this and tell that student to put the prop back where it belongs or help them by taking it there themselves.

Video/Audio Feed in the Dressing Room/Green Room: This is one I wished I had much earlier in my career. Once I got it figured out, it was a game changer. I hooked up a camera facing the stage to a wireless HDMI transmitter, then hooked up a tv to the corresponding wireless HDMI receiver in the dressing room. From then on, the students who were still in the dressing room were able to see and hear exactly what was going on onstage and would know much more accurately when their cue was coming up.

End of Show Notes: Some people like going off script, but I'm not one of those people. Even if you are one of those people, always pre-write your post-show notes. At a minimum, write an outline and keep it in your pocket just in case. You do *not* want to forget anybody when you go through the thank yous. You do *not* want to let the seniors down, or anyone else who deserves extra recognition. Even if you give the same post-show speech at each of your multiple shows, keep it on hand because you don't know what your state of mind will be when you get up there.

So those were all of the stressors from the introduction story. Now here are a few more tips to help on performance night:

Food: Provide food for your students on show day so that it is not something they have to worry about. They need to show up two hours before curtain, which is usually around 5/5:30. You don't want them late to call time and you don't want them having to worry about ordering something during the process. For three shows I usually did three different meals: pizza for the opening, sandwiches for the Saturday matinee, and chicken for Saturday night.

No Eating in Costume: Ever.

Costumes Ready: Every costume needs to be laid out and ready to go for every show. This is especially important if you have multiple shows back-to-back. Students usually just throw their stuff off and chuck it into a corner. Insist that they must hang up their costumes properly before they can leave.

Makeup or No Makeup: If you don't know how to do makeup, don't do makeup. No makeup is better than bad makeup.

Show Speed Run-Through: Before the show starts, the hour-and-a-half before warm-ups, have the cast do a speed run-through the show. This is where they blurt out the lines as fast as they can. It helps with short-term line memory and confidence.

"Thank You, Five": If you are not aware of this common theatre phrase, it is where a stagehand or the director calls the time until "places." "Five (minutes) until places!" The response from everyone who hears this call is, "Thank you, five." It's not just for five minutes, it's for any amount of time, or the house is open, or we are holding, or even for "places." The reason we have everyone say it while repeating the amount of time is so that they physically say the number or the call, and therefore it guarantees that they heard the information and are now aware of it.

Calm Intermission: During intermission, stay calm. Don't be too hyped up because that energy can take away from the energy onstage in Act 2.

Water: Make sure they are drinking plenty of water all day of the show, before the show, during the show, during intermission, and after the show. Hydration is king.

No Sodas: Insist on "no sodas after lunch on show days." The syrup can coat your voice and the carbonation can make you burp. Water water water instead.

Show Day Schedule

Now here is a to-the-minute schedule of what a show day will look like to continue to provide advice for you while also giving you a timeline of when things should be happening. This timeline will be running under the assumption that: (1) The show starts at 7 pm; (2) The show that is starting is the opening night show; (3) There will be at least one show the following day; and (4) The show is a two-act musical production. If any of these things are different, adjust the schedule accordingly.

8:00 am (11 Hours to Curtain): Once you arrive at the school, get to the performance venue and make sure everything is in place, and most importantly, that the AC and/or heat is on and working.

12:00 pm (7 Hours to Curtain): During lunch, go check the venue again. Also, go visit the cast and crew at lunch and check in on them. Remind them no sodas after lunch. Remind them of their call time.

4:00 pm (3 Hours to Curtain): School is out, and although it is one hour until call time, some students, like you, won't be going home. So, head on over to the green room/dressing room to be there for the students who need to stay at the school. Have cards or board games on hand for them to pass the time. Make sure they are conserving their energy.

4:45 pm (2 Hours and 15 minutes to Curtain): The food arrives either by restaurant delivery or a parent helper. Get the food set up and ready for the students to eat since they need to eat before putting on their costumes.

5:00 pm (2 Hours to Curtain): Call time for the cast and crew. Insist that all students must be there at or before call time. Any tardiness should be noted. Students start eating.

5:15 pm (1 Hour and 45 minutes to Curtain): Students and helpers begin makeup and hair.

5:30 pm (1 Hour and 30 minutes to Curtain): Turn on the sound, lighting, and all other tech systems and do a system check.

5:45 pm (1 Hour and 15 minutes to Curtain): If they haven't done so already, students need to begin putting on their costumes and getting ready for mic check.

6:00 pm (1 Hour to Curtain): Mic check. Concessions start setting up. All students with mics head to the stage, and the sound tech makes sure their mic is working and on. Ticket personnel arrives and is briefed.

6:05 pm (55 minutes to Curtain): Music sound check. Have all students with mics now do a full sound check with one of the songs from the musical.

6:10 pm (50 minutes to Curtain): Dance check. Perform a tough dance from the show to get things warmed up and to test if the mics are secure.

6:15 pm (45 minutes to Curtain): Student 20-minute warning to have all makeup, hair, and costume done and on and ready. Prop check. Every student who handles a prop goes and makes sure it's in its 'prop'er place. Concessions start popping popcorn.

6:25 pm (35 minutes to Curtain): Check in with concessions, ticketing, and any other helpers who are on hand to make sure they are good and don't need anything and don't have any questions.

6:29 pm (31 minutes to Curtain): Begin the pre-show entertainment, which will usually involve turning on music or beginning a video/picture slideshow. Turn on the stage camera for the dressing room tv.

6:30 pm (30 minutes to Curtain): Open the house. Doors open and those that have been waiting can enter and begin the ticketing and program process. The director makes sure everything runs smoothly for the first few minutes.

6:35 pm (25 minutes to Curtain): The director joins the cast and crew in the green room/dressing room. Deadline for the actors to be done with makeup/hair/costume. Begin pre-show warm-ups. Stretch the body, warm up the voice, and relax the mind. Traditional legacy rituals also happen during this time. End with a prayer and/or speech.

6:55 pm (5 minutes to Curtain): The director returns to the theatre to (hopefully) find a nearly full house. Check in with concessions and ticketing again. Do another systems check. Make sure the booth has their scripts and everything they need.

7:00 pm: GOTCHA. Do we start the show right at 7:00 pm? NO. Never start a show right on time. Why? Because people are late. People are always late. No matter the time of day, what day, where, traffic, or anything. There will always be late people. Starting the show a few minutes late to accommodate for this is better than those late people coming in after the show has already started and distracting everyone. This is the five-minute hold buffer. Dim the lights to indicate everyone should make their way to their seats. The pre-show entertainment should be wrapping up. Concessions should be shutting down while also setting up for intermission.

7:05 pm: Pre-show announcements. This can differ from show to show, but generally, the director will come up to greet the crowd and welcome them to the show. This can also be a pre-recorded announcement, or not included at all. If not included, have your buffer be longer to accommodate the lost passage of time here.

7:10 pm: Curtain. The show begins. Concessions are being shut down. Ticketing stays at their post for the late arrivals.

8:30 pm: Intermission. Concessions are back up and running. Get some intermission music going, or even another slideshow (or the same slideshow). Check in with the students in the dressing room. Make sure they are conserving their energy. Handle any issues that cropped up in Act 1. It's never too late to give acting advice and to encourage the students' success.

8:45 pm (ish): Intermission is almost over. The length of intermission is more often than not based on your bathroom situation. If you have a single stall for each gender, it's going to be longer. If you have multiple stalls and multiple bathrooms, it should go rather quickly. Once the bathroom lines are back down and mostly everyone is back to their seats, dim the lights and go call places. Concessions shut down.

8:50 pm (ish): Act 2 Begins

9:30 pm: The Show Concludes: The director comes onstage for post-show announcements, thank yous, tributes, and more. The director also informs the parents what the students will be doing so far as costumes and leaving are concerned. Ask the audience for help in cleaning up the area around them and getting it ready for the next day.

9:35 pm: Cast with families. After the remarks are over, the cast is encouraged to visit with their families and friends in costume to get pictures, etc.

9:40 pm: Post-Show Reset: Actors return their props. Actors hang up their costumes. Everything gets reset to its proper place to prepare it for the next show. Stagehands set up the stage for Act 1 Scene 1.

9:45 pm: Students can leave. Once they are done with their costumes and what they need to do, they can leave to go with their families and get a full night's rest.

10:00 pm: Close It Up. Once everything has been reset and everyone has left, the director shuts it all down, closes it all up, and gets ready to return in the morning for show two. The director goes to get a well-deserved full night's rest.

Key Takeaways

1. Many things can go wrong on a performance day. Have contingency plans in place to avert these problems, including backup costumes, an emergency costumer, makeup and hair helping hands, and providing a live video and audio feed to the green room.
2. For performances, provide the audience with pre-show entertainment, intermission entertainment, and concessions.
3. Follow a show day schedule that ensures that you and your students are fully prepared and ready for the show, including having call time two hours before curtain, food for the students, mic, music, and dance checks, pre-show warm-ups, and traditions that last about 20 minutes, and time to reset everything before the next show after this show.

17

Theatre Class

Have you ever seen the movie *Harry Potter and the Order of the Phoenix*? If not, you can look up the classroom scene where Dolores Umbridge first takes over the Defense Against the Dark Arts class. It's a perfect example of what *not* to do in a theatre classroom.

In the scene, Umbridge immediately sets a rigid tone – desks are in perfect rows, students are expected to follow Ministry-approved curriculum, and the focus is entirely on reading theory from a textbook. There's no movement, no application, and certainly no practicing of the actual magic they're supposed to be learning. Any time a student challenges this approach or asks for something more practical, they're quickly shut down. The message is clear: Memorizing information is more important than understanding how to use it.

This type of classroom, sadly, exists in some theatre programs too. Students sit at desks every day, reading from outdated textbooks, completing worksheets, and taking written tests on vocabulary and history – never once getting out of their chairs to act, rehearse, or perform. It's theatre taught as theory only, with little to no actual theatre being done.

Now compare that to Professor Lupin's class in *Harry Potter and the Prisoner of Azkaban*. Same subject, completely different approach. Lupin clears out the desks, gets the students on their feet, and walks them through practical exercises with a focus on experience and application. The students are engaged, active, and learning through doing – not just listening or reading. That's what a theatre class should look like: filled with movement, games, rehearsals, performance projects, and exploration. It's hands-on, immersive, and reflective of what theatre truly is – a living, breathing art form.

In this chapter, I will dive into the theatre arts curricular classroom. I will give you examples of games, projects, and performances to liven up your classroom and to make your students better, more well-rounded thespians. So that, in keeping with the Harry Potter analogy, you will be able to have your class be less like Umbridge's and more like Lupin's.

The Four Quarters

Covering all of what can be done in theatre class in one chapter is going to be impossible. I'm going to have to narrow it down to more general ideas and suggestions, and you can adjust based on how many classes you have and what level they are at. What works for some might not work for others. You might have your theatre class five days a week for an hour a day. You might only have them two days a week for 45 minutes per class. You might be a high school theatre teacher teaching Theatre 1, Theatre 2, Technical Theatre, and Advanced Theatre. You might only have one class for all of the high school, the same class every year. The great thing is that great resources are out there to help with theatre class curriculum, project ideas, game instructions, and more. Many books are dedicated to teaching theatre well, and I highly recommend looking those up and adding them to your repertoire. Aside from that, I'll let you know what worked well for me and what I've seen done well in other places.

My theatre classes, if they were year-round, were separated into four quarters. This was regardless of what grade level I was teaching.

The four quarters were separated as follows:
- Quarter 1: Basics, Fundamentals, Improv, Skits, Comedy
- Quarter 2: Fall Class Production – One-Act Comedic Play
- Quarter 3: Projects, Monologues, Scenes, Drama
- Quarter 4: Spring Class Production – One-Act Dramatic Play

Quarter 1: This is where we would cover warm-ups, voice projection, stage directions, stage presence, improv, pantomime, ensemble work, and more. This would be an emphasis on the basics and the fundamentals. Now, if you have only one theatre class and the same students come back to it year after year, you will need to make these units different year after year, perhaps even creating a four-year rotating schedule so that they don't re-do the exact same things all the time. We would of course fill the classes with games and activities as well. It is important when we play games to always discuss the games afterward and what they taught us about theatre.

Quarter 2 and Quarter 4: This system was based on the premise that they were able to perform a play twice a year, once in the fall and once in the spring. The good thing about this is that all of the rehearsals are curricular. In most cases, the performance would be extracurricular preferably, but the performance can also be a presentation during school to stay away from other activity conflicts. I believe that there is *nothing* in theatre class that is better at getting a student to learn and experience theatre than actually doing a production from start to finish. It teaches them the whole gambit of theatrical productions.

I would have them perform a comedy in the fall and then a drama in the spring. This is because I would say to them: It's easier to make an audience laugh than to make them cry. That is true to an extent, and they will most likely be more comfortable starting with a comedy anyway. They would be one-act productions so as to not bog them down with too much during their class. However, if you have an extraordinary amount of time and talent and want to do a full-length production, go for it.

Because they were class one-acts, I usually didn't charge at the door for them. However, I would still have concessions and a donation bucket, which would go to the theatre program or to cover the costs of the show.

For your more advanced classes, this is where you can delve into student-directed productions.

Quarter 3: This quarter takes us past the basics and into practical application by way of projects. There will be a section later in this chapter to give you lots of ideas for projects to do. This is also the chance to dive into serious acting, monologues, and competition-based theatre.

Curriculum and Textbooks

In this chapter's introduction, I basically told you not to use a textbook. However, sometimes it is unavoidable. Some schools require a textbook-based class. Some newer teachers need more of a roadmap to follow. Some need textbooks to have lessons for the substitute. Some even keep them around for punishment. One of my colleagues I interviewed for this book said: "I have a new textbook. I only bring it out when they are in trouble, they hardly see the book."

For whatever reason, you might need to have a textbook around.

After all of my interviews, the overwhelming majority, if they had to pick one textbook, picked *Basic Drama Projects*. It is a great textbook: easy, concise, and filled with great projects, skits, and ideas. However, if you do teach a textbook-based class year after year, it's important to keep the textbooks rotating so that you aren't teaching the same things to the same students year after year. Some other recommended textbooks are: *Stage in a School*, *Introduction to Theatre Arts*, *The Art of Theatre*, *Theatre, Art in Action*, and *Theatre: The Lively Art*.

Some schools require paper tests for grades instead of performance grades. Most of these textbooks come with great teacher editions and workbooks that have helpful paper tests already made for you.

There are, of course, hundreds of other theatre-based books that you can count on to fill up the rest of your curriculum. These focus solely on activities, games, projects, and improv. Here are some of the most recommended examples to add to your shelf: *Theatre Games for the Classroom*, *Theater Games for Rehearsal: A Director's Handbook*, *Places, Please! An Essential Manual for High-School Theater Directors*, *Everything about Theatre!*, *Drama Games & Improvs*, and *101 Comedy Games for Children and Grown-Ups*.

If you are at a school that requires theatre in some form, in other words, some students chose theatre because they had to or didn't want to choose something else, then sometimes some kids don't want to be there. That is especially true with a required credit course like Theatre I for some high schools and middle schools. Don't punish them. Don't make them miserable. Teach them the fun stuff. Keep them engaged. You never know what diamonds in the rough will be in there. You never know what unseen passions you'll ignite.

Games

There is no way I'd be able to list and explain the games that I have done in my theatre classes over the years. A lot of the books in the previous list have dozens and dozens of games that are a wonderful resource to pull from. A quick Google search, AI search, or colleague ask will yield great results as well. There is no shortage of games that teach theatre concepts, but let us start there. Do not waste time in class. In most cases, you won't have the theatre kids as long as you want. Either the classes aren't long enough, the classes aren't enough days of the week, or they don't last throughout the year. It does the students and you a disservice if you play games just to play games or play useless games. There should always be a *theatrical reason* to play that game. Don't worry, it doesn't eliminate a lot of them out there. But even if it has a theatrical reason, don't just play the game and move on. Discuss what the game was about. Talk with the students about why you played it, what they learned, and how it applies to the big picture.

Unless you are working on a production or major project, for a regular class I usually played at least one game per class right at the beginning. It got the kids excited to know we'd be kicking off the class with something active and fun. Also, always have a game in your back pocket if you end the class early. If you are done with your lesson with 5–10 minutes to spare, don't waste class time by letting them read or look at their phones; have a backup game ready to go and have them playing until the bell.

Always keep track of how long it takes to explain each game and how long it takes the kids to get the hang of it. If it's a quick in, quick out game, you can pull those out often. But if it's a new game that is sort of complicated, make sure you have enough time to get into it.

Other tips for playing games in theatre class:
- Be enthusiastic! Your energy will set the tone for the entire class. Show your students you're enjoying the process.
- Encourage all students to participate, even if they're hesitant. Offer modifications or alternative roles if needed.
- The emphasis is on the journey, not the destination. Celebrate effort, creativity, and collaboration.
- Highlight specific things you see students doing well, rather than just generic praise.
- Feel free to adjust the rules or add variations to keep things interesting and cater to different learning styles.
- Occasionally, let students choose or suggest games they'd like to try. This fosters engagement and ownership.
- Be patient. It might take a few tries for students to feel comfortable participating fully.
- Vary your games. Use a mix of games that focus on different skills and aspects of theatre.
- Connect to the curriculum. Relate the games to the plays or techniques you're studying for a more cohesive learning experience.

Projects

Although there is a wealth of theatre game ideas out there, there aren't nearly as many major project ideas. They can mostly be found in textbooks, but there are hardly any separate books on the subject.

Here is a list of some of my favorite projects that have worked well over the years:

Radio Broadcast: Plan, write, and record a traditional radio broadcast including characters, call-ins, and other cliché radio show fixtures. The "performance" is the recorded broadcast being played for the class.

Video: There are all kinds of video-recorded media out there you can do with your theatre classes. There is no shortage of ideas. Just a few are a shot-by-shot remake of a scene/music video, a comedy video connected with the comedy play, a recorded version of a student-written work, and more.

Student Teacher: This is a unit that teaches theatre teaching. You spread all of your theatre textbooks, books, and resources out on a table and the students research, plan, write, and teach a 20-minute theatre lesson.

Student-Written and Student-Directed Plays: Getting into theatre writing is always great fun and often yields excellent work. Then seeing the students take that writing and direct it onto the stage is even more rewarding.

Puppets: Create your puppets, write a puppet show, and perform the puppet show.

Masks: Create your masks, write a face-less show, perform the show with masks and no dialogue.

Stand-Up Comedy: Study and research stand-up comedy acts, write your own, and perform it onstage for the class.

Original Musical: Write your own musical that lasts for 10–15 minutes. Includes three songs: one real song with real lyrics, one real song with original lyrics, and one original song. Include lines, props, costumes, and choreography.

"The Funniest Skit Ever Performed" Project: With three group members, 5–7 minutes, completely original ideas, the only premise is the prompt "The Funniest Skit Ever Performed."

Comedy Joke Writing: Writing original jokes based on common premises including a knock-knock joke, a city motto, a dear sir or madam letter, and a riddle.

Poetry Slam: Write poems in various forms including haiku, limerick, and Shakespearean sonnet, then perform them for the class poetry slam style.

Monologue Slam: Same as above. Write an original monologue and then perform it.

Key Takeaways
1. Although classes can differ from school to school, the four-quarter system – 1: basics, 2: comedy one-act, 3: projects, and 4: drama one-act – has proven to work well in different environments.
2. If you need to use a textbook for whatever reason, find a good one that matches your philosophy and curriculum, and try not to use the same lessons year after year if the same students are returning.
3. There is no shortage of theatre game ideas out there, but make sure there is a theatrical reason for the game and an educational debrief with the students about the game and how it ties in with their theatre craft.
4. Projects can be excellent ways to put theatre knowledge into practice, including projects that involve writing, acting, and performing in front of others in many different ways using many different media.

18

Other Performance Opportunities

It was my first year at the charter school, my first year of teaching. Any teacher's first year is an overwhelming experience; don't let anyone tell you differently. I was struggling to get a band program going, grow a choir program, and start a theatre program. But on top of all of that, my administrators, at the beginning of the second semester, told me: "Oh yeah, we almost forgot, in the last couple of years we have had a district-wide talent show, and you're the director of that now." So, on top of everything else I was doing in that overwhelming year, I just had a massive production placed on my shoulders. I would have never thought of a talent show as a production I would do there, but because it had been done before, it had to be done again. I did some research as to how it had been done in the past and tried to copy the good things and improve on the things that needed improvement.

I titled it "(School Name Here)'s Got Talent," gave it a Hunger Games/Caesar Flickerman theme, and put it on. In that first year, I had exactly 20 people from kindergarten to 12th grade sign up (no audition), and those 20 people performed anything from singing to magic to a karate demonstration. That show was a success, and I actually quite enjoyed putting it on. I took notes on what to improve for the following year and continued the tradition for the years I was there.

Fast-forward four years later, and it is my final semester there. The show had become so successful and liked throughout the district that the one show turned into four shows! One semi-final show for every level campus (elementary, middle, and high) and the top five acts, scored by judges, made it to the fourth show, the district-wide final. These shows included auditions, videos created by the teachers of each campus, live audience voting, 'Ten-Second Teacher Talents,' and a judging panel of teachers from the respective campuses.

In just four years, I took a show that I hadn't even planned on doing and made it the biggest show that the charter school had ever seen. Sometimes shows placed unexpectedly into your lap are not necessarily a bad thing.

In this chapter, I'll dive into that talent show and many other different types of performances that you can put on at your school and how to implement them within your program. I'll also let you know about many various ideas for alternative performance opportunities for your production casts, performance opportunities out in the community, and other ways to enhance the theatre program year after year. Then finally, I'll go over some of the many opportunities that students can take advantage of during the summer, and what we as directors should do to keep their flame of interest in theatre burning bright for years to come.

Various Opportunities

Following is an exhaustive list of theatre opportunities that I put together from things my students have done in the past, things I've heard about, and great ideas from my theatre director colleagues interviewed for this book. Some of the opportunities involve the school, whereas some are solely up to the student. However, it is your responsibility as a theatre director to make sure they are aware of all of their options and provide them with as many opportunities to participate in theatre as possible.

> **Advertising/Preview Performances:** At a major school event, usually a concert, within a month of opening our show, I would have our cast perform something at that event to preview the show. If it was a musical, we would perform a song, sometimes with choreography; if it was a play, we'd perform a scene. This can be done at concerts, games, cafeterias, dinners, fundraisers, and more.
>
> **Concert Prelude:** Sometimes for music concerts, music directors will have prelude performances in the 30 minutes leading up to the concert starting. This can also be a great opportunity to highlight your theatre shows or actors.
>
> **Go to Performances:** Community theatre shows, regional theatre shows, traveling Broadway shows, and other area school shows. There are dozens of shows within driving distance of you each school year. Every show doesn't need to be a field trip or school trip, but make sure

you post the calendars and flyers from those theatres so that the students are aware of theatre performances happening in town.

Talent Show: As mentioned in the introduction, a talent show is a great, all-encompassing event where you get the opportunity to see student talent in many forms. It won't be just singing and acting, there will be magic, martial arts, juggling, ventriloquism, and more. The show can be competitive with prizes, or just an exhibition of talent. It can have a theme like the Hunger Games or The Price is Right, or it can go without a theme. It can have a charismatic host who does their own Oscar-like bits between acts, or it can just be someone saying, "next up we have Suzie on the Ukulele!" This is a great cross-district, multi-level event.

Agents: A few students I've had in the past have sought representation to get them more opportunities, in the hopes of working their way up to tv or movies. Make sure you teach your students about exercising caution when seeking an agent, as some agents will try to take advantage of the student financially. Otherwise, it can be a great opportunity for students to rise in the industry and find work.

Commercials: Businesses all around towns and cities are looking for talent for their commercials. Some post about them, and some you just have to ask around about.

Casting Calls: There are regional casting calls all the time for television and Hollywood movie productions. Keep your eye out for them on social media, and if your students are interested in that industry, encourage them to go out for them.

Community Theatre: I cannot recommend community theatre enough for your students. Community theatre, compared to school theatre, is "big time." Bigger shows, bigger audiences, bigger stages (in some cases). Most community theatres do six shows a year, most of which involve youth roles. Although it's tough to have students in a community theatre show while your show is going on, it is not impossible.

Regional Theatre: If you live in a big city, you likely have a regional theatre. Sometimes they are seeking youth actors for some of their shows. It is hard to break into that realm, but the right audition at the right time could lead to great opportunities.

Theatre Club: Starting a theatre club gives students an opportunity to exercise theatre games, activities, monologues, and plays outside of class or production.

Veteran's Day/Memorial Day: These are great opportunities for monologues or readings from theatre students.

Dinner on the Diamond: This is a good fundraiser on the baseball field. There are nine innings, and every inning is a different performance. Inning 1 is the national anthem, inning 4 is a comedy sketch, and so on.

Theatre Showcase: Put together different scenes from different plays.

Improv Groups: Fun, funny, and almost always a good money-maker. If you have the time and the students to do it, do it. A school improv troupe can be a great legacy item that lasts through the years, with new students wanting to join year after year.

ITS, International Thespian Society: This is a theatre service organization. They get service hours for helping with your theatre program. Provide opportunities for students to serve by having them come in to help organize before the school starts. They get rewards for hours of service.

Student-Directed One-Acts: This is an opportunity for more performances by students, while also training for the directing side of things as well.

Youth Theatre Programs: There are programs and community centers out there that have acting classes, workshops, and productions tailored for students.

Drama Festivals: Regional and national drama festivals offer opportunities for student-produced one-acts to compete and receive feedback from adjudicators.

Monologue Competitions: Many organizations host monologue competitions for students, allowing them to showcase their acting skills in a solo format.

Reader's Theatre Performances: Libraries or community centers might host reader's theatre events where students can perform dramatic scripts without full staging.

Historical Reenactments: Local historical societies or museums sometimes involve students in theatrical reenactments, offering a unique performance experience.

Volunteer Performances: Hospitals, senior centers, or community events might welcome student performances of short scenes, songs, or monologues.

Play Race: Split students into groups, where they all get the same script and the same amount of time to put on the same play. A great speed-theatre opportunity.

Karaoke Tournament: It is just as it sounds, karaoke, but tournament style! There is a bracket and the audience votes for the winners to advance.

Silent Film Re-enactment: Choose a classic silent film and have students create a live performance with sound effects, music, and physical comedy to complement the visuals.

Black Box Theatre Experiment: Transform a small, black box space into a sensory experience. Play with light, sound, and minimal props to create an immersive and atmospheric performance.

24-Hour Play Festival: Challenge students to write, rehearse, and perform a short play within a 24-hour timeframe. This promotes quick thinking, creativity, and teamwork.

Mythology Mashup: Combine elements from different mythologies or fairytales to create a one-of-a-kind performance. Students can rewrite familiar stories with a modern twist or create a whole new mythological world.

Historical Reimagining: Select a historical event and reimagine it through a playful or satirical lens. This can be a great way to explore social commentary or hidden facets of history.

The Summer

Let's look at three theatre students from three different schools and what their directors expect of them. Let's call the first one Bill, the second one Sam, and the third one Harry.

Bill has a director who does not have any expectations for him over the summer. The director doesn't like his job that much and wants as much time away from it as possible before school starts back up in August. Bill's director also doesn't assign any work over the summer because he doesn't want to deal with it or grade it right when the school year starts. Bill also is not aware of any theatre opportunities in town happening during the summer because, you guessed it, his director didn't bother looking them up and telling the students about them. Bill has a summer that is completely void of theatre. Although his flame of interest in theatre was bright after the spring production, that flame is now a dim flicker because between the spring production ending and the fall production beginning, four whole months went by. Bill loses some interest in theatre and decides to join the school's athletics weight training program during the summer because he has nothing else to do and his friends are also in that program. He fills the void left behind by the theatre with athletics and decides to join the football team. Bill decides not to audition for the fall production.

Sam has a director who has moderate expectations for him over the summer. Although Sam's director does need a break, they sacrifice a week of their summer to plan, host, and direct a theatre camp at their school. Sam attends the camp and has a wonderful time. Sam is also assigned just a bit of work over the summer, but not an excessive amount. His director wants him to read through the fall's one-act competition play to become familiar with it, to go to a production in town and bring back the ticket as proof for a completion grade, and to write a one-page essay on his thoughts on the production for another grade. Sam's director also informed all of the students, including Sam, about several theatre camps in town as well as some community theatre opportunities. Sam's director encourages Sam to take advantage of one or two of these opportunities if he has the time and interest. Sam decides to audition for the community theatre's summer musical. Sam's summer is filled with theatre but not overfilled. Sam still gets a break and some rest, but also keeps his flame of theatre interest burning bright.

Harry has a director who has excessive expectations for him over the summer. Harry's director never takes a break and thinks that the summer is actually a great time for more theatre opportunities and work. Harry's director hosts two school summer camps, one for plays and one for musicals, both of which are required for any student who wants to be in the fall production. Harry is assigned lots of work over the summer: four essays, reading the first three chapters in next year's textbook and answering all of the questions in each chapter, and memorizing his lines for the one-act competition play, as casting happened before school ended. Harry's director not only tells their students about the summer theatre opportunities in town, but they also expect Harry to get into the community theatre production, sign up for another in-town theatre camp, as well as a university theatre camp four hours away. By the time the first day of school rolls around, Harry feels like he hasn't had a break at all. He has not adequately rested from theatre and is not excited about the coming semester, let alone the whole year and the following summer. Harry's flame of interest in theatre is burned out. He will end up quitting theatre by the spring semester and chooses no other extracurricular activity for fear of that much work over the summer again.

The summer during theatre is a Goldilocks situation: not too little, not too much, just right. We, as directors, want to aim to be like Sam's director.

I will say that my colleagues interviewed for this book differed wildly when it came to what to do and not do during the summer. Some said not to do anything at all. Some said do some. Some said do a lot. There are pros and cons to all three philosophies. At the end of the day, it is up to your time and energy and your students' time and energy.

Here are just a few of their thoughts on summer:
- "I think kids should be kids, allow them to be free, that's when they appreciate things, absence makes the heart grow fonder."
- "If you require too much, you push them away."

- "Stay in communication with the core group, and check in on them. 'Thinking of y'all.' Check in with all of them. This is the play I'm thinking of."
- "They should be reading plays. If you're one of those who knows your next season, give them a script. What roles are available? Look ahead to help out with other design or tech things. They can give suggestions."
- "Should not sit around all summer being lazy doing nothing. Hit the gym, 30-minute exercise routine."
- "I'm very big on breaks, but again, at a small school, encourage two-week theatre camps."

Most of the 'other theatre opportunities' in the first section of this chapter still apply during the summer, so I will not reiterate those. However, for this summer section, I will talk specifically about two kinds of summer camps: ones that you/the school hosts, and then all the others.

School-Hosted Theatre Camp

I've had a lot of success with these in the past. The good thing is they don't have to have too many frills. You don't have to go all out on them. The students are looking for things to do during the summer sometimes, and the parents definitely are. One year, I even had an upperclass student, who was going to seek theatre as a career, direct the theatre camp under my supervision. Our format was just one week, five days, six hours a day. In that time, we would: rehearse and perform a 10-minute play, rehearse and perform a full musical choreography number, design handmade shirts, play games, do activities, do arts and crafts, and more. You can provide different camps for different ages.

Here are some other tips from my own experience and some of my colleagues' experiences hosting their own summer camps:

Theme: Choose a theme for the camp (e.g., fairytales, musicals, improvisation).

Curriculum and Activities: Develop a clear curriculum with a mix of acting exercises, scene work, improvisation games, and culminating performance activities. Adapt activities to fit different age groups.

Space and Resources: Utilize your school's facilities effectively. Reserve a performance space, classrooms for workshops, and storage for props and costumes.

Safety and Supervision: Ensure a safe and supervised environment. Develop a safety plan, have first-aid supplies readily available, and maintain appropriate student-to-staff ratios.

Marketing and Registration: Spread the word! Promote the camp through school announcements, flyers, posters, and social media. Set deadlines for registration and offer early-bird discounts.

Camp Vibe: Set a positive and inclusive atmosphere. Encourage teamwork, creativity, and respect for each other's ideas.

Variety Is Key: Incorporate a variety of activities to cater to different learning styles. Use games, movement exercises, and storytelling alongside traditional acting techniques.

Guest Artists: Consider inviting guest artists for workshops or master classes. This can offer students exposure to professionals and different areas of theatre.

Camp T-shirts and Swag: Create a sense of community and belonging with custom camp t-shirts or other branded items.

Field Trips: Organize optional field trips to see professional theatre productions or visit museums related to theatre history.

Staffing: Recruit enthusiastic and qualified staff members who are familiar with working with children. Consider involving drama club members or theatre students as assistants.

Parental Communication: Keep parents informed through emails, camp newsletters, and a dedicated camp website. Provide information about schedules, activities, camp policies, and performance details.

Technical Aspects: If your camp involves a final performance, secure assistance with sound, lighting, and set design/construction. Consider involving students in these aspects where appropriate.

Offer Scholarships: Consider offering needs-based scholarships to ensure accessibility for all students.

Showcase Performance: Plan a culminating performance for students to showcase their work, inviting parents and the school community. This provides a sense of accomplishment and celebrates their efforts.

Other Theatre Summer Camps

There are so many theatre camps out there if you look hard enough. Some will be in your town, some will be down the road, some will be across the state, and some extraordinary ones will be across the country. Theatre camps outside of your own can be excellent on a college resume, especially if they are seeking a major that involves performance and theatre. It is important to let students know the college and career benefits of theatre camp early in their high school career because if they go the summer of their junior or senior year, it'll be too late.

There are excellent benefits to the student in going to theatre summer camps, including continuing to develop their acting skills, exploring different theatre styles outside of what their school does, gaining more confidence and self-expression, finding new friendships within the theatre community, learning from professionals in the field, supplementing their classroom learning, building more good theatre memories, and more.

Here are some ways to seek out theatre camps and find great ones near you:
   The American Theatre Wing (https://americantheatrewing.org) maintains a database of summer theatre programs across the country.
   The Theatre Communications Group (https://circle.tcg.org) offers a resource page with summer theatre programs.
   State and Local Theatre Organizations: Many states and cities have their own theatre organizations that might list summer camps on their websites or newsletters.
   Online Directories: Websites like https://www.ussportscamps.com or https://www.ycamps.org allow searching for summer camps by location, age group, and keywords like "theatre" or "drama."
   Social Media: Follow local theatre companies, schools, and arts organizations on social media platforms like Facebook and Instagram. They might advertise or promote summer camps.
   Colleague Connections: Connect with other theatre educators in your area. They might be aware of summer camps offered by their schools, local organizations, or summer arts programs.
   Professional Theatre Companies: Contact your local professional theatre companies. Some offer summer programs for students, or staff might have connections to other camps.
   Arts Education Departments: Check with your city or state's arts education department. They might have listings or grant programs for summer arts programs, including theatre.

Lastly, here is some advice for you to help with your students' journey in finding and going to theatre camps. By providing resources, connections, and proactive guidance, you can empower your students to find enriching theatre summer camp experiences that ignite their passion and hone their skills.

   Financial Aid Opportunities: Many camps offer scholarships or financial aid. Encourage students and their families to research such options to find affordable camp experiences.

Consider Options: Discuss different types of summer camps with your students (e.g., performance-focused, technical theatre, musical theatre). Help them find options that fit their interests and skill levels.

Host Information Sessions: Dedicate a class session or school meeting to discuss summer theatre camp opportunities and guide students on finding the right program.

Post Flyers and Information: Put up flyers with summer camp information on school bulletin boards or in common areas. Promote upcoming camp deadlines and registration details.

Offer Support With Applications: If students need assistance with applications or scholarship essays, offer guidance and support during class time or office hours.

Key Takeaways

1. There is no end to the different kinds of other performance opportunities that you can provide for your students for theatre. Some include a talent show, theatre organizations and clubs, workshops and festivals, re-enactments and showcases, community and regional theatre, and professional acting work.
2. For the summer when school is out, the key is to not make your students do too much while also not just letting them do nothing. Find that perfect middle ground and provide opportunities for them to gain knowledge, skills, and experience in theatre throughout the summer.
3. Direct your own theatre camp at school for different age groups that has a theme, set curriculum and activities, enough space, safety, a great vibe, and a showcase performance at the end.
4. Go online to seek out the many great theatre camps that are out there, and then be sure your students are aware of these opportunities so they can take advantage of their many benefits.

Conclusion

Legitimacy and Excellence

It was the spring of my fourth year teaching in the private school. My program had been successful and was growing year after year. We had just performed the big spring 3rd–12th grade musical, but I had no idea what production we would be doing in the fall. I got the inspiration for the idea in a very surprising place. I was going to a theatre performance at another private school in town. The director was a friend of mine whom I met in community theatre, so I wanted to support him while also seeing what the theatre program at a similar school to mine was like. The show I was seeing was a custom show he called *A Broadway Revue*. It was a compilation performance of several different songs from Broadway musicals. As a Broadway musical fan, I was rather excited.

Continuing the story about the other school's *Broadway Revue* would have never happened. Going out into the world to other schools and theatre organizations can spark ideas for you and your program. You don't know what you don't know. I would have never known a review of Broadway songs was even an option as a production had I not seen it for myself.

Unfortunately, the performance was very disappointing. It lacked so much of what made legitimate theatre legitimate and excellent theatre excellent. If you read the intro for the "Tickets, Programs, and Advertisements" chapter about the school play with the little red ticket paid with cash, etc., this production was that example. Here is some of what I didn't like about that production:

- Couldn't get tickets beforehand, only at the door
- Only cash
- No real ticket, just a red raffle ticket

- No program
- Seats were first come, first served
- No concessions

Once the performance started, the beginning announcement made me learn that the performers were made up of the director's friend, four theatre classes, two middle school classes, and two high school classes. These were all students who signed up for curricular theatre, and they were made to sing and dance at an extracurricular public performance. There is a very big difference and a wide gap between the students who sign up for theatre class as an elective and those who choose to do it extracurricularly. Those in elective classes are in general not as excited and enthusiastic about all aspects of theatre as those who choose to do it in their free time. Some just choose it because they don't want to take choir (don't want to sing publicly *hint hint*) or art (don't think they can draw). So, a majority of the performers looked like they'd rather be anywhere else than onstage singing and dancing publicly. Now, don't get me wrong, there were also very enthusiastic and talented students who performed that night, the ones who were gung-ho about theatre, but they were the minority, and the ones who didn't like it overshadowed the ones who did. (If you read the chapter on Theatre Class, you'll know that I am not against having the theatre class/elective perform, but I'm saying here that there is a huge difference between performing a straight one-act play publicly and a big two-act musical publicly.)

The students were just wearing 'concert blacks,' meaning black pants and black shirts. They were not standard either; they were just asked to wear whatever black clothes they had at home. Some wore black jeans while others had black slacks. Some donned a black T-shirt while others went with a polo shirt. There was no standard. There were no costumes or additions to the concert blacks, and they just kept their non-matching uniform the whole time.

The performance was basically a concert, not a theatrical production. There was little to no movement onstage. The performer(s) would get up onstage for their song, stand there, and sing it like a choir performance.

Two upperclass student 'hosts' introduced each act, but they did not have a script or set lines at all. They were improvising and all of their remarks were off-the-cuff all night. Unfortunately, this led to a cringy blend of awkwardness and amateurism. It took away from the legitimacy of the show.

Lastly, the performances of the singers were not strong. There were a few stand-out solos and one big group unison song that was done well, but other than that, the songs were weak and not done to a high standard.

There were a few other issues that night, including with their lighting setup, audio, music, and the director's extemporaneous remarks (more on those things in their respective chapters). But as you can see, I walked away very disappointed.

That production was not *legit*. That production was not *excellent*.

No matter how small your community, school, or cast is: always always always strive for legitimacy and excellence.

Through my disappointment, I only had one thought on my mind driving away from that school that night: "I could do that. My students could do that. We could do that. And we could do it much much better than they did." There is nothing like a bad performance to make you fired up to make a better one.

Thoughts started to form in my mind. Thoughts turned into ideas. Ideas turned into a proposal to the admins. An approved proposal turned into a script. That script turned into the greatest production I have ever directed in my career, *The Broadway Revue*. I certainly took my concerns and worries about the other school's performance and made sure that they did not happen to mine. I turned their lack of legitimacy and absence of excellence into our legitimacy and excellence. I, of course, had pre-ordered select-seat tickets, and the tickets and programs the likes of which I described in the "Tickets, Programs, and Advertisements" chapter. All of the performers were auditioned extracurricular students, not forced classroom students. Although they were in concert blacks: (1) they wore matching pants and matching shirts provided by me (guys wore one style, girls wore another); and (2) for each song, the performers would put a costume on top of their concert blacks, which gave each character within each song even more personality. I made sure it wasn't a concert – each song was a theatrical performance with blocking and choreography as if it were plucked right out of the show the song was from. Although the 'host' was a senior student, he had a set script to follow to studiously and properly introduce each section of songs rather than improvised banter. Lastly, I made sure that the performances were strong. If they were not going to be strong or the students performing the song would not be up to excellent standards, the song was cut. We rehearsed for two months and created a massive two-and-a-half-hour musical extravaganza: 50 songs from 30 musicals.

Audience members that night admitted that they forgot they were at a small private school theatre performance, and likened it to the excellence found in community or even professional theatre.

Working toward legitimacy and striving for excellence in everything you do in your theatre program will take everything to the next level.

"Excellence in all things, always." This is the motto of my programs.

Don't accept anything less than excellent. Don't expect anything less than excellent.

Within my program, I created the "Three Pillars of Excellence." They were the first sections of the program's handbook that discussed how to achieve excellence in all things.

Some people think that talent is the only thing standing between them and being in a production. In theatre and in life, you will find: Talent. Isn't. Everything. Students in a theatrical production must be on their best behavior and be responsible as well. The Three Pillars of Excellence in any theatre program refers to the three attributes that determine whether they can strive for the highest and reach excellence: Responsibility. Behavior. Talent.

> **Responsibility:** A student in the theatre program must be responsible at all times, including before rehearsal, during rehearsal, after rehearsal, and during the shows.

Students should adhere to the following guidelines for excellence in responsibility:
- Bring your script to every rehearsal.
- Keep your script intact.
- Don't lose your script or leave your script behind.
- Show up on time.
- Show up every time.
- Stay the whole time.
- Inform the Director of any conflict as soon as possible.
- Use a pen during rehearsals to write down any directorial notes and changes.
- Don't leave anything behind after rehearsal.
- Take care of your microphone: getting your mic from the mic closet, handling it properly, never setting it down, never wrapping the cord, putting it up properly.
- Clean up after yourself during and after rehearsal.
- Bring your assigned costumes, makeup, and hair products on the assigned day, leaving them at school until the shows are done, and taking them with you when it's over.
- Memorize your lines by the assigned line memorization day.
- Memorize your songs and dances by the assigned song/dance memorization day.
- Be in your spot, "places," or room when you are supposed to during the run of a show.
- Turn in any paperwork, signatures, money, or anything else to be collected on time.
- While not being actively worked with, work on lines, songs, dances, or help others with lines, songs, and dances.

- Show up to the Production Workday.
- Show up to the Post-Production Strike Day.
- Keep up with your schoolwork, homework, studying, projects, tests, and classes to remain passing without any fear or closeness of failing.

Behavior: A student in a theatre program must be on his/her best behavior at all times, including before rehearsal, during rehearsal, after rehearsal, and during the shows.

Students should adhere to these guidelines for excellence in behavior:
- Don't talk while the director is talking.
- Don't be on your phone while the director is talking.
- Don't bring your phone, food, and/or drink onstage.
- Don't distract others.
- Keep your hands to yourself.
- Don't touch props, costumes, or mics that are not yours.
- Don't "play" with props.
- Don't add any unnecessary drama.
- Don't touch, go through, mess with, and/or take anyone else's personal property.
- Listen to the director, follow the director's notes and guidelines and what the director asks you to do.
- Obey right away, all the way, with a happy heart.
- Take criticism well and humbly. Do not get upset with notes or criticism.
- Listen during "notes" even if they are not yours.
- Be quiet backstage when you need to be, quiet in the dressing room when you need to be, and quiet onstage when you need to be.
- Do not tell other students what to do and what not to do when it is not your job or place to do so. Worry about yourself.
- Do not yell at, insult, get frustrated at, or otherwise demean other students in the production.
- Do not act as if you are more talented, higher, or in any other way better than someone else.
- Don't openly question or disparage the director's decisions with casting, scenes, or the production.

Talent: A student in the theatre program must strive to improve his/her talent, including before rehearsal, during rehearsal, after rehearsal, and during the shows.

Note: The expectation is not that only 100% talented, the absolute best, flawlessly talented students are accepted into the theatre program. The expectation is that every student in the theatre program strives for the highest, strives for excellence, and is always working on improving his/her craft of acting, singing, and dancing to the best of his/her ability 100% of the time.

Students should adhere to these guidelines for excellence in talent:
- Recite your lines as the director asked you to.
- Remember your blocking, your entrances, your exits, your stage business, and everything you are supposed to do, say, sing, and dance when you are onstage.
- Take the director's notes, and adhere to them the next time you do the scene/song/dance.
- You do not need to be asked twice.
- Be always improving your scene/song/dance.
- Be loud. Project your voice to the appropriate stage volume with/without a mic.
- Your lines need to sound *real*. Lines cannot sound monotone like they are being read out of a book or fake (unless the script calls for those things).
- Sing with a full voice.
- Sing on key.
- Sing melody if you have melody, and sing the correct harmony if you have harmony.
- Dance with energy, determination, focus, and a character-appropriate expression on your face.
- Dance the dance moves your director asked you to.

And lastly, before we wrap up: How do we combine that excellence in your theatre program with the legitimacy of that theatre program? How do you reach legitimacy? Where do you even begin? What does it look like to have a 'legit' production?

Your plays have to have a certain look. It can't just be cardboard and markers. It's gotta look good, gotta look right, and gotta have believable characters. You have to have an eye for what looks good/legit and what doesn't. It takes experience. Go to every theatre program in town. See the decorations, see the sets, see the props and costumes. Some you'll be genuinely impressed; some you'll be disappointed. Stay away from stuff that could disappoint your audience and stick to things that will impress them.

If you do one great show a year, that's better than three mediocre shows a year. If you only have the time, resources, and energy for one, then sink all of your guts into a good one. A famous quote from the character Ron Swanson in the tv show "Parks and Recreation" applies here: "Never half-ass two things, whole-ass one thing." You should never settle for a mediocre show. You should never see the time, money, resources, and energy that will go into it, know that it won't turn out as well, and still proceed. Either find a way to make it great, or don't do it.

You don't want to do a high school production; you want to do a good production. Just put on good theatre. You want your audience members to come up to you and tell you that they forgot they were at a school production. Although it is 14, 15, and 16-year-olds up there, their characters should be so convincing that they seem like their adult characters genuinely. There should be no settling for the word "For . . ." What I mean by that is you and your audience members should never say "That was a good production FOR a high school production," or "That was pretty darn good, FOR middle schoolers." It should just be good. It should just be pretty darn good. Don't qualify it. You as the director should not strive to make a good production for your school level; you should always strive for a good production period.

One director colleague of mine stated that social media nowadays is part of what makes you legitimate. We try to be relevant to social media until we are perceived legitimately by the community. Make theatre department accounts – Instagram, Facebook, and X – add accounts to your personal accounts if you have them, reach kids. As of now, Instagram is the way to go, the way to reach the kiddos. If your program has social media accounts like the big boys, then you'll seem just as legit as the big boys.

Know what good theatre is. Know what your version of good theatre is. This is another aspect of being a great director: you need to have an eye for this stuff. If at every theatrical production you go to you are blown away by how good it is, you need to raise your standard, you need to raise your thoughts on what 'good' theatre is. There is bad theatre out there, no doubt about it. You need to know what is bad, why it is bad, and what makes it bad. Then do everything in your power to do the opposite in your program.

If you set a bar for your program, and the program reaches that bar, always raise the bar. Don't ever be content. Don't ever settle or say that the mountaintop has been reached. There is always a higher to go, and there are always better ways to do it. If your program reaches the goals you have set, then set higher goals and go again.

What does my audience expect? The parents' bar is way too low. In some cases, the admin's bar is way too low. Most parents are just happy that their kid is up there doing something. The program could stink, and they would never know because they are too focused on Junior up onstage. The admins could not care less sometimes. Sometimes they are too focused on money or sports to worry about whether the show is actually good. They are usually good with something – as long as it exists! Don't lower your bar for them. Don't say, "Well, the parents' bar is low, so mine will be too," or "The admins don't care if this is good, so what's the point of putting more effort in?" Their bar is usually too low. Yours needs to be too high. Strive for the highest. Don't stoop to their level.

It's a culture of excellence you are looking for, and the culture of self-improvement is all about that growth mindset. If you are starting a new theatre program, growth is always the mindset: You are just trying to get a building and your first students within your first show. But if you are at an already established program that has won all kinds of awards, you might think to yourself, where can I go from here? There's only one way to go and that's downward. Not true. Never true. Always have a growth mindset. Explore other avenues of theatre, uncharted territory for your program. Are y'all already excellent at dramatic one-act plays? Great. Now try comedies. Are y'all already good at fantasy musicals? Great. Do a real-world subject. If you are 'done' growing in one area, find another area in which to grow.

Come in with no drama and lots of excitement. You are the change champion. You are the excitement captain. The students, parents, and admins will feed off of your mood and your excitement (or lack thereof) for the program. Don't bring your own personal drama into it. Don't be nonchalant about big changes in your programs. Be excited, exude that excitement, and spread it like wildfire.

Getting buy-in from your students is crucial. If they are invested in it, then excellence will follow. Getting investment happens by showing them that you care about them more than just what project they are working on.

Excellence and legitimacy are not destinations on a map, but rather constellations guiding our theatrical journey. Each program, each production, and each performance becomes a brushstroke on the ever-evolving canvas of theatre. The pursuit of excellence reminds us to strive for creativity, innovation, and potential, while legitimacy acknowledges the rich tapestry of traditions and improvements that weave together the theatrical world. Ultimately, the magic of theatre lies in the space where these two forces intersect – where excellence breathes life into the established, and the legitimate embraces the daringly new. In this ongoing quest, we find not only validation, but also the profound privilege of contributing to a living art form that has the power to move, inspire, and illuminate the human experience.

For Product Safety Concerns and Information please contact our EU
representative GPSR@taylorandfrancis.com
Taylor & Francis Verlag GmbH, Kaufingerstraße 24, 80331 München, Germany